ARCHITECTURE, ARCHAEOLOGY and LANDSCAPES:

Resources for Historic Preservation in Unincorporated Cobb County, Georgia

by Darlene R. Roth, Ph.D.

Photographs by Darlene R. Roth Ph.D. and S. Ralston Cox
Frontispiece Photograph by Jim Richardson
Illustrations by Gregg A. Coyle

Editorial Assistance by Linda Barnes Cater and S. Ralston Cox

ARCHITECTURE, ARCHAEOLOGY and LANDSCAPES:
Resources for Historic Preservation in Unincorporated Cobb County, Georgia

Published on behalf of the citizens of the County
by the Cobb County Historic Preservation Commission
Cobb County, Georgia

Members of the Cobb County Historic Preservation Commission
since its inception in 1985:

Linda Barnes Cater
Frank D. Duncan
Richard J. Hutnik
Don M. McAfee
James F. Morris
Dr. Philip L. Secrist
Sally D. Thomas
Robert F. Webb
Glenda A. Willoughby

S. Ralston Cox, Historic Preservation Planner
Cobb County Planning and Zoning Department

This project was financed in part by funds from the National Park Service,
U.S. Department of the Interior, through the
Georgia Department of Natural Resources, Historic Preservation Section.
Additional funding for this project was provided by
Governor Joe Frank Harris' discretionary fund.

Publication was made possible by funds appropriated by the
Cobb County Board of Commissioners

Library of Congress Catalog Card Number 88 - 62643

ISBN Number 0-9621120-0-3 (hardcover)
ISBN Number 0-962110-1-1 (softcover)

COBB COUNTY BOARD OF COMMISSIONERS

1985 - 1986

Earl E. Smith, Chairman

Emmett L. Burton, Eastern District

Barbara E. Williams, Eastern District

Harvey D. Paschal, Western District

Joseph C. ("Butch") Thompson, Jr., Western District

1987 - 1988

Earl E. Smith, Chairman

Emmett L. Burton, Eastern District

Thea J. Powell, Eastern District

Harvey D. Paschal, Western District

Charles C. Clay, Western District

Harriet L. Smith, Western District

No true secrets are lurking in the landscape, but only undisclosed evidence, waiting for us. No true chaos is in the urban scene, but only patterns and clues waiting to be organized . . . . Each [city] reflects the ideas, traditions, and energies available to its citizens in past centuries, as well as at this moment. Each landscape and townscape is an intricately organized expression of causes and effects, of challenges and responses, of continuity and, therefore, of coherence. It all hangs together, makes sense, fits one way or another -- for good or bad, loosely or tightly. It has sequences, successions, climaxes. It reveals patterns and relationships forming and reforming.

Grady Clay
Close-Up: How to Read the American City   (1973)

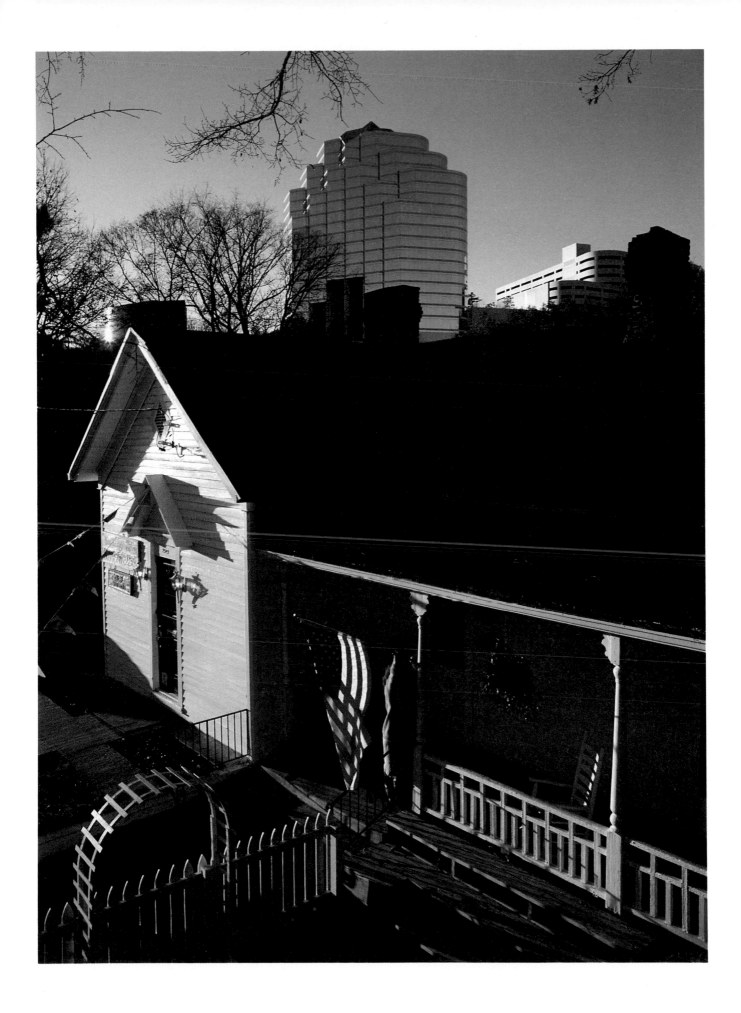

TABLE OF CONTENTS

Preface
Methodology .... *xi*
Acknowledgements .... *xiii*

THE THREE FACES OF COBB 1
Introduction 3
The Land 3
Names on the Land 3
    Preservation Assessment 5
Landscape I: Forests And Indians 6
    Early Populations 6
    The Creeks and Cherokees 7
    The Landscape Legacy 9
    Preservation Assessment 11
Landscape II: The Agrarian Past of Cobb County 11
    Demographic Trends, 1840-1940 11
    Agricultural Patterns, 1840-1940 13
    Antebellum Landscape Characteristics 13
        The Farmscape 14
        Early Industrialization 20
        The Roads 21
        Communities and Communal Nodes 21
        Preservation Assessment 26
    The Civil War Landscape 28
        Preservation Assessment 31
    The New South Landscape, 1870-1940 31
        The "Urbanization" of Cobb County 32
        Railroad Developments, 1880-1910 35
        Industrialization, 1870-1940 37
        New South Agriculture 41
        The Modernization of Cobb County 42
        Preservation Assessment 46
Landscape III: Sunbelt Suburbanization 53
    Landscape Effects 53
    Historic Elements of the Modern Changes 54
    Preservation Assessment 59

VERNACULAR ARCHITECTURE IN COBB COUNTY 61
Introduction 63
Single-Pen Styles (One Room) Log House, 1820s to c. 1860 64
Double-Pen Styles 67
Hall and Parlor Houses, 1840s to c. 1890 75
I-House 80
Massed-Plan Hall and Parlor, late 19th Century to 1920s 82
Folk Victorian and Railroad Houses, 1870s to 1940s 85
    Pyramidal Hip-Roofed Houses, c. 1870 to 1910 85
    Victorian "L" or "Bent" House, 1870 to 1940 92
    Early Twentieth Century Houses, 1910s to 1940s 96
Farmsites, Barns and Outbuildings 100
Rural Institutions 103

COBB COUNTY SITES LISTED ON THE NATIONAL REGISTER OF HISTORIC PLACES
AND THE COBB REGISTER OF HISTORIC PLACES 107
    Introduction 109
    Braswell-Carnes House 113
    J. H. Carmichael Farm and General Store 113
    Israel Causey-Maxham House 116
    Andrew J. Cheney-Newcomer House 118
    Coats and Clark Thread Mill and Village (Clarkdale) 118
    Gilgal Church Battlefield 123
    Glover-McLeod-Garrison House 125
    Johnston's River Line 126
    Kennesaw Mountain National Battlefield Park...................... 129
    William Gibbs McAdoo House 133
    Robert Mable House and Cemetery 134
    Midway Presbyterian Church and Cemetery 135
    Sope Creek Ruins/Marietta Paper Mills............................... 137
    Concord Covered Bridge Historic District: 139
        Concord Covered Bridge 140
        Ruff's Mill 141
        Miller's House 142
        Rock House (John W. Rice Summer Cottage) 142
        Concord Woolen Mills and Millworkers' Village 145
        Gann-Love-Hill House 148
        Martin Ruff Homeplace and Cemetery 149
        Railroad Trestle 151

THE GEORGIA HISTORICAL MARKER PROGRAM 153

HISTORIC SITES INVENTORY 185
    Introduction 187
    District 1 191
    District 16 196
    District 17 216
    District 18 236
    District 19 244
    District 20 264
    Incorporated Areas... 274

PRESERVATION FINDINGS AND OPPORTUNITIES.. 283

Bibliography 289

LIST OF MAPS

Incorporated Areas .... *xii*
Cobb County Location Map 2
Indian Trails and Indian Villages 8
Militia Districts 22
Crossroad Communities 24
The Civil War in Cobb County 29
Railroads in Cobb County 34
National Register and Cobb Register Sites 110
Kennesaw Mountain National Battlefield Park 130
Historic Sites Inventory:
    Cobb County District Index Map 190
    1st District 191
    16th District, northwest quadrant 196
    16th District, northeast quadrant 197
    16th District, southwest quadrant 198
    16th District, southeast quadrant 199
    17th District, northwest quadrant 216
    17th District, northeast quadrant 217
    17th District, southwest quadrant 218
    17th District, southeast quadrant 219
    18th District, western section 236
    18th District, eastern section 237
    19th District, northwest quadrant 244
    19th District, northeast quadrant 245
    19th District, southwest quadrant 246
    19th District, southeast quadrant 247
    20th District, northwest quadrant 264
    20th District, northeast quadrant 265
    20th District, southwest quadrant 266
    20th District, southeast quadrant 267

Note: Photographs and illustrations are placed throughout this volume, and are not listed separately here.

PREFACE

Methodology

The Cobb County Historic Preservation Commission contracted with Darlene Roth & Associates to prepare a comprehensive survey of Cobb's historic sites, requiring the following scope of services: the preparation of a written introduction to the history of Cobb County to cover known prehistoric sites, known Indian sites and history, pioneer family and settlement documentation, church and school history prior to 1935, and waterways, roadways and other major geographical features. In addition Dr. Roth was asked to prepare an historic sites inventory of unincorporated Cobb County which would include known archaeological sites, residential sites from 1832 through 1935, industrial and mercantile sites from 1832 through 1935, including the Bell Bomber Plant, Civil War lines, railroad and trolley lines, cemeteries, and natural geographical and landscape features.

Dr. Roth conducted the survey in the following manner: 1) compiled all known information from prior surveys of the county and other sources, including the Bicentennial Survey of the county conducted by Dr. Philip Secrist, the State of Georgia Historic Preservation Section's survey of the county's architecture conducted by Ted Bessette, projects under current environmental review under Section 106 of the National Historic Preservation Act, cemetery studies conducted and partially published by the Cobb County Genealogical Society, the site files of the Cobb County archaeological survey office, and other information voluntarily provided by citizens of the county; 2) read standard historical sources on Cobb County, North Georgia, and the Piedmont region to establish developmental and architectural trends which would apply to the county; 3) conducted research on a limited number of specific topics and sites (such as the Bell Bomber Plant) as needed for the survey report; 4) conducted a windshield survey of the county to confirm the continued existence of previously identified sites and to identify classes of structures not previously identified (most especially vernacular residential architecture and industrial and commercial sites); and 5) prepared the necessary documentation on the sites to meet State of Georgia Historic Preservation Section and National Park Service standards for architectural and historical surveys, locating the sites on USGS topographic maps, photographing them and providing a brief architectural description.

Dr. Roth prepared the inventory of sites as the first part of the completed report, compiling the sites by district and land lot number into a list which could be logged into the Cobb County computer system. Each architectural site was evaluated according to a set of criteria implying the known value of the site to the county as an historic resource. Included in the computerized inventory were all the categories of information listed above plus county recreation areas, historical markers, communities and municipalities (including "lost" crossroads and early trading centers), important Indian trade routes, and sites in the county already listed in the National Register of Historic Places.

The consultant prepared a narrative to accompany the inventory which places the historic and prehistoric resources within the context of demographic and economic growth of the county, its agrarian character during the historic period, and which analyzes the effects to the landscape of the demographic and economic changes in the county. This portion of the narrative is included as the section entitled "The Three Faces of Cobb." In addition, the narrative includes a discussion of the rural architecture in Cobb County, showing generic building styles for homes, schools, and churches; it is included as the section entitled "Vernacular Architecture in Cobb County."

INCORPORATED AREAS

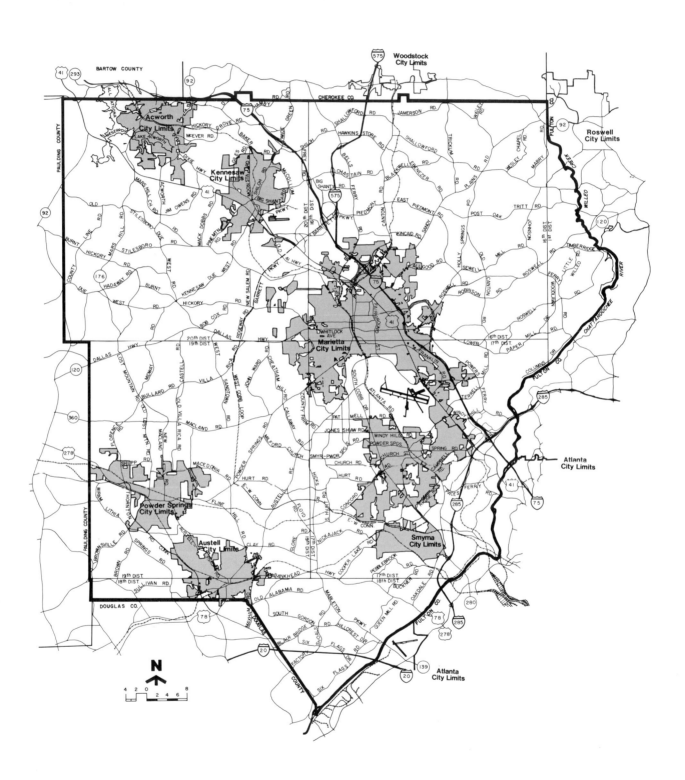

While incorporated areas are mentioned throughout, this study is devoted almost entirely to unincorporated Cobb, which had not heretofore been included in a detailed study. The Cobb County Commissioners, the Historic Preservation Commission, and professional county planning staff are using the inventory as a planning tool designed to effect the short-term and long-term preservation of historic resources.

Acknowledgements

Any project that has been "in process" for more than three years has many people to thank when it is finally complete. One problem in properly acknowledging those who have contributed to this publication is that many who have been a part of the project have moved on to other responsibilities. The editors sincerely apologize if anyone has been overlooked here.

Bethanie C. Grashof of the Center for Architectural Conservation, College of Architecture, Georgia Institute of Technology graciously created the conceptual drawings from which Gregg Coyle of the University of Georgia School of Environmental Design crafted the vernacular architecture illustrations. The text of the National Register nominations on file at the State of Georgia Historic Preservation Section were used to provide much of the historic information included in the chapter on the National Register sites. The authors of this research were usually not identified, but Maurie Van Buren of Historic Preservation Consulting (Atlanta) and Dale Jaeger of Jaeger/Pyburn (Gainesville) deserve special thanks for their research on Clarkdale and the Concord Covered Bridge areas, respectively.

Many people gave freely of their time and energy. Florrie Corley, Jim Corley and Dr. Tom Scott all agreed on very short notice to read and edit the text; all offered sound criticism for which the editors are most grateful. Doug Davis of the Cobb Geneological Society shared unpublished and published cemetery information which added greatly to the accuracy of the historic sites inventory. Karen Lawrence, a very patient professional photographer, took the time to work with the printing of each photograph so that photographs taken by different amateurs look their best.

The editors would like to extend their special thanks to the many Cobb County employees who worked long hours to ensure that this publication was of high quality and would be a source of pride for all Cobb County residents. Regina McGarvey and Vivian Barnett typed, retyped and corrected endless drafts of the entire report. Lesley McHugh helped us stay on budget and was always helpful in finding a way through the bureaucratic maze. Roswell Story and Debbie Tatum were patient with us when the bidding process didn't go as we thought it would. John Moeller and Dave Robbins were invaluable in helping us to negotiate schedules and prioritize when necessary. All the employees of the Cobb County Planning and Zoning Department are also due our thanks for taking care of all our other responsibilities while we focused our attention on this publication.

Without the expertise and assistance of Jeffrey C. Beckham and Damon L. Gensel we could never have published this volume. We owe them more than our thanks for working to high standards when less would have gone undetected.

THE THREE FACES OF COBB

Americans have no urban history. They live in one of the world's most urbanized countries as if it were a wilderness in both time and space. Beyond some civic and ethnic myths and a few family and neighborhood memories, Americans are not conscious that they have a past and that by their actions they participate in making their future... Without a sense of history, they hammer against today's crises without any means to choose their targets to fit the trends which they must confront, work with, or avoid.

Sam Bass Warner, Jr.
The Urban Wilderness (1972)

Georgia and the United States

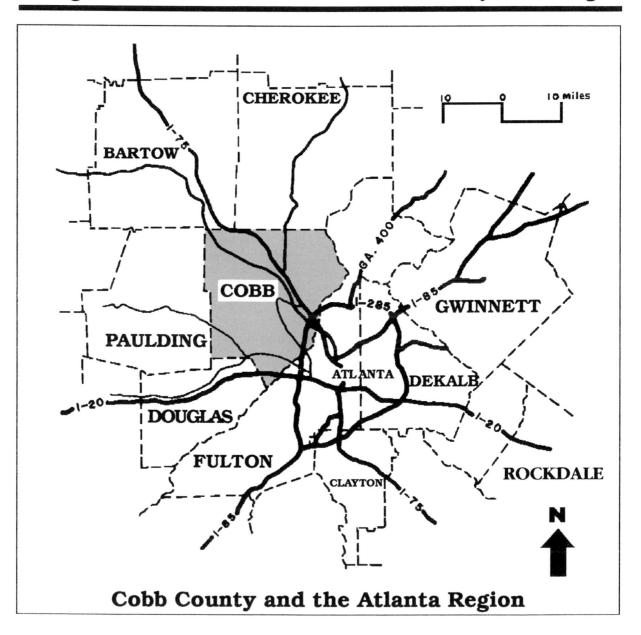

Cobb County and Georgia

BLUE RIDGE

PIEDMONT

COASTAL PLAIN

CHEROKEE

BARTOW

10   0   10 Miles

COBB

GWINNETT

GA. 400

285   85

PAULDING

ATLANTA   DEKALB

I-20

DOUGLAS

20

FULTON

ROCKDALE

CLAYTON   75

85

N

Cobb County and the Atlanta Region

INTRODUCTION

There are three landscapes in Cobb County, three "faces" visible on the terrain, one superimposed over the other; they represent the prehistoric (Landscape I), the historic (Landscape II), and the contemporary (Landscape III) periods. While the contemporary scene almost obliterates the two older landscapes, there are traces of them remaining for the sensitive eye and the informed mind to see. As people have lived on this land, worked it, and built over it, they have changed the face of it with varying results. Together and individually, the inhabitants have created different visual effects knowingly, intentionally, as well as unconsciously. Accordingly, the accumulation of man-made shapes on the land is a vast resource for education, cultural enrichment, and human understanding. Contemporary landscapes are a collection of landforms and structures to support economic and social endeavors. What remains from the first two landscapes provides an opportunity for choice today; both are disappearing rapidly under the pressures of new and forceful land uses. Cobb County residents may now decide how best and how much to preserve of what is left of Landscapes I and II as a conscious, continuing legacy of Cobb County history for future generations. This report is intended as a tool to support those decisions. It is not a history of the county. This report is an interpretation of that history, which addresses itself to the material evidence of the past as seen in the buildings and structures, patterns, roads and artifacts from the three different "faces" of this place.

THE LAND

Cobb County's 346 square miles are located in the northwest section of Georgia, across the Chattahoochee River from Fulton County and the City of Atlanta. Physiographically, the county belongs to the Upper or Northern Piedmont, a section of the southeastern United States stretching from the Carolinas to Mississippi characterized by hilly terrain and fertile soils along narrow and numerous creek beds. At one time, the Piedmont area housed trading centers, hunting grounds, and settlements of Indian populations; later, it was the seat of the cotton culture of the South. Currently, the Piedmont area contains most of the South's urban and industrial centers. The Upper Piedmont section is hillier than the Lower Piedmont, and has somewhat less desirable growing conditions such as less fertile soils and shorter growing seasons; the latter factors significantly influenced its settlement as well as its success or failure as an economic region.

Cobb County slopes north gradually, its surface broken by ravines. Creeks and streams flow into twelve drainage basins, most of which empty into the Chattahoochee and all of which find their way to the Gulf of Mexico. Lakes Allatoona and Acworth are the largest bodies of water in the county. Lake Allatoona is formed by the damming of the Etowah River in Bartow County with Lake Acworth being formed by the damming of Butler and Proctor Creeks. Other lakes and pools have been created with small agricultural dams, private dams, and drainage controls. All are man-made. The plateaus between ravines are raised up by a string of mountains crossing the county in a line that runs northeast and southwest from the major mountain, Kennesaw Mountain; the latter is found in the heart of the county midway between Marietta and the town of Kennesaw.

NAMES ON THE LAND

The first mark local inhabitants make on the land is a name. Naming stakes a claim on the land, identifying a specific spot in an undifferentiated wilderness. Some of the ancient names in Cobb County have survived, and their origins are preserved in legend and custom. One such name is Kennesaw, so called for an Indian chief of the same name or an anglicized pronunciation of Gansagi, itself a Cherokee adaptation of an older Indian word, Conasagua. Sope Creek is allegedly named for Old Sope, a Cherokee hermit who somehow avoided evacuation in the Indian removals of 1838. Noses, Allatoona, and Nickajack, also are Indian names or derivatives. Other names reflect observations made by early settlers about the elements in their environment such as in Rottenwood, Mud, and Sweetwater Creeks and Brushy or Pine Mountains. Two road names in Cobb County, Sandtown and Shallowford Roads, are English names referring to Indian sites. Other roads were named by the settlers, the first developers in Cobb County, who built them, including Howell, Pace, Johnson and McLain.

As long as people continue to build anew on the land, they will continue to name and rename its parts. The names in themselves reveal the tastes, preferences, identities, and concerns of the people who do the naming as well as of the times within which the names appear. Smyrna in Cobb County was named after one of the ancient Christian churches in Asia Minor at a time in the early nineteenth century when revivalism swept across America in great waves. At the time, Smyrna was a non-denominational religious campground, barely a community, where Protestants of differing belief systems could worship together. The name Smyrna appealed to both a belief in the unity of early Christianity and the pioneer character of the Biblical Smyrna and the Georgia community of the same name.

The "tents" at Marietta Campground. Similar campgrounds existed elsewhere in Cobb County, most notably in Smyrna.

Commemorative names tell less about a place than about the sentiments of the people who live there and their response to a momentous event or a famous person. Cobb County was named after Thomas Cobb, an influential statesman and judge in North Georgia, who never resided in Cobb County but was known and revered here. The county was formed two years after Cobb died while his memory was still fresh enough for the citizens of the county to choose it as their primary collective, political, and social designation. With equal honor the county seat, Marietta, was given the diminutive form for Cobb's wife, Mary.

The names across Cobb County's geography are one of the historic resources of the county. Several issues surface which reflect choices that developers, neighborhood groups, planners, educators, and community leaders have to make. They include: (1) whether old names are retained, removed, or replaced; (2) whether the circumstances of their naming is remembered officially; (3) whether new names evoke old traditions and environments; (4) whether the metaphors behind the names on Cobb County land are conscious parts of local wisdom; and, (5) whether the names of geographic elements ever indicate more than location. Some of the oldest and some of the newest memories in the county rest in the names of its communities, roads, subdivisions, streams and hills.

The tabernacle at the Marietta Campground, a Methodist revival campground in operation since the 1830s. Undoubtedly, the original Smyrna Campground would have resembled this one.

Preservation Assessment

There is no "keeper of the names" in Cobb County, and very little official record of what the names have meant except for some very old and important places. Such an activity is normally undertaken out of curiosity and love by local historians interested in the history of place names. If such a person exists in Cobb County, this would be a good time for him or her to step forward. In cases such as Sandtown Road, where the name of the object, in this case an important secondary Indian and early settlement trading path, is all that is left of the original element, the county might undertake a marker program to indicate the route. Some creativity is called for outside the realm of the familiar roadside tablet. Such a route designation might be painted on street surfaces, attached to street lighting, added to sidewalks, or otherwise indicated in the other street furniture. Likewise, the old ferry sites (Paces, Johnson, Howell, Bells, etc.) where only the names exist, could receive some additional attention, especially as the areas along the Chattahoochee are more intensely developed. At a minimum, a county record could be prepared of the rationale behind the name selection of new developments in the county. There would be at least a memory of names being selected during this period of development for the enlightenment of future generations.

LANDSCAPE I: FORESTS AND INDIANS

Early Populations

Archaeologists estimate that people have been living in the area now defined as the State of Georgia for at least twelve thousand years. There are traces of civilizations, even of the earliest ones, but aspects of those early environments are not readily recoverable; biologically, the land has changed too much. Twelve thousand years ago, parts of continental America were still under ice, and plant life in this region as elsewhere was far less varied than it is today. Bulky beasts roamed the land, such as mastodons, mammoths, giant beavers, ground sloths, and musk oxen whose bones and replicas may now be seen at the Fernbank Science Center in Atlanta. These animals were hunted by the inhabitants, called Paleo-Indians, for several thousand years.

The Paleo-Indians, like their successors, lived in harmony with the natural cycles of the land and the physical elements which composed it; they roamed freely, stopping wherever there was food, such as fish, game, nuts, berries, and water, while living in small bands and setting up camps on a seasonal basis. Their abodes were impermanent; they lived in caves, or rock shelters, always near a water source. Structures, if they were built at all, were of natural materials which decayed with time. The remains of these civilizations are chiefly their tools, such as simple quartz scrapers and projectile points, and scatterings from the work areas in which the tools were made.

Between approximately 5,000 and 3,000 B.C., the early peoples lived in the Archaic Period of development. During this period, life was much as it had been for centuries but with some improvements; pottery was invented, more elaborate and varied tools were fashioned, and they lived in huts made of poles, hides or brush. The Archaic peoples still lived in bands, although in larger numbers than before and in seasonal camps, which were also larger than they had been in earlier times. They buried their dead in circular graves near their huts, and added mussels to their diet.

The Woodland Period of development (c. 1,000 B.C. to 400 A.D.) brought notable changes in the life patterns of the Indian civilizations. In addition to the hunting and gathering activities they had always undertaken, the Woodland Indians now cultivated some plants. They were organized into tribes and became less nomadic; they lived in established, permanent, and widely scattered villages and buried their dead in mounds. Some of the most notable archaeological sites in Georgia date from the Woodland Period such as the Ocmulgee and Kolomoki Mounds and the Rock Eagle rock effigy at Eatonton. Artifacts from the Woodland Period are more numerous than from earlier periods and include bows and arrows as well as other tools which were more refined, decorated pottery, village refuse, and burial artifacts. They made ceremonial effigies and they used copper, galena and hematite.

The Mississippian era began about 800 A.D. and ended in the mid-1500s when Europeans first started to explore territory on the east coast of North America. The Mississippian Indian populations settled into large, permanently established, fortified villages, and sustained themselves with well-developed agricultural enterprise in which native plants such as corn, squash and beans, were farmed along major creek and river bottoms. The villages were trading centers among the various Indian groups and ultimately became the sites for contacts between the Indians and the first European explorers. The Mississippian cultures constructed temple mounds, plazas, and earth lodges; their villages were colorful places, decorated with native materials such as reeds and shells. Cultural artifacts from these civilizations are the most plentiful of all the early groups and include such items as village remains, ceremonial mounds, refuse piles, tools, pottery, ornaments, and weapons.

Once the Europeans began spreading their authority into the Americas, the Indian civilizations were heavily influenced by European technologies. They adopted European tools and weapons and learned to ride and breed European horses. Once European settlement began to occur, the Indians learned the European alphabets, agricultural practices, and housing styles. As the Europeans expanded their domains, the Indians lost their lands, their burial and religious grounds, their freedom to hunt at will, and their jurisdiction over tribal affairs. Some tribes lost more than their styles of living. Susceptible to European diseases, they became ill from smallpox, diphtheria and syphilis.

When the first explorers wrote of their adventures in the Americas, they created the first written records of the early Indian civilizations. These rare documents and the official records of colonial and eighteenth century federal government interactions with Indian tribes constitute the best descriptions of Indian civilizations in existence. They are, however, partial and conflicting.

Hernando de Soto is popularly credited with being the first European explorer to pass through Georgia and the Carolinas. It is now generally agreed that when he made his trek in 1540, he did not come through the northwest section of Georgia which includes Cobb County. Had de Soto come to what is now Cobb territory, he would have encountered tribes of Mississippian descent and culture. The Cherokees were the last of the tribes to move west of the Chattahoochee. At the time of de Soto's journey, the Creeks may have been as far north as the Chattahoochee, but they, too, were relative latecomers to what is now Cobb County. In fact, these later Indian groups moved into northwest Georgia about the same time the English were settling along the coast in Savannah.

The Creeks and Cherokees

According to some testimony, the Creeks settled in Cobb County in the 1700s. With the arrival of the Cherokees after the treaty of 1819, they were forced south, back across the Chattahoochee River. From 1819 until the Cherokees were removed from Cobb County, jurisdictional disputes erupted among the Indians and between the Indians and whites. All of these disputes ended by working to the advantage of the whites. The Indians signed several treaties throughout the eighteenth century (in 1773, 1783, 1785, 1791, and 1795) and the early years of the nineteenth century (1804 and 1819), ceding more and more land to the American settlers. From the Cherokees' first relocation into northwest Georgia until 1838, when Georgia took possession of all Cherokee lands left within her borders, relations between the two cultures, native and settler, ranged from strained to violently hostile.

The federal government facilitated economic activity in the Indian territory and the state government fostered white settlement. The frontier, and this included Cobb County, was not tame. Local authorities sought to impose order not only by keeping the peace, but also by included mapping the territories, improving transportation routes through them, regulating trade through the territories, and keeping records of occasional white citizens who "happened" to settle there.

INDIAN TRAILS AND INDIAN VILLAGES

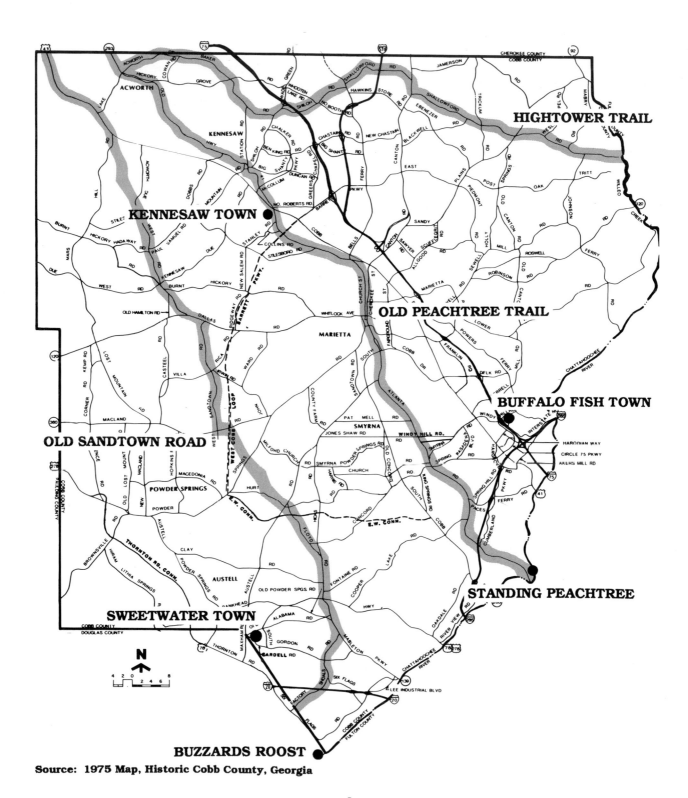

Source: 1975 Map, Historic Cobb County, Georgia

The Indian villages in and near what is now Cobb County were important points for trading and negotiating. The old Creek town, Standing Peachtree, occupied territory on both sides of the Chattahoochee at the mouth of Peachtree Creek and was the entry point to the Cherokee nation from the Creek nation, a strategic location for white commerce with the Indians. Three other towns within the present borders of Cobb County served Indian trading necessities; they were Sweetwater on Sweetwater Creek, Kennesaw Town on Noonday Creek, and Buffalo Fish Town, located 16 miles southeast of Marietta. Buzzard's Roost, so-called by the federal government in 1821 (also known as Sandtown) was another important trading center on the Chattahoochee.

When gold was discovered in the Cherokee territory near Dahlonega in 1828, adventurers and prospectors flocked to the area, encroaching on Indian lands. In 1830, Georgia claimed the Indian territory in its entirety, designating it as Cherokee County of the State of Georgia rather than the "nation within a nation" which it ostensibly had been. The land was surveyed, carved into 40-acre gold lots and 160-acre farm lots. In 1832, the state held a lottery to dispose of the Cherokee lands to eligible white citizens, chiefly those who had been in the State of Georgia for a specified number of years. In the same year, the state divided the old Cherokee lands into five smaller counties, one of which was Cobb County. With gold and land to gain, settlers, speculators, and prospectors poured in.

The first attempts to remove the Indians totally from nothwest Georgia occurred in 1830 when vigilante groups raided Indian properties, forcing the Indians to relocate. During the lotteries, the lands were actually passed to the whites with the Indians still on them. The Cherokees refused to voluntarily abandon their properties in 1834, even while they offered to cede another portion of their holdings to the State of Georgia. In 1835 they finally ceded all their lands, though there was much opposition to the treaty among the Cherokee people. Officially, that nation never endorsed the treaty it negotiated with the United States. It did not matter--Georgia did not recognize the Cherokee Nation. When the treaty was made effective in 1836, the Cherokees were given two years to evacuate on their own accord and some 2000 did so. The rest, more than 17,000, were rounded up in 1838 by the United States Armies under General Winfield Scott and removed bodily to Oklahoma. The trek lasted from June of 1838 to March of 1839; more than 4000 of the Indians perished along the way. A handful of stragglers escaped the removal, but the Indians' lives, including their villages, towns, houses, ceremonial mounds, burial grounds, trade routes, fields, and deer foraging areas were all left behind, and were eagerly confiscated or plundered by the citizens of Georgia.

Landscape Legacy

Landscape I in Cobb County ended when its Indian inhabitants were incorporated into the Cherokee Removal of 1838. No more Indian influences exerted force into the economic, political, social, or the geographic patterns in the county. The Indians had dealt gently with the land, settled it sparsely, co-existed with its creatures amiably, and their impact was slight compared with the earth-moving capabilities of white industrialized generations.

The primeval landscape which existed twelve thousand years ago is gone. It can be found, if at all, in geological formations and fossils. The hills and streams of Cobb County are what remain of this. The aboriginal landscape viewed by the first European visitors exists in several forms. There are, however, few places where remnants of this landscape are visible to the naked eye. Presumably, the forested areas in Cobb County today somewhat resemble the forests which the Cherokees left in the nineteenth century, but not the forests which the earlier Indian cultures knew. During the earlier ages, hardwood forests receeded because pine trees, lighter in seed and faster growing, replaced themselves more quickly than did the oaks and hickories. An important landscape element which remains from the aboriginal eras, though hardly in its original form, is the system of Indian trading routes which white settlers converted from single-file pathways to horse paths to wagon roads. In turn, several of these Indian trails were improved by state and federal governments, i.e. mapped, cleared, and graded, then widened, paved and bridged. Several contemporary roads in Cobb County reiterate, but do not exactly follow, the first transportation routes through this section of Georgia.

Two routes are of primary importance to Cobb County: (1) the New Echota Trail (known commonly in the Atlanta area as the Peachtree Trail) and (2) the Hightower Trail. New Echota ran north and south between Chattanooga (Ross's Landing) and Standing Peachtree on the Chattahoochee. State Route 293 (old Highway 41) and State Route 3 roughly follow this route. Shallowford Road follows the original route of the Hightower Trail as it wound through the county.

The Cherokees opposed the federal government's use of these trails as military roads. In the 1820s they were to be turned into turnpikes as part of the system of federal roads being built across the eastern United States. Another Indian trail through Georgia, known as the Old Echota Trail, became what is now known as the Unicoi Turnpike. This ran east and west across the mountains from Old Echota in Tennessee to the headwaters of the Tugaloo. Traces of this can be found in White County and elsewhere in Northeast Georgia. Just how extensive and how successful the federal road-building program was in Georgia is not well documented. It has been supposed that only one of the three proposed military roads, the Unicoi, was finished. But a rock-walled road bed, similar to the rock-walled traces of the Unicoi Turnpike, is located in Cobb County near Shallowford Road in District 16. This leads us to believe that the Hightower Trail was at least partially turnpiked.

Keheley Mound. Recent archaeological investigation indicates that this may be an agricultural rather than an Indian mound.

Preservation Assessment

Most of the evidence of the prehistoric landscape is archaeological; it lies beneath the soil, invisible to the onlooker. These are the resources which could provide information about civilizations ranging from 150 to 12,000 years ago; as such, they can only be discovered by means of excavation by professionals trained in the field of archaeology. The Cobb County Archaeological Survey Section under the Department of Transportation presently operates an ongoing program of archaeological survey and recovery on county and private property in association with all manner of projects. They have documented archaeological sites throughout the county which correspond with all of the aboriginal periods of development. Though other locations may be better known in the public mind (such as New Echota and Etowah Mounds), Cobb County is rich in archaeological resources.

From the archaeological findings, it is known that Cobb County itself, not just the northern section of Georgia in general, was occupied continuously for 10,000 or more years before Europeans made any contact with Georgia Indians. The archaeological resources of the county, therefore, would contribute considerable knowledge about all of the aboriginal groups. County staff estimates that evidence of the early inhabitants could be found in literally thousands of places in the county, and that hundreds of significant aboriginal sites do exist within its borders. Since the Chattahoochee River as well as the southern and southwestern portions of the county constituted an important border between Indian groups and a trading zone as well, these areas are likely to be particularly sensitive archaeologically and potentially most revealing about the aboriginal cultures which lived here.

LANDSCAPE II: THE AGRARIAN PAST OF COBB COUNTY

For more than a century, the character of unincorporated Cobb County was entirely rural in nature and agricultural in economy. Between 1832 when the county officially opened for white settlement, and 1943 when the Bell Bomber Plant moved the county into the mainstream of 20th century industry, rural Cobb County was typical of similar places across the southern states. During this period the county, like the rural South in general, stayed essentially unchanged although it was not unaffected by modernizations such as electricity, sewer services, trolleys, and automobiles.

The county grew slowly during its century of agrarian existence except for two periods: the settlement years between the middle 1820s and the 1840s and the decade of the 1870s following the Civil War. During these two phases of growth, the population increases were sudden and large; otherwise, they were incremental and insignificant in their impact on county resources.

To illuminate the changes in the landscape over this period in Cobb County, it is useful to divide the period from 1832-1943 into three different phases. Each phase is marked by economic, social and political forces which altered the landscape but which did not undo the dominance of agriculture in the economy or white supremacy in the social-political structure. These three phases are characterized by (1) the first white settlement and early development; (2) the Civil War and its aftermath; and (3) the influences of the "New South" (mechanization, urbanization, and industrialization).

Demographic Trends, 1840 - 1940

The population figures for Cobb County, taken from the decennial federal census data, reveal several important facts and trends about Cobb County development. First, the population figures substantiate the three-part breakdown of the county's agrarian century; during each of the phases, a different demographic phenomenon was at work. During the period of time 1830-60, Cobb County grew very rapidly; during the Civil War years, it lost population; and during the remaining years, 1870-1940, it grew at a relatively slow and steady pace.

POPULATION STATISTICS

Census Year	Total*	% Change	White	Black	Black % of Total
1834 est.	1,576	n/a	--------	-------	-----
1840	7,539	+378%	6,630	909	12%
1850	13,843	+84%	11,568	2,275	16%
1860	14,242	+28%	10,410	3,819	26%
1870	13,814	- 3%	10,593	3,217	23%
1880	20,748	+50%	14,734	6,012	28%
1890	22,286	+ 7%	15,510	6,774	30%
1900	24,664	+10%	17,334	7,328	29%
1910	28,397	+15%	20,977	7,418	25%
1920	30,437	+ 7%	23,677	6,645	22%
1930	35,408	+16%	28,787	6,540	18%
1940	38,272	+ 8%	31,990	6,280	16%

*Includes foreign born and non-white citizens, which are not separately enumerated here.

From an estimated 1,576 persons in the early 1830s, Cobb County quadrupled in population by 1840, the first year the county was enumerated separately in the national census. During the 1840s, the county grew another 84 percent from 7,539 persons at the beginning of the decade to 13,843 persons in 1850. During the 1850s, the rate of new settlement slowed, and the population increased by only 2.8 percent, or from 13,843 to 14,242 persons. It is important to note that this increase is largely due to the addition of black people in the county. In 1850, there were 2,275 slaves in Cobb County; in 1860, there were 3,819. Blacks still did not constitute a racial majority in the county, nor were their numbers as large a proportion of total population as they were in the coastal areas in Georgia or in the counties along the Lower Piedmont. The slight shift in racial balance in Cobb County does imply that the county was becoming more dependent upon the economic system of slavery even though cotton had not yet become an important cash crop.

During the 1860s, the decade of the Civil War, Cobb County lost aggregate population. There was a slight increase in the white population (from 10,410 people to 10,593) but a loss in black population (3,819 persons in 1860 to 3,217 in 1870) caused the overall three percent drop in population.

Between 1870 and 1940, the county population grew more steadily and slowly. Except for the 1870s, the county population never increased by less than seven percent nor more than sixteen percent. In the 1870s, the county regained and then surpassed its pre-Civil War population figures among both blacks and whites. In 1870, the county's population stood at a low of 13,814; in 1880, it had grown to 20,748. By 1890, the accumulated demographic data of Cobb County indicated the county's aggregate growth, its racial ratios, and the major periods of development before and after the Civil War. As part of the "last frontier" in Georgia, carved from Cherokee County and the Cherokee Cession of 1835, Cobb County was settled by whites very late in the early history of Georgia; otherwise, it conforms generally to the rises and declines in state development for those counties which were agriculturally based.

Agricultural Patterns, 1840 - 1940

Some idea of the persistence of the agricultural economy in Cobb County is illustrated in comparisons of agricultural statistics for 1850, 1890, and 1930, with census data selected at forty year intervals throughout the century of farming. No differentiation is made between black-owned and white-owned farms; the historic data does not make such a differentiation.

In 1850, 52,697 acres of land were cultivated in Cobb County, not quite one-third of the total land area. Farm lands were valued at $743,237. There are no comparable figures for manufacturing values in the same year; however, in 1870, when Cobb County had 60 manufacturing establishments, these were valued at $535,400. By that time, farm lands had increased in value, despite the war, to $1,238,766. Before the Civil War, corn, wheat, and oats were the primary agricultural products. Little cotton was cultivated in Cobb County before the war compared with other counties. The average farm size is not given in the 1850 census; however, there were about 1,200 rural households and 52,697 improved acres in the county. Each family would have worked about 44 acres of its entire holdings, on the average. The bulk of undeveloped land was left forested.

In 1890, farmers produced more than ten thousand bales of cotton and nearly three thousand tons of cotton seed. Corn was still heavily produced at 318,738 bushels in 1850 to 347,786 bushels in 1890. At this time, the average farm was 86 acres in size, and there were 2,080 farms operating on 98,240 cultivated acres, more than twice the amount under cultivation in 1850. Fifty-one percent of all farms were operated by farm tenants rather than owners. If anything, Cobb County became more agricultural rather than less after the Civil War, while in other places in the nation as well as the Southeast, the forces for urbanization and industrialization were more dominant.

In 1930, there were 3,233 farms in Cobb County, down from an all time high in 1920 of 3,698. Seventy-five percent of the county land was being farmed, and a wide variety of cash crops were produced such as dairy products, fruit, poultry, stock, trucked items for local consumption, and specialty crops. Nonetheless, 2,600 of the three thousand farms were categorized as cotton producers. The average farm size was 49 acres, a little more than half the size of the average farm in 1890; one third of all Cobb County farms contained fewer than 50 acres. An additional 20 percent of the farms contained more than 50 acres, while only ten percent of all county farms had more than 100 acres. Nearly 62 percent of Cobb County farms were tenant operated.

Farm tenancy and sharecropping systems had worked to reduce the size of the average farm; by 1930, the national economic depression, the havoc of the boll weevil, and declining cotton prices combined to erode the viability of southern farming, including Cobb County. The value of local farms decreased from 15 million dollars in 1920 to slightly more than eight million in 1930, at which time fully one-third of the county's farmers were in debt. Over the next twenty years, agricultural cultivation declined. By the late 1940s, only half the county was in farm land, and of this fewer than 30,000 acres were in actual cultivation. More than 100,000 acres of former farm land lay idle and abandoned, in pasture, or in woodland. The number of farms also decreased by half.

Antebellum Landscape Characteristics

There are four important elements to the antebellum landscape, which shaped the face of the county, traces of which today constitute parts of the county's historic resources. These four elements include: (1) the farmscape with all its components such as the buildings, associated fields, fences, and boundaries; (2) the industrial structure such as factories, mills, and the early railroads; (3) the road systems which developed; and (4) the communities which developed in the rural sections of the county and which functioned as social, religious, or economic nodes for clusters of population but which did not become population centers or towns.

The Farmscape

The first white inhabitants in Cobb County were traders and prospectors who moved through the county in the 1820s. These pioneers seldom created permanent settlements or left much development behind them. In the 1830s, when the county was carved from the Cherokee lands of Georgia, the permanent settlers moved in, usually just one step behind the land speculators. These settlers, of English, Scotch-Irish, and occasionally German descent, came from two migratory sources. They originated from the Great Pennsylvania Wagon Route which ran from the middle states through Virginia and the Carolinas into Georgia and Tennessee. Most of North Georgia was settled by first or second generation migrants along this route. The other source of population was the coastal areas of South Carolina and Georgia, directly up the rivers and then, after 1840, by the railroad. These settlers moved wherever the land was cheap and fertile, and then moved on when the soils were exhausted. They farmed, intent on subsisting, not on building centers or culture or commerce.

Hyde farm, which has been in continuous operation since the 1830s.

The house at the Hyde farm.

Outbuildings at the Hyde farm.

Their farming methods were often careless and exploitative and they abandoned lands as quickly as they settled them. The land they found in Cobb County was fertile; this is especially true for the lands along the bottomlands of the Chattahoochee, which were estimated to be worth more than twice as much as any other lands, upland or creek bottoms, in the county. According to gazetteer writer George White, who in 1849 published *Statistics of the State of Georgia,* Cobb County offered the settlers an excellent opportunity to grow corn, wheat, and cotton successfully.

In a few decades, many of the original pioneers moved on to the rich lands of the Mississippi and the Tombigbee. With their departure, the abandoned farm house became a feature of the county landscape. The sight of vacant farm houses and empty, often eroded, fields was still in evidence when General Sherman came through Cobb County in 1864, and these structures are often delineated on his maps of the area. Abandoned farms were plentiful after the Civil War, when blacks migrated from the southern counties to urban areas in the 1870s. In the 1910s, the boll weevil emptied even more farms, as did the Great Depression in the 1930s. Consequently, vacant farm houses have been part of the landscape from the first decades of Cobb County.

The land lotteries tended to spread out the population, and the settlers scattered over the countryside on their full or partial land lots. This settlement pattern produced small isolated farm sites scattered randomly over the land, some near roadways and trails, some not. In most instances, the farms came first, and then the roads.

The main barn at the Hyde farm.

Each farm site would have consisted of a small clearing for the house and outbuildings, with marker trees and close-by kitchen gardens, fenced-in fields, and woodlands. The home would have at first been a crudely constructed log house with hand-hewn, probably squared logs. The larger the farm, the more dwellings and outbuildings and the more sizeable the fields; however, the components were alike. The grounds around the house and outbuildings would have little or no landscaping. There were no lawns, foundation plantings, and at first few ornamental plants.

Powers Cabin, one of the few standing pioneer cabins in Cobb County. Hewn logs have been covered with planking. The second chimney served the kitchen shed addition to the main part of the house.

The creation of the first sawmills facilitated construction of all buildings; the timber no longer had to be worked on the site, but could be bought already cut and worked. The railroads further facilitated construction by stretching the market range for the pre-worked timber of any sawmill. Cobb County, because of the presence of the Western and Atlantic Railroad from the beginning of the early 1840s, had access to the Tennessee interior and the coast of Georgia, as well as access to a dependable transportation route cutting diagonally across its own territory. Log houses were still being built in the isolated reaches of the state, including backwoods sections of Cobb County, until the outbreak of the Civil War; however, frame structures were preferred and were known to be built in the county from 1840 and on, possibly as early as the late 1830s.

Since the early settlers preferred to remain mobile, their structures were sturdy but not very permanently constructed. Likewise, their fences, split and stacked rail, lacked the permanence of rock walls in other parts of the country. A chimney built of fieldstone instead of clay-banked wood indicated that a family was rooted; the chimney was often the most permanent structural element on the farm. The houses were simply styled, fashioned along construction patterns which in some cases were centuries old. The most common sequence appears to have been a single room structure made of logs replaced by (or absorbed into) a linear, multi-room structure with the rooms all in a row, or stacked, two-by-two on top of each other. After the railroads were completed, it was common for the settlers to cover log structures with sawed wood and to install floors and ceilings where there had been only earth and exterior roofing. More finite description of architectural styles can be found within the architectural chapter of this report. It was the tradition in this part of Georgia to fence in the fields and let the livestock roam freely. Open ranges and fenced fields with four-to-six foot high fences were the norm and presented a far different landscape from that in the middle and northeastern states where, livestock pens were fenced and fields were left open.

One of the few field bridges left in Cobb County, this bridge is constructed of planks laid over logs.

An outdoor privy, an architectural form rarely found today in Cobb County.

The Tritt family farm complex is a hundred year-old farm site.

The house at Tritt farm.

Early Industrialization

Though an agricultural county, the area grew up with industrialization. When the county was formed in 1832, the cotton gin had been in use for three decades, the steam engine was being adapted to boats and railroad engines, and the United States was in the midst of a transportation revolution; the latter opened up much of the country and made it accessible for both settlement and development. Federal, state, and local governments were sponsoring canal projects, railroads and turnpikes. Private corporations were active as well. Cobb County was not without influences from transportation and industrial interests throughout its early history, but it was not fully transformed by the industrializing forces. In the late 1830s and the early 1840s, local mills were set up to serve agricultural needs for processing grains. At the same time, several important local manufacturing establishments were also founded along creeks in the county where the water supply was sufficient to run water-powered wheels and grindstones. In 1849, gazetteer George White reported that there were 21 grist mills and an equal number of sawmills in the county; in addition, he noted there were "merchant mills" on Sope Creek. The factories were located in Roswell, Lebanon (near Roswell), and along Sweetwater, Nickajack, and (as mentioned) Sope Creeks. The Ruff-Daniell mill complex, along Nickajack Creek, now comprises part of the Concord Covered Bridge Historic District (the first such designated district in the county). Also, the ruins of the Sope Creek Mills, which consisted of paper, grist, and sawmills, an associated village, and a nearby distillery, are listed on the National Register of Historic Places.

The early mill sites were all quite similar. The complex usually nestled alongside a creek in a narrow valley with the long side of a rectangular, multi-storied building parallel to the creek. The head and tail races would run out from the mill to the creek and dam. The building itself was wood or brick, usually on a stone foundation; the wheel itself was made of wood. Often a village, or at least the owner's farm complex, was associated with the mill.

Sawmills were often not water powered and sometimes were portable. With either horsepower or manpower, they could be transported through the woods and set up in temporary logging camps with only the crudest sort of shelter erected for the loggers.

Ferry services and improved roads either preceded or accompanied the factory developments and increased settlement in the county. Settlement in turn created the need for mail coach and stage lines. County historian Sarah Gober Temple, in *The First Hundred Years*, cited efforts to establish coach and mail routes during the years 1835 to 1841 between Marietta and places such as Decatur, Cassville, Cumming, Barnesville, Dahlonega and Canton. These routes would have tied in with routes to other parts of the state. Neither Mrs. Temple nor later historians seem to have determined which of these and other proposed stage and mail routes through Cobb actually were established; some certainly were, and discovering their routes and stopovers offer a challenge for future researchers.

Of all the transportation developments, however, the most important was the railroad. When the first railroad was completed through the county, it offered alternative locations for factories besides creek and river sites. After 1846, when the Western and Atlantic Railroad was complete through the county, though not all of the way between Chattanooga and the Georgia coast, industrial developments in Cobb County began to appear in small railroad towns such as Acworth, Big Shanty (later Kennesaw), and, of course, in Marietta. The rural industries which remained, many of which were revived after the Civil War, were not as successful as the railroad-served factories. In fact, the entire pre-war factory development in Cobb County never dominated the economy, served only local markets as opposed to regional or national ones, and never employed more than several hundred workers altogether. They were there to serve the agricultural and domestic interests of the county, not to redirect them.

According to the county's first chief historian, Sarah Gober Temple, author of *The First Hundred Years*, there was mining activity in the county as well; however, sufficient amounts of ore were not found to justify much large-scale mining, as in the area of Dahlonega. It was not until less precious ores were mined later in the nineteenth century that Cobb County had any mining activity of any size. Like the other industries, mining was no competitor to farming in the county's economy.

The Roads

When the county was formed in 1830, there were perhaps a half dozen important trading routes running through the county, and myriad footpaths. Many of the trade routes show up on the 1832 survey plats as mentioned earlier: Peachtree Trail, Sandtown Trail, and Shallowford (Hightower) Trail are among these. The first wagon routes, used by the settlers for both migration and trade, followed the Indian trails and the topography. These ran in east-west directions primarily. Other roads were built by the settlers as they needed them, which did not necessarily lead to central destinations but followed the topography from farmhouse to farmhouse as well as from farmhouse to the nearest other road. The roads often converged on each other in a haphazard manner. They began as regular paths for commerce and communication, and they belonged to the men and women who carved them out of the forest and rock. The roads were themselves a wilderness, barely cleared, unpaved, with puddles or dust holes, pits, stumps, and rocks as well as impossible curves and snags. They existed primarily to serve neighbors who lived at some distance removed from each other, but they were not designed to be particularly friendly to the tourist, the traveler, or the stranger. According to Robert Healy, the roads themselves, along with the courthouses, the early post offices, the churches, and the warehouse/trade centers, were important centers for cultural interaction; along with the other nodes, they fostered migration, visitation, communication, religion, family visitation, peddling, private hostelry, and bartering. They did not always have to lead anywhere for they were themselves destinations.

There was a tendency for the early roads to follow the section and land lot lines, which follow the compass points; such section line roads can still be found in Cobb County. These roads include all or parts of the following: Corner Road, Lost Mountain Road (but not Old Lost Mountain Road), Old Villa Rica Road, Allgood Road, Macland Road (beyond Villa Rica Road), Terrell Mill Road, Old Canton Road, portions of Holly Springs Road, portions of Johnson Ferry Road, Holt Road, Hill Road, Sullivan and James Roads, Clay Road (the western parts), Hurt Road, Hawkins Store Road, Greers Chapel Road, Bells Ferry Road, and portions of Trickum Road. Other old roads can be identified in the county not from their configuration but from their names and association with early transportation and other industrial enterprises; examples are all of those marked "ferry" or "mill" road. Some early farm roads were named for the family who owned them, such as McLain Road and Kirk Road; however, road naming for individuals continues even today in the county and is not an indication of land use patterning so much as of land ownership.

Communities and Communal Nodes

The self-sufficiency of southern farms, especially in areas where there were full-scale plantations, precluded the development of villages and towns as the main center of population. People lived, by and large, in separate and isolated farmsteads, which were capable of sustaining life, providing most needs, and some small luxuries. Farms were not clustered into small communities in proximity, such as in Europe and England where farm houses were grouped together along the road while the fields were scattered; instead, in the South, both farm houses and fields were scattered. A "village", subsequently, could be comprised of a single landowner's holdings, especially if he functioned as a miller or post master, and members of his extended family lived nearby. Wherever there was a gristmill, a blacksmith shop, or a church, there were the makings of a "community." The few shops were mostly general stores which grew out of milling and blacksmith operations; there were no inns to speak of.

MILITIA DISTRICTS

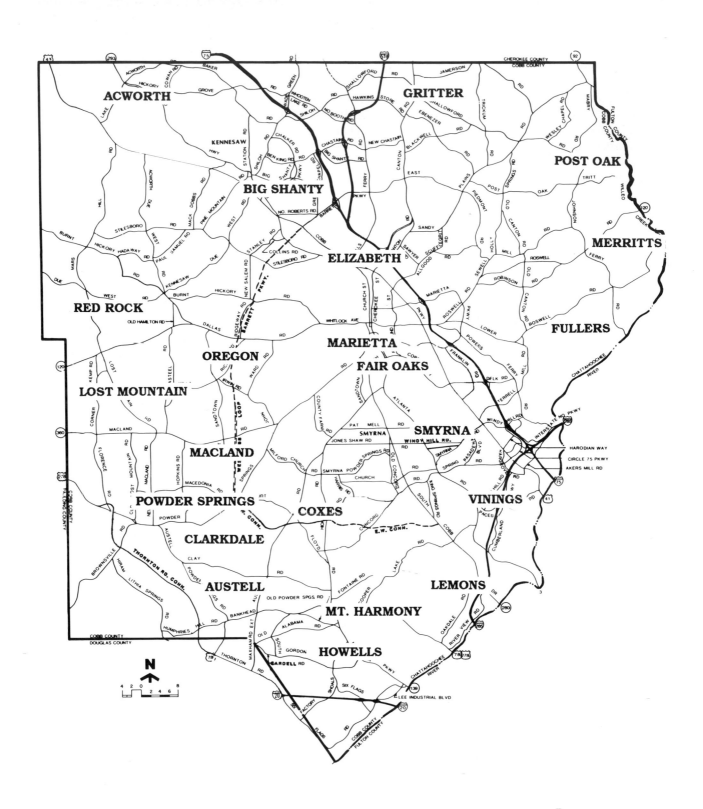

Cobb County was no exception to this pattern, except along the railroad, where true towns and villages were more likely to develop. Even along the rail line, it was not inevitable that every stop would become a major population center. Vinings is a good example of how small a railroad stop could be until well into the twentieth century.

In most cases, the "neighborhood" in Cobb County consisted of the entire militia district or at least the 100 original militiamen and their families who petitioned for the political unit to be organized. Militia districts grew out of a colonial practice. As soon as 100 heads of households were located in an area, a militia district was organized as a defensive zone, expected to form a "home ground" defense. One district provided one militia unit. As the population grew, a new militia district was formed to protect 100 households. In later years, militia districts became population census enumeration areas, and in some areas they became voting districts. Occasionally, the name of the district remained as the sole community identifier when no other element was appropriate.

Lost Mountain Crossroads Community at Dallas Highway, Lost Mountain Road and Mars Hill Road.

The names of the districts were taken either from a prominent place within the district, such as Marietta, Powder Springs, or Lost Mountain, or from one of the originators, such as Coxes, Merritts, Howells, or Lemons. The families spread themselves throughout the district, relating to whatever communal nodes existed within it, such as churches, smithies, crossroads, parade grounds, or religious campgrounds. These "uncentered" places, as John Stilgoe has described them, served very large geographic areas. According to historian Joan Sears' work, which covers the development of towns in North Georgia, trade was carried on among farmers who were also the local masons, carpenters, and justices of peace as well as blacksmiths and post masters. A village was created when a critical concentration of non-farm tasks and structures coalesced to include a tavern, a doctor, a lawyer, a hotelier, craftsmen, and store owners. What was sold in the village were the things the farmers could not make for themselves, such as rifles, iron tools, and a few luxuries. Generally, the farmer stayed on the farm and did not venture into town unless absolutely necessary.

CROSSROAD COMMUNITIES

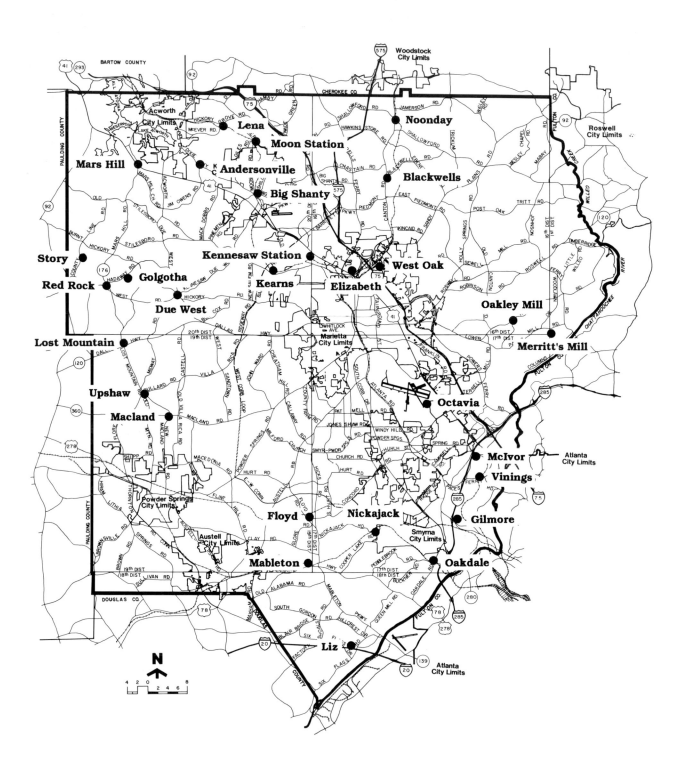

In 1849, George White recorded several post offices located in Cobb County. These included Marietta, Powder Springs, Acworth, Golgotha (Gilgal Church Community), Roswell (now in Fulton County), Lebanon (once located near Roswell and also now in Fulton County), and Mill Grove (possibly the Nickajack community). White did not mention the militia districts and, therefore, missed a major organizing feature of this and other Georgia counties.

The nature of these "non-village" communities can be ascertained from some contemporary descriptions, such as White's study and local lore. The Due West community, a very old pioneer community, was founded at the point along the Alabama Road due west along Coffee's line, which separated the Creek Indian Lands from the Cherokee Indian Land. Coffee's line was located due west of the Shallow Ford on the Chattahoochee. This was the furthermost settlement point in Creek country prior to the official opening of Cobb County. The community formed itself around several pioneer families including the Kemps of Sandtown Road, the Goodwins on Acworth Road, the Davises on Burnt Hickory, and the Darby Family on Marietta Highway. Vinings was inhabited in the 1830s, but did not have a post office until Hardy Pace moved his post office from his ferry site in 1839. Undoubtedly, he anticipated trade coming through with the railroad, which was under construction. Coxes District is another illustration; it consisted of almost everything which is today in South Cobb, from Mableton south to the Chattahoochee. In 1840, according to Harold Glore, there were seventy families including a total of 501 inhabitants; of the latter, 59 were slaves. The majority of the residents were farmers with only nine occupied in some kind of manufacturing; these made boots and shoes, cotton goods, flour and meal, leather goods, paper, saddles, harnesses, and woolen goods. In all of Coxes, there was not one "center" of commerce. Mableton was a small collection of families, barely a crossroads village, and not the commercial point it became later when the railroad was built through it.

The Old Pavilion House, Vinings. The Pavilion was built near the Vinings Spring by the railroad. It was used for entertainment and refreshment by visitors who "took the train out" from Atlanta to the country.

The Nickajack settlement on Nickajack Creek with its factories, constituted a community, according to the definition here, as did the Sope Creek community; the latter was actually incorporated as a town for a short period, beginning in 1859. This pattern of uncentered, villageless, or barely nodal communities has persisted throughout the nineteenth century into the twentieth. A school, a roadside business, a railroad siding, all could serve as a magnet for a community. The Lost Mountain community is a case in point; the militia district here was formed relatively late. Lost Mountain post office appears on Civil War maps, and the store has been serving the local populace for a century at least.

4040 Building, now Old Vinings Inn Bar, Vinings. This structure has also served as a community store with gas pumps, as a retail specialty store and as antique shops. It was originally designed to be used for apartments.

Preservation Assessment

There are two basic types of historic resources which date from the antebellum period, i.e., from the first settlement to 1860. These include the ruins of the early factories and the remaining early farm houses, including log houses and frame houses built in early folk and vernacular types. There are only a handful of free-standing log structures; they are very rare in Cobb County. There are possibly 200 early house forms in the county, not all of them built before the Civil War. These early types, such as I-houses, hall and parlor houses, and double-pen houses in several variations, constitute the best of Cobb County's early rural architecture, and as a group merit historical identification. Many of these are in good repair as they have been continuously occupied for a century or more; some are dilapidated, others are so heavily altered that they are barely recognizable. The mills and factories, which have not been demolished, lie in ruins. Most were rebuilt after the Civil War, but did not flourish. The most singular examples are at Sweetwater Creek (just outside Cobb County and owned by the Georgia Conservancy), and in Roswell (now in Fulton County), but the collection of structures in the Concord Covered Bridge Historic District is undoubtedly the most representative of the characteristics of early mill development in Cobb

The Solomon K. Pace house, Vinings. The Pace plantation was burned during the Civil War and this structure dates in part from immediately after the war.

The Carter-Vanneman homeplace, Vinings. Surrounded by magnificent oak trees, this house is central to the character of the remaining village atmosphere.

County. The ruins definitely deserve protection; they contain the potential for archaeological investigation. No known sawmills and few early mines remain; either would offer significant information on the county history if located.

The roads, even though in some instances their names have been changed, remain as roadways in the county today. Although improved, by widening and regrading in many cases and paving in almost all cases, the roads still follow the general routes of the originals. Some of the earliest wagon routes and Indian trails might be marked as such, since their early names have given way to the highway numbering systems and much of the original topography removed. There are only rare instances in the county where a true, narrow and unpaved rural road can still be found. McLain Road and parts of Hyde Road are examples. If rural essence in its totality is a preservation objective in the county, at least one such road, as part of a larger farm landscape, should be protected.

The Civil War Landscape

The stories of Civil War encounters in Cobb County have been extensively told in other histories, and it is not the purpose here to reiterate the details of each battle, skirmish, or entrenching; rather, the intention is to evaluate the whole in its effects on the landscape in unincorporated Cobb County and the potential for historic preservation.

There are several important points to make about the war in Cobb County, which are relevant to the remnant resources: (1) the intensity of battle and the level and frequency of the encounters made Cobb County one of the major battlefield centers in the war; three of the eight major battles fought on the march to Atlanta were fought on county soil; (2) Cobb County was in itself a strategic target during the war because of factories and the railroad; and (3) Cobb County provided natural defenses in its mountains (Kennesaw, Pine and Lost Mountains especially) and in the Chatta-

Restored farmhouse at the site of the Battle of Lattimore's Farm.

THE CIVIL WAR IN COBB COUNTY

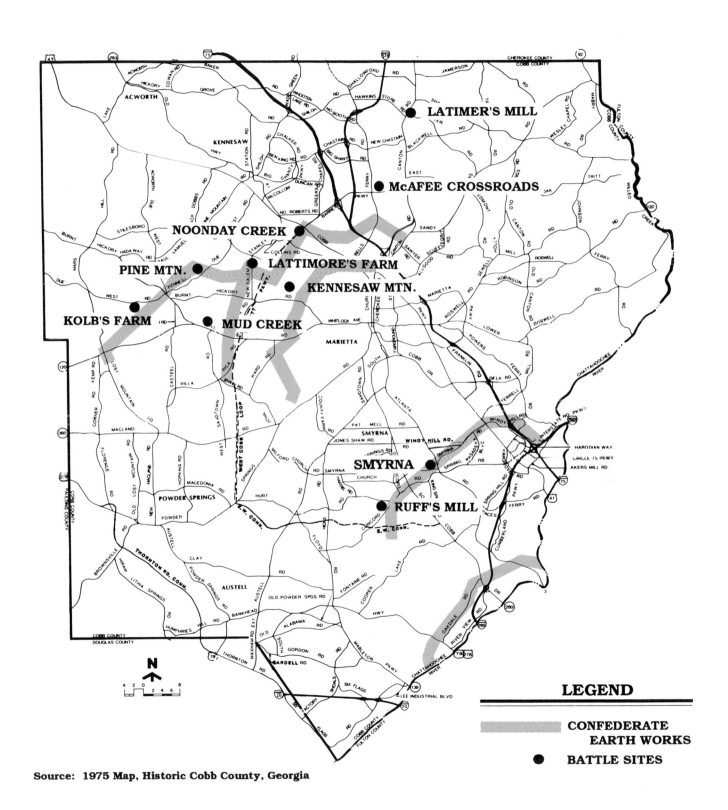

Source: 1975 Map, Historic Cobb County, Georgia

hoochee River. In 1862, Andrews Raid occurred in the county. Military activity occurred in the summer of 1864 between June 4, when General Sherman entered the county, and July 9, when Confederate General Johnston evacuated his defenses along the Chattahoochee, leaving the county in Sherman's hands. A calendar of events during those few weeks proves the intensity of the confrontation.

On Saturday, June 4, 1864, Sherman set up his first headquarters in Cobb County; the next day he moved toward a deserted Acworth; there were skirmishes down Sandtown Road and Acworth-Kennesaw Road. By June 7, the railroad above Acworth was repaired, and a Federal garrison was established at Allatoona. On June 9, Sherman set up his headquarters at Big Shanty, while the Confederates were stretched out in a line which ran between Lost Mountain, Gilgal Church, Due West crossroads, and the Western and Atlantic Railroad line, with signal stations at Lost Mountain, Pine Mountain, and Kennesaw Mountain. On June 14, the Federals took Pine Mountain. On the fifteenth, in "one grand skirmish extending from along a front of eight miles", to use the words of historian Sarah Gober Temple, the Battles of Gilgal Church, Pine Mountain and Noonday Church occurred. On June 16, the troops engaged each other at Lost Mountain, and on June 17, the Federals occupied Lost Mountain and also fought the Battle of Mud Creek. On June 18, the opposing forces met in the Battle of Lattimore's Farm, bringing them close to Kennesaw Mountain. On the 19th, there was skirmishing at the base of the mountain. On June 22, the armies fought the Battle of Kolb's Farm. Between the 10th of the month and the 27th, there was continuous skirmishing in the eastern portions of the county, with the Federal troops moving toward Roswell. Between June 27 and July 3, the Federals assaulted the Confederate defenses on top of Kennesaw Mountain, including the Battle of Cheatham Hill nearby. On July 4th, fighting continued at Smyrna Campground and at the Ruff Mill. On July 5th, Johnston retreated to his entrenchments along the Chattahoochee while the Federal forces occupied Vinings. On July 6, the Federal troops burned the Roswell mills and factories. On July 9th, Johnston evacuated his position and Cobb County was under the control of General Sherman. On the 15th of July, Sherman removed the factory workers from Roswell and Sweetwater and shipped them north to detention camps. On the 16th, he occupied Marietta, the county seat.

The effects of the Civil War on the landscape were twofold: (1) the destruction of material and buildings because they were targets of war or merely in the way of the fighting, and (2) the construction of wartime landforms such as earthworks, fortifications, breastworks, and entrenchments. Primary targets were the railroad and the factories. All of the factories were burned and had to wait for the end of the war for rebuilding at private expense. Since such reconstruction took place in most cases, none of the ruins of the antebellum industries are found today as they were before the war. The railroad was rebuilt largely at Federal expense because it was the supply route for the occupying forces. The re-creation of the rail line gave this northwest sector of Georgia, from the border to Atlanta, an advantage in reconstruction after the war, but it also allowed thousands of homeless Georgians access to the towns along its rails, creating serious health and welfare problems in Atlanta and its surrounding territories, including Cobb County.

Nonetheless, the farm culture was devastated and agriculture rendered unsuccessful due to social, transportation, and communication breakdowns. Agricultural historian Willard Range estimates that it took two decades for the pre-war levels of corn crop production to be regained. Cotton cultivation recovered more rapidly, in approximately 15 years; however, since Cobb County had not participated extensively in cotton cultivation before the war, its "recovery" was tantamount to a new agricultural direction. Real and personal property values ultimately increased again, but historian Temple reported a decrease in land values after the Civil War of almost one million dollars and an eight million dollar decrease in all property, including more than two million dollars in slaves. Some of the results have already been implied elsewhere, chief among them being the breakup of the larger plantations into smaller ones and an overall decrease in the average size of the individual farm. The wartime destruction also caused about a twenty-year delay in the development of large-scale industries; it was not until the 1880s, with the placement of new railroad lines through other sections of the county, that local manufacturing expanded.

The county was left not only with the rubble of its own foundations but also the refuse of war chiefly in the form of abandoned earthworks and material. The extent of these earthworks is indicated by the sheer size of the Civil War historic sites already recognized in Cobb County; they include remaining trenches of Johnston's River Line (listed in the National Register of Historic Places and the Cobb Register of Historic Places), the trenches associated with the Gilgal Church Battlefield site (listed in the National Register of Historic Places), and trenches at the Kennesaw Mountain National Battlefield Park, itself a National Register site.

Preservation Assessment

The Civil War impact on Cobb County is history written on the face of the land. The series of actions and counteractions, which constitute one major section of the march on Atlanta, have the highest level of historic significance of anything which has ever happened in the county. This fact is already recognized by the presence of a National Park devoted to one of the battles fought in Cobb County, by the number of sites in the county which have Civil War associations and are designated historic sites in the National Register of Historic Places (Johnston's River Line and Gilgal Church Battlefield), by the number of historical markers denoting troop movements and engagements, and by other assorted Civil War related sites such as the Little General Museum in Kennesaw. The Bicentennial Survey of historic places in Cobb County conducted by Dr. Philip Secrist identified nearly three dozen sites related to the Civil War as historically significant places in the county.

The Civil War military actions were fought primarily in western Cobb County, in Districts 20 and 19, sections of the county which until very recently were not programmed for large-scale suburban development. The Civil War battlefields, as well as older structures which may have been standing at the time of the war, could well exist in undisturbed peace. Today, however, development pressures are increasing in west Cobb County, and these areas are in danger of being lost. Despite heavy pillaging by Civil War buffs and treasure seekers, each one of the battlefield sites still has potential for important archaeological recovery; each one contributes something to the full story of Cobb County during the war, which is much more considerable than the Battle of Kennesaw Mountain alone can tell. Yet, except for Kennesaw Mountain Battlefield Park and its ancillary units, none of the Civil War sites are currently protected from contemporary encroachment. The battlefield lands are largely in the hands of private owners and as such are protected as long as the owners respect their history -- only the Johnston's River Line has, to date, been designated as a county site. No county designation protects other Civil War sites. Those listed in the National Register of Historic Places have no protection from private development and only limited protection from federally licensed or subsidized projects.

The New South Landscape, 1870 - 1940

Between the end of the Civil War era and the United States' entrance into World War I, the history of Cobb County reflects both national trends towards urbanization and industrialization and regional trends towards agrarian persistence. The county experienced moderate growth throughout these decades except for the period immediately following the Civil War, as noted earlier. The addition of more railroad lines in the county created more incentives for industry to develop along the tracks, accounting in turn for some of the population increases in the county's railroad towns. During the same years, other modernizations came to Cobb County, such as electrification, sewers, the telephone and the automobile. It was, however, the middle of the twentieth century before these modern features were found extensively in the rural sections of the county. The effects of all these forces on the landscape were varied. Most obviously, there were more and different kinds of structures on the land, some new configurations to the towns (street grids following the railroad tracks, for example) and for the first time on such a large scale, topographic changes from culvert cutting for roads and rail beds. The scale of buildings to the land remained relatively unchanged. Until the 1940s, the largest building in the county was probably not more than four stories tall nor wider nor deeper than a half city block.

The "Urbanization" of Cobb County

In the 1870s the county population grew from 13,814 people to 20,748, an increase of 50 percent over the 1870 figure and of 45 percent over the 1860 pre-Civil War high. The population lost during the war years was regained and surpassed in numbers. In the same decade, the black population nearly doubled in actual numbers (from 3,217 persons to 6,012) and increased as a percentage of the total population as well (from 23 percent to 28 percent). In 1890 Cobb County's black population was 30 percent of the total and the highest it has ever been in the county's history. Two factors probably account for the increase: (1) the availability of work in the rail towns, and (2) the increase in cotton production in the county.

Black history in Cobb County is like black history everywhere in that it is primarily anonymous. To date, most black history in the county refers to black history in Marietta and larger towns, which lie outside the scope of this study. What is known is that black farming communities were formed after the Civil War and during the period of late 19th century agricultural expansion. These outlying communities were centered in their churches, scattered across the county, like Mt. Zion African Methodist Episcopal Church.

The population was not only increasing in size; however moderately, it was also shifting from countryside to town. This shift, an urbanizing redistribution of the population, can be measured in several ways, beginning with the development of the towns themselves. Though most of the Cobb County towns have pre-Civil War origins, their corporate entities date from the 1870s and 1880s, when they received town charters from the state. Marietta was incorporated in 1834, Acworth in 1870, Smyrna in 1872, Powder Springs in 1883, Austell in 1885, and Big Shanty (as Kennesaw was called) in 1887.

Between 1880 and 1940, the Cobb County towns grew at a faster rate than the county itself. Between 1880 and 1900 the towns grew by 104 percent while the county as a whole grew only 18 percent; between 1898 and 1920 the equivalent figures were 49 percent for the towns and 23 percent for the county. Between 1920 and 1940 town growth abated; during this period the entire county grew 25 percent and the towns 26 percent. The loss of Roswell to Fulton County in 1933 is reflected in that decrease; without Roswell, Cobb County was more rural.

Another way of looking at the urbanization of the county is to consider the town population as a percentage of the total county population. In 1880, the population of the five separately enumerated towns that year (Acworth, Marietta, Kennesaw, Roswell, and Smyrna) constituted 16 percent of the county's population. In 1900, Powder Springs and Austell were included in the separate township enumerations, and the urban population increased to 27 percent. By 1920, this figure rose to 49 percent and by 1940 to 50 percent. In 1940, even though 75 percent of the land was in farms, half of the population, according to the U. S. Census that year, lived in towns.

These towns, however, were little more than villages. They served as market, political, and educational centers for their militia district populations, and if they had banks, they were financial centers as well. Austell, Marietta and Roswell had banks in the late nineteenth century, but the others did not until the twentieth century. Since the town of Roswell and the militia district were co-terminus, Roswell appears to be the most "urbanized" of all the county listings. Austell also had a high percentage of its population in town, i.e. never less than 64 percent between 1900 and 1940. Kennesaw (Big Shanty) Militia District and Powder Springs were the most rural of the

TOWN POPULATION

	1880	1900	1920	1940
Acworth Militia District	1821	2294	2875	3042
Acworth Town	633	937	1370	2077
% of Militia District Population in Town	35%	41%	48%	68%
Austell Militia District	n/a	1017	1490	1912
Austell Town		648	997	1631
% of Militia District Population in Town		64%	67%	85%
Big Shanty Militia District	1463	1399	1584	2071
Kennesaw Town	244	320	254	352
% of Militia District Population in Town	17%	23%	16%	17%
Marietta Militia District	5461	7814	13468	14958
Marietta Town	2227	4446	10232	12298
% of Militia District Population in Town	41%	57%	76%	82%
Powder Springs Militia District	1978	2017	1814	2017
Powder Springs Town	n/a	262	301	489
% of Militia District Population in Town		13%	17%	24%
Roswell Militia District	1180	1329	1588	n/a
Roswell Town	1180	1329	1440	
% of Militia District Population in Town	100%	100%	91%	
Smyrna Militia District	1087	1185	2802	2882
Smyrna Town	259	238	1791	2110
% of Militia District Population in Town	24%	20%	64%	73%
Total County Population	20748	24664	30437	38272
% Urban	22%	27%	49%	50%
% Increase for the County	—	18%	23%	25%
% Increase in Urban Population	—	104%	99%	26%

districts, with no more than a quarter of their populations residing in town. Other militia districts (e.g. Gritters, Merritts and Post Oak) had no communities large enough for the census to count them as separate entities, even though Vinings, for example, had long been recognized as a village. Mableton also achieved incorporated status during this time.

Marietta was the only significant population center, and it was still a small town. In the sixty years between 1880 and 1940, its population nearly doubled resulting in a total population of 8,000 persons. Smyrna was a small town of a few hundred people until after the Atlanta-Marietta Interurban Railway line was constructed. There was a great deal of residential development in the Smyrna area and all along the railroad in the 1900s and 1910s, but the overall effect was more that of suburbanization than urbanization of Smyrna. It became not so much a cultural and economic center as a bedroom community for both Marietta and Atlanta. Austell and Acworth, despite large percentage increases in their populations, remained small towns with 1,600 and 2,000 inhabitants respectively. Powder Springs and Kennesaw were also relatively small, with a few hundred residents each at the beginning and the end of the period (1870 - 1940).

RAILROADS IN COBB COUNTY

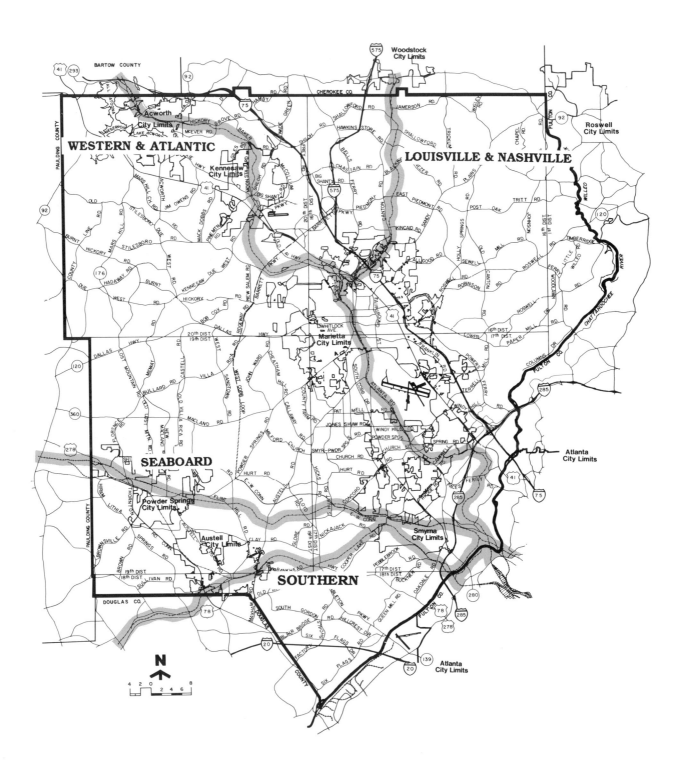

Railroad Developments, 1880-1910

The addition of three more railroad lines running through Cobb County accounted for an increase in industrial activity along the rail lines as well as the growth in railside communities. The importance of the railroad can be seen in the single fact that by 1910 all towns and communities of any size whatsoever were located along the major lines which ran through the county. These included Acworth, Kennesaw, Marietta, Smyrna and Vinings on the Western and Atlantic, Austell and Mableton on the Southern, and Powder Springs on the Seaboard Coast (now CSX) line.

The rail line which runs through Austell was planned in the 1850s but it did not become reality until the 1880s. In 1880 the Georgia Pacific Railroad, as it was called, came under the directorship of Civil War General John B. Gordon, who saw the system completed between Birmingham and Atlanta. In the 1890s the line was taken over by the Southern Railroad system, established in 1894. The Seaboard Coast line, completed in 1904, also connected Atlanta and Birmingham and was designed to compete with the Southern line through Austell.

One of several wood trestle railroad bridges still standing in Cobb County, this one is over Cooper Lake Road.

The third of the new lines ran from Marietta north. The Marietta and North Georgia line was chartered in 1885 connecting Marietta with the mineral resources in North Georgia; the latter consisted chiefly of marble and copper according to Sarah Gober Temple. The line was begun in 1870 to connect Marietta, Canton and Ellijay and was subsequently completed to Jasper in 1883. It was taken over by the Atlanta, Knoxville and Northern in bankruptcy proceedings and ultimately the line was completed to Tennessee. The importance of the railroad to the development of Cobb communities lies in the establishment of the town, now a community, of Elizabeth which lies at

A view of the south side of Marble Mill Road in Elizabeth.

Marble Mill Road, Elizabeth

the juncture of the Western and Atlantic and the old Atlanta, Knoxville and Northern line running north to Ellijay. Marble Mill Road, named for the marble works which grew up at the end of the railroad line, is the main residential street in Elizabeth, running between the mill (since then totally lost, except for a chimney, in the maze of a chemical factory now on the site) and the railroad (which bisects the street). The Louisville and Nashville line took over the Atlanta, Knoxville and Northern line in 1904 and Elizabeth continued to be a railroad community for the Louisville and Nashville workers.

The impact of the railroads is evident in other ways too. The configurations of some of the town streets, for example, reflect the importance of railroad frontage to their development. The main streets in Acworth, Mableton (old section) and Austell all parallel the railroad tracks. The railroads also brought a host of new and different structures into the county such as depots, sidings, trestles, bridges over the tracks, service buildings, station signs, crossing signs, rail yards, workers' housing and miles of tracks.

Industrialization, 1870-1940

According to historian Dr. Tom Scott, the industrialization which came to Cobb County in the latter decades of the nineteenth century was not the "salvation" people had hoped it would be. The factories which were built produced a small low-wage working class who were somewhat better off than tenant farmers but not as well off as landowners, and a small upper class of prosperous businessmen. Cobb County industry did not produce any multi-millionaires or dominant local patriarchs such as the Callaway family in Troup County, who profited from the mills in LaGrange, Georgia. In 1870 there were 21 manufacturing establishments in Cobb County including seven leatherworks, seven sawmills, two cotton manufacturers, three woolen goods factories, one flour mill, and one paper mill. The value of manufactured goods already slightly exceeded the value of agricultural products as expressed in $846,000 as compared with $811,000. In a few decades, the discrepancy between the valuations grew; in 1890, there were 60 industrial establishments producing $834,548 in goods while agriculture produced goods valued at $753,550. Both figures are relatively low for 1890, a reflection of business depression for the manufacturers and low cotton prices for the farmers. By 1940, the county was producing manufactured goods worth more than twice as much as the value of agricultural products, or six million dollars as opposed to 2.9 million dollars.

Textile manufacturing became the most important industry in Georgia and the largest employer among local industries in Cobb County. By 1900, the county had six textile mills besides the factories in Roswell. There were, however, greater concentrations of textile mills in Richmond, Clarke, Muscogee and Upson Counties than in Cobb County. In the 1880s one third of all the local mills were grist mills, with the sawmills and blacksmith shops being next in importance; however, by 1900 the focus of enterprise was on cotton goods production. Also the location of the mills had generally shifted from creekbeds to towns, especially Marietta.

The Perkerson Mill, though not a textile mill, offers a good example of the kind of transition in location and market which was taking place. This mill was founded in the early days of Cobb County as a grist mill; it was bought nearly 20 years after its founding in 1851 by John S. Perkerson who moved to Cobb County from DeKalb County. At the time Perkerson bought it, the mill was a one-man operation, according to the family history of the place. The mill was burned during the Civil War and rebuilt in a larger building on Sweetwater Creek. In time Perkerson added a wheat mill, a saw mill, and a cotton gin to the original corn mill. After the first railroad line was completed through south Cobb, the mill flourished despite the fact that cotton cultivation in the area was leaching the soils and silting Sweetwater Creek making the waters very sluggish. The mill owner had a small branch operation built in Austell, powered by a gasoline engine; in 1928 the entire operation was moved to Austell. The mill was sold by the family in 1962 and closed permanently in 1975. In 1979 the buildings were demolished.

Marble Mill Road, Elizabeth

Marble Mill Road, Elizabeth

The early twentieth century did more than move mills like the Perkerson mill from a creek to a community; it brought with it expansions of all sorts. The 1910s brought the highest cotton prices since before the Civil War, and the greatest period of prosperity among Cobb's farmers that they had had in decades. The proximity to cotton supplies, the cheap available labor supply, and low political impediments brought northern textile companies into the South to establish new profit centers. Cobb saw at least two such developments by the Clark Thread Company, which bought the old Acworth hosiery mills in 1904, and in 1932 built Clarkdale, one of the last planned mill communities in Georgia.

It should be noted that the number of types of manufacturing establishments increased between 1870 and 1890; thereafter, the number decreased up to 1940. Meanwhile, the size of operations increased. In 1890 there were 60 establishments and the average number of employees was twelve persons. This is an increase over the 1870 figure of 21 establishments employing the same number of people per factory. In 1920 there were only 35 recognized manufacturers in Cobb County with an average of 57 employees. By the end of the period, the farmer/carpenter/miller concept as a single enterprise was all but extinct.

This water tower is all that remains of the hosiery factory at "Socktown," a 1930s industrial site at Furniture City.

Clarkdale. Side view of the **factory** buildings before 1980s renovation.

Clarkdale. A view of a street in the management section of the village.

New South Agriculture

Between the end of Civil War and the turn of the twentieth century, Georgia and the other southern states persisted as agricultural dominions in the face of agricultural depression. Farmers grew corn and cotton with the former for local consumption and the latter as a cash crop. The very low cotton prices from the end of the Civil War to the 1910s negatively affected area agriculture. Meanwhile, some of the energies of the state were directed toward manufacturing. The value of manufactured goods exceeded that of agricultural goods as early as 1870. However, the State of Georgia still attempted to upgrade its agricultural technologies and to educate its farmers. According to historian Willard Range, between 1865 and 1900 Georgia, both publicly and privately, tried to build new land management and labor systems and to become more scientific in its land cultivation. These efforts were partially successful. Various forms of crop sharing, land rentals, and land tenancy were introduced. Sharecropping and tenancy extended to landless whites as well as to former slaves. Directly after the Civil War, 65 percent of the population of Cobb County were classified as one kind of farmer or another. Most rural blacks were tenant farmers; the percentage of black-owned farms was very low. It was the typical pattern that the owners were white and the tenants were black.

Despite low prices, aggregate wealth in the county increased. The value of farm lands doubled between 1870 and 1890 from one to two million dollars. The per capita figure for taxable property of all kinds rose as expressed in a 23 percent increase between 1880 and 1890. At the same time, tenancy rose. By 1900, more than half of all Cobb County farmers were tenants rather than owners. The rise in tenancy was accompanied by an enormous growth in population. Historian Dr. Tom Scott found that only 22 percent of all heads of households who were in the county in 1880 remained there in 1900. This means that nearly 80 percent of the population turned over in that twenty-year period, a turnover of populace causing at least as great a disruption in the county's cultural continuity as the abolition of slavery. The growth in tenancy was also accompanied by a decrease in the average farm size. In the state, the average farm size dropped from 338 acres after the Civil War to 117 acres in 1900. In Cobb County, indicative of the smaller landholdings in the Upper Piedmont, the average dropped from 112 acres to 72 acres in the same period.

The number of owner-operated farms dropped as well; there was widespread absenteeism among owners. Immediately following the Civil War, it was the norm for an owner to live on and operate his own farm in Cobb County. By 1900, it was common practice for the owners to live elsewhere and for tenants on shares or other farm laborers to work the farms.

Ironically, the absentee ownership pattern would have encouraged commercialization by distancing the owner from a personal relationship with his land. Scientific procedures such as terracing, crop rotation, soil testing, and the use of fertilizer were put forth and made popular through agricultural journals and societies. The State Department of Agriculture was established in 1874 for the purpose of bolstering agrarian activity in Georgia. Its efforts were assisted by a whole series of activities at the county level. The Cobb County Agricultural Association, which sponsored county fairs and exhibits, was one such support group. This organization was formed in 1870 and held fairs for the express purpose of improving agricultural pursuits in Cobb County.

Agricultural reform, however, never achieved status as a major political force in Cobb County, according to both Temple and Scott, although the Grange, the largest southern farm reform organization, was active here.

A kind of reform arrived after 1900 as cotton prices increased, permitting local farmers to make capital improvements on their lands, purchase new machinery and subscribe to more modern competitive technologies. Diversification of crops also increased after 1900. Two decades of farm prosperity ensued, since 1911 and 1914 were bumper crop years for the whole state. Cotton was again "king" for awhile; more and more farmers planted it. Almost simultaneously with the rise in cotton prices, the boll weevil made its appearance, its larvae hatching in the cotton seeds and destroying them. The weevil arrived in Georgia in 1913; between 1919 and 1924, it began to do disastrous damage to Georgia cotton. During World War I, the farms of Cobb County, as elsewhere in Georgia, began to lose workers to the Army. Blacks left the farms in large numbers, and the War Department encouraged people to grow chickens and produce eggs rather than cotton. By the mid-1920s, Georgia's cotton yields were the lowest they had been in fifty years. By 1930, Cobb County farmers produced 18,000 bales of cotton, only 8,000 bales more than they had produced forty years earlier.

During the Depression, more cotton was produced than could be sold. Hundreds of farmers abandoned their fields, and thousands of acres of farmland reverted to pine forest. In the 1930s, the absolute number of farms decreased as did the acreage under cultivation in the county except for the largest commercial farms (over 1,000 acres) and the smallest farms (under three acres), used for family subsistence. Meanwhile, the percentage of cropland per active farm increased. There were fewer farmers, but the ones that remained were working harder.

Some farmers turned to dairy products, cattle farming, truck farming, peaches and other orchard crops, and specialty crops as sources of cash. Only dairy products and cattle ranging reached measurable proportions and persisted. During the depression and the Second World War, the federal government put limits on cotton growing and encouraged "banking" cotton land for subsidy. More than 300 acres in Cobb County were banked. By 1950, cotton cultivation in Georgia was all but dead. Of the 2,000 existing farms, only 165 grew cotton. The remainder of the farms were in livestock and dairy products, poultry, field crops, and cash grain production. An additional 100,000 acres of agricultural land was idle, lay in pasture, or had reverted to woodland. The long agrarian era was ended.

The Modernization of Cobb County

The attributes of modern society came to Cobb County before the end of the last century, i.e. to Marietta. Historian Temple tracked the signs of progress in this manner. First, electric street lights were introduced in Marietta in 1889, sewerage in 1896, and the first telephone in 1898. These tools and utilities of the modern age did not penetrate rural Cobb County at this time. The county residents did, however, benefit from the rural improvement programs of the Great Depression which included electrification, road refinements, sewers, and farm assistance of various sorts. Installation of utilities and sewers as well as road improvements are being carried out in the undeveloped sections of the county today.

The most important feature of modernity affecting the rural part of the county was the better roads program. The systems of paved streets and highway interconnections again focused on Marietta. In 1917, Marietta had the streets around the city square and one block in each direction away from the square paved. Between 1917 and 1921 the city carried out a more extensive program of paving. Beginning about the same time, the county began a federally subsidized program to improve (grading, widening and paving) highways through the county. The first to be paved were the Bankhead Highway, the Dixie Highway (State Route 3), the Canton Highway, and parts of Dallas and Austell Roads. By 1934, there were 50 miles of paved roads in Cobb County; few miles were added until after World War II.

The adoption of the automobile, the truck, the tractor and other gasoline-powered farm equipment put pressure on local governments everywhere for good roads. The adoption of the automobile had other effects as well; it brought with it a whole host of new structures to the

An early gas station, now featuring modern pumps.

Twentieth century roadside commercial buildings.

landscape such as service and filling stations, free standing gas pumps, garages and tourist homes, auto and parts dealerships, parking lots and driveways, and vehicular bridges over creeks, railroad tracks, and the Chattahoochee River.

The final feature of modernization to come to Cobb County during its agrarian period was the suburb. The first suburbs followed rail and trolley lines. Commuters between Cobb County and Atlanta took the railroad. By 1905, the Atlanta-Marietta Interurban Railway was in operation. This was a singular transportation development in Georgia since it traversed a largely rural area to connect two cities and it was the largest development of this kind in the southeast. Also, each stop on the trolley line generated residential development. In addition, much housing was built along the trolley route, which paralleled modern Route 3 through most of the county, between 1900 and 1930. The trolley ran until just after World War II, when the rail line was abandoned in favor of bus service. The former trolley stops are still well known places in Cobb County, though some have since disappeared. They include Jonesville (a black community absorbed into Dobbins Air Force Base), Fair Oaks, Mozley, and Belmont (absorbed into Smyrna), Smyrna, Gilmore and Oakdale, as well as Conways and Woodlawn (absorbed into commercial developments around Plant Atkinson). Log Cabin Road is part of the pattern of interconnecting suburban streets and the trolley line. Carmichael's was a trolley stop on Log Cabin Road.

The right-of-way for the Atlanta-Marietta Interurban trolley line is still visible along parts of Atlanta Road and Log Cabin Road.

A house along the Interurban Trolley Line on Log Cabin Road.

A house along the Interurban Trolley Line on Log Cabin Road.

Preservation Assessment

The older sections of Mableton reflect most of the forces for change operative during the historic period of Cobb County's past. There is the antebellum Mable House, other mid-nineteenth century houses along Church, Peak and Center Streets, one large altered Victorian mansion, a sprinkling of commercial store fronts on the main street facing the railroad tracks, some early twentieth century bungalow houses, a wooden vehicular bridge over the tracks, and some assorted early commercial buildings on the south side of the tracks. Furthermore, most of the very contemporary development is located south of Bankhead Highway.

There are a number of manufacturing sites in Cobb County. The old pre-Civil War mills, which were rebuilt and are now in ruins, have already been mentioned. Reflective of later developments would be Clarkdale, an exceptionally well preserved mill community, which has been listed on the National Register of Historic Places. The Glover Machine Works is a perfect example of the late nineteenth century industrial development and the ties it had to both local towns and railroad construction; this parcel of land was annexed to the City of Marietta in March of 1986 and is no longer under the jurisdiction of the county.

A house on Oakdale Road.

A house on Oakdale Road.

Marble Mill Road in Elizabeth has been mentioned as an important railroad community. The street contains examples of housing from the mid-nineteenth to the early twentieth century in a heterogencous mix ranging from large Victorian homes to small two or three room workers' cottages. Aside from the architecture, the street still bears the landscape imprint of early railroad construction with its uncurbed, dome-shaped, barely paved and tree-lined streets.

There are some remnants of early automobile-related structures, but most of the best examples of tourist homes and service stations are either gone or located within the Cobb County municipalities. There are no known tourist cabins or bungalow style motels along the early highways with any architectural integrity left to them. Most have been demolished or modernized beyond recognition.

Few historic bridges are left in Cobb County, either those constructed for early cars or field bridges which farmers used to get their tractors from the roadway to the fields over a creek or stream. In addition, there are only remnants of bridge piers for the highway developments in the 1930s, since virtually all of those early highways have been more recently improved (widened and repaved).

There are scores of incidental farms, farm structures, and rural residences, the generic styles for which are covered in the architecture section of this report. Two excellent examples of complete, working farm complexes which date to the late nineteenth century are the Tritt Family Farm on Post Oak Tritt Road and Hyde Farm.

The wooden vehicular bridge across the Southern Railroad tracks at Floyd Road, Mableton.

Late nineteenth century pyramidal hip-roofed house with Queen Anne style gables, Mableton.

Service building behind a residential structure in Mableton.

A hall and parlor style house on Center Street, Mableton.

A hall and parlor style house on Center Street, Mableton.

Glore House, an altered classical revival mansion in Mableton.

A pyramidal hip-roofed house on Front Street, Mableton.

Early twentieth century commercial structures in Mableton.

An early twentieth century commercial structure in Mableton.

LANDSCAPE III: SUNBELT SUBURBANIZATION

Cobb County is currently experiencing a population and building boom. Less than 40 percent of the county now remains undeveloped, or untouched by modern highrise commercial buildings, office parks, shopping malls, or suburban subdivisions. Since the mid-1970s, single-family subdivisions have accounted for the majority of the growth in the county. Later additions include shopping malls, apartment complexes, condominium developments, office towers, and suburban mixed use complexes involving retail centers, offices, and hotels.

Cobb County is a primary example of the kind of changes which have been taking place across the Southeast and Southwest since World War II. During this time, the entire southern region has been undergoing revolutionary land use changes and unprecedented growth. In recent years, intense competition over the land has developed, as the prime locations for population growth are also perceived as prime locations for airports, industrial plants, forestry, agribusiness, and commerce. In some areas, there are renewed (and more intensive) rural uses for the land such as poultry farming, soybean, peanut, and cattle production in the place of more traditional crops. At the same time, the center of national forestry interests has shifted from the Northwest to the Southeast, and forestry wishes to occupy the same land spaces as farming. Competition also comes from new and large industries including highly technical computerized communications and manufacturing. Furthermore, the population increases have produced intense pressure for housing services, shopping, transportation provisions, and commercial outlets. Tourism is placing increasing demands on the region, since the metropolitan Atlanta area serves as a major convention and tourist destination. The Atlanta area also serves as a major hub of automobile and air traffic, providing easy access to Cobb County as well.

The population statistics are telling. In 1940 Cobb County had a population which slightly exceeded 38,000 people. By 1980 the figure came to nearly 300,000 people. Furthermore, the Atlanta Regional Commission estimates that Cobb County will have a population of over a half million people by the year 2000. There are now, as a result of the demographic increases, several major population centers in Cobb County including the Marietta-Smyrna corridor, East Cobb (unincorporated but heavily populated), and South Cobb around Mableton and Austell. Still, Cobb County is not "urbanized" in the normal sense of being organized primarily into cities. The bulk of the county population lives in non-urban, but also non-rural (i.e. non-farm) circumstances. According to the County Data Book, 77 percent of the county population lived in unincorporated areas in 1980. Historically, Cobb County has never been a "citified" place; it still is not.

The implications of the rate of growth in Cobb County on the landscape are considerable. According to Robert Healy, author of an insightful book about contemporary land use in the South, the built-up uses drive out the rural uses of the unrelenting. The "centerless" places of the past are replaced by "faceless" places of the present as brick ranch houses replace farm houses, subdivisions fill in the green spaces, linear sprawl pushes out the roadside nodes and crossroads trading centers, and widened highways alter the setback relationship of all buildings to the streets and roadways. Healy suggests that a traveller returning south after a forty-year absence would hardly recognize the landscape.

Landscape Effects

The changes in the landscape are numerous and almost too obvious to enumerate. First there is the old agrarian landscape which now exists in remnants and pieces. What was once functional now appears "quaint" and irrelevant, useless and expendable. Reminders of the old systems appear scattered across the land, including sagging barns (often behind 1950s ranch houses), derelict tenant houses, and a few stands of ancient trees missing their homesteads. All of the sites and representative architectural specimens cited so far appear in the county. The effects of the automobile are prominent. They include new garages next to old farm houses, widened streets, an extensive highway system criss-crossing the county, pavements and parking lots everywhere, decentralized shopping, traffic lights, mobile homes and trailer parks. The relationship of the land and buildings has changed in three ways: (1) the land is much more densely occupied now, as can be seen in the places which have buildings and roadways on them which were previously open space; (2) the scale of the buildings is larger when compared to anything else which appears on the landscape such as trees or people; and (3) land holdings are much smaller while buildings are much larger than was the case during the agrarian past. In suburban developments, five acres is a large holding and not uncommon, as compared to even the smallest farm holding of forty or so acres in the past. Houses, however, are much larger as a rule than they used to be with more square footage and more rooms. The number of bedrooms (four per average house in the county's new subdivisions) equals the total number of rooms in pioneer homes. Swimming pools and tennis courts are frequently seen in multi-family complexes and are not uncommon in single-family housing areas. Two other changes in the landscape are more ironic in their effects. One, the appearance of the forested areas of the county, which are probably similar to the piney forests which the Cherokee and Creek tribes were accustomed to seeing, though today's forests are not aboriginal. Two, a current trend to build houses in "nostalgic" architectural styles, which evoke early colonial (Williamsburg, especially) and Victorian house forms and details, lends visual amenity and pleasure to some of the latest subdivisions and an occasional commercial development. These late designs indicate a new awareness of architectural traditions, if not local Cobb County or southern regional traditions. The village of Vinings is a noteworthy example.

Historic Elements of the Modern Changes

The establishment of the Bell Bomber Plant just south of Marietta is viewed by many as the single precursor to the modern Cobb County. In 1941, Cobb County purchased 600 acres of land for a municipal airport to rival Candler Field, now Hartsfield International Airport, in Atlanta. Named Rickenbacker Field after the World War I flying ace, it was constructed by the Army Corps of Engineers in 1941 and 1942. In 1943 the Federal government leased space to the Bell Bomber manufacturers for the assembly of B-29 bombers during World War II. The plant was active for the duration of the war but closed shortly thereafter. At its peak, 29,000 people worked near a city with fewer than 10,000 inhabitants. According to James V. Carmichael, the first director of the airplane works plant, Bell opened up in one "fell swoop" a viable, year-round, full-time, good wage opportunity for the entire county and catapulted Cobb County into the twentieth century. When Bell abandoned the plant shortly after World War II, thousands of workers were laid off; a similar prosperity was not felt again by the county residents until Lockheed Aircraft Corporation out of Burbank, California, took over the Bell plant in 1951 during the Korean conflict. Since that time, Lockheed has continued to be the largest employer in the county and one of the most important in the fifteen-county Atlanta metropolitan area.

There were other new developments beside the Bell Bomber Plant which were important in their own right. One such development was the penetration of Cobb County by utility interests in the twentieth century. The direct effects of this development are both visible and invisible. Cobb County is a major center for gas line connections for the whole of northwest Georgia. It was also, from the 1910s and 1930s, a center for electric power production. The first electric power installation was at Morgan Falls on the Chattahoochee River between Cobb and Fulton Counties; this was completed as a hydroelectric plant in 1904. In 1930 Plant Atkinson, a coal-generated electric power plant, was built on Cobb County soil. The early interest in energy development in the county is most dramatically represented by the multi-purpose impoundment of Lakes Allatoona and Acworth achieved when the Army Corps of Engineers dammed the Etowah River in

Bartow County and Butler and Proctor Creeks in Cobb County. The engineers were commissioned to improve flood controls, water supplies, and electrical energy sources. Their programs for the improvement of the internal waterways (which still continue today) had significant predictable results, and some unpredictable and unprogrammed by-products. One of the latter was the re-introduction of tourism to Cobb County.

Inside the original Bell Bomber Plant.

The administration building of the Bell Bomber Plant, now Lockheed-Georgia.

Factory "A", the 19-acre main plant for the Bell Bomber installation, now Lockheed-Georgia.

A converted 19th century farmhouse which now serves as an officers' club for Dobbins Air Force Base.

Cobb County has been a tourist destination from its earliest days when the waters of the various springs, such as Lithia Springs in nearby Douglas County, attracted people for cures and vacations. The history of the other springs in Cobb County is not well known, but Blue Springs, Collins Springs, Powder Springs, and other waters in Marietta all drew visitors. The attractions of North Georgia destinations continued to draw tourists until the early part of the twentieth century when the automobile expanded the range of vacation travel. A new type of tourist appeared in the form of the Dixie Highway travelers and the roadsters of the 1920s who were passing through the county on their way to somewhere else. In later decades, the irrigation programs of the Farm Security Administration and the United States Department of Agriculture created small impoundments such as ponds and small lakes, which were used for drainage and water retention primarily for agricultural purposes. They unintentionally became swimming holes, picnic grounds, and camping spots for the populace at large. The greatest of these local lakes was Allatoona, created in the 1940s. Prior to that time, the idea caught on in Cobb County that such a site, engineered for economic production purposes, could also serve as an intentional recreation area. The result of that insight produced weekend resorts, such as Bishop Lake in East Cobb, a 1936 subdivision designed to be a settlement of small cottages encircling a small artificial lake. The Depression kept Bishop Lake from complete development; houses were subsequently constructed there in the 1930s, 1940s and the 1950s. The idea was still being used in the 1960s when Paces Lake subdivision was built in Vinings. Other areas fostered summer camps and hideaways for business and religious institutions. One major camp was the Boy Scouts of America's Camp Burt Adams, located on the land presently occupied by Cumberland Mall. The idea is perpetuated in such popular tourist attractions as Whitewater and Six Flags Over Georgia.

Bishop Lake.

One of the early cottages at Bishop Lake, which was built when the lake was a weekend resort.

Preservation Assessment

Though it would seem that the modern era in Cobb County could not produce historically significant sites, in fact, some of the origins of the modern developments must be considered historical. They include such places/items as the original Bell Bomber plant, Bishop Lake and similar developments, and possibly, the early electric power plants. Contemporary developments offer the opportunity, not only to preserve what came before, as in these instances, but to create new buildings which incorporate some of the historic architectural and landscape traditions of the past. The reminiscent architecture of some of the subdivisions would indicate that this is not either impossible or unrealistic as a design alternative.

In 1972, the Department of Planning and Zoning in Cobb County adopted a new land use plan which held among its multiple objectives a goal to "preserve the archaeological and architectural heritage and environmental quality of Cobb County." In 1985 the Cobb County Historic Preservation Commission was established with several missions; one of these was the provision for the "protection, enhancement, perpetuation, and the use of places, districts, sites, buildings, structures, and works of art having a special historical, cultural, or aesthetic interest or value." Among the specific authorities of the Preservation Commission are the preparation of an inventory of all the properties within unincorporated Cobb County deemed worthy of a designation as historic properties. In accordance with that authority and that mission, the present report is presented as the result of a year-long survey of properties, published histories, public records, and prior surveys of historic properties within the county, and a compilation of all available information on historically, architecturally, and archaeologically significant places in the county.

The Vest-Hodge House in Vinings is an example of a Victorian "L" house adapted for commercial use.

VERNACULAR ARCHITECTURE
IN COBB COUNTY

How can we live without our lives?
How will we know it's us without our past?

John Steinbeck
The Grapes of Wrath (1939)

INTRODUCTION

The preservation of older buildings and structures deemed to be of historical value to the county requires some consideration of the architectural styles they represent, the relative value of their architectural forms, and the integrity of the architecture as it is presented in the contemporary condition of the structures. "Styles" refers to the forms and details which adhere to certain types of buildings (most notably houses) during certain periods of time; "integrity" refers to the retention of original materials and shapes in the building as it appears today. The question of architectural value is interpreted here to signify the relative frequency or rarity of a particular house or other building form found within the boundaries of the county itself.

The architecture in unincorporated Cobb County may be deemed to be historic if it falls into the period between the first white settlement and World War II, when an agricultural-based economy dominated county affairs. The buildings, therefore, are rural in nature such as county churches and schools, farm houses with barns, cribs, and other outbuildings as well as assorted roadside structures. These structures are usually not large or heavily ornamented; instead, they are plain and relatively small in size. They typically do not evoke great wealth and are not pretentious, nor do they entertain the eye with ornamented surfaces, elaborate bric-a-brac, or porches. Generally, they lack false and broken roof lines, balustrades, turrets, wings, towers, pediments, bay windows, and classical columns. Instead, they belong to the mainstream vernacular building traditions of the southeastern United States, and remind the viewer not so much of impressive and extraordinary events as they do of daily life and mundane activity. This is the architecture of survival more than of pleasure and represents hard work and public anonymity at a time when the center for working, living, and playing was the individual farmstead. Some building forms predominate among the architectural remnants of the past in the county; accordingly, it is the purpose of this report to help Cobb County residents as well as visitors to become familiar with the styles to provide a step toward recognition and appreciation of Cobb County history and its rich architectural heritage.

The predominant historic house shapes are listed below: (1) the early "single-pen" house (more commonly known as the pioneer log house); (2) two forms of the mid-nineteenth century "double-pen" house called the saddle-bag; (3) the hall and parlor forms; (4) several turn-of-the-century folk Victorian or "railroad" house styles such as the pyramidal hip-roofed house and "L", or "bent", house shape; and, (5) the ubiquitous bungalow and "temple" form houses of the early twentieth century.

The vernacular, non-professional, non-fashionable style in architecture extended to other buildings besides dwellings. Churches, schools, warehouses, roadside stores, barns and outbuildings all reflect the basic values of shelter and function with a minimal attempt to show stylish faces to the world.

The architecture of rural Cobb County, an indigenous architecture, evolved from the requirements of the locality such as available materials, siting needs and climate, as these were affected or impacted by external realities. Such influences included: (1) individual preferences and know-how in building construction brought in by the settlers; (2) the existing link via the railroad with the whole of the eastern seaboard and transatlantic trade allowing for the introduction of new ideas and technology of building; (3) the effect of the Civil War on local demographics and local residential patterns; and (4) the establishment of suburbs and subdivisions in Cobb County as early as 1905 due to the growth of Atlanta as a New South metropolis in the twentieth century. Throughout the history of Cobb County the local building pattern generally persisted with its tendency toward relatively small, modestly styled wood frame buildings.

SINGLE-PEN (ONE ROOM) LOG HOUSE
1820s to c. 1860

Typical front elevation, above, and floor plan, below, of a single-pen house.

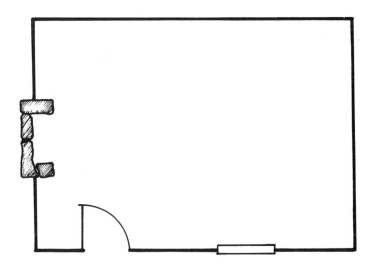

In remote areas, the log house of southern legend and history was still being built until the outbreak of the Civil War; however, it is likely that in Cobb County this had already been replaced by frame construction using locally milled planks at that time. Frame houses were more economical, and both platform and balloon framing were widespread across the United States by the 1840s. In the Southeast, where timber was plentiful, inexpensive and easily accessible, small-cut lumber was also common. Specifically, in Cobb County, where sawmilling existed from the first days of the county's formation, building logs did not have to be hand-hewn; instead, they were cut to size either on site (with a portable saw mill) or at a permanent mill and brought in by rail and/or wagon. Accordingly, the log building tradition in Cobb County is relatively short; it began late because of the late settlement of the northwest section of Georgia and it ended early due to the early presence of rail transportation and local mechanic technologies. Furthermore, it was the practice for home owners to add on to the original log structure with planked and framed construction, to install cladding or some other form of siding over the logs, or to replace the logs altogether with new construction; the log structures were often reused for more primitive purposes such as outbuildings or firewood. Lastly, many log houses were simply abandoned to the elements in favor of more finished, more "civilized" buildings. Consequently, pure examples of log construction are very rare in Cobb County. There are probably not more than half a dozen free-standing, one-room, hand-hewn, squared-and-notched-log constructed "pioneer" houses which have not been altered beyond recognition; even some of the better examples, such as the Powers-Jackson Cabin, have had additions put on them as recently as twenty or thirty years ago.

These early log houses should not be confused with the log "cabin," which is a twentieth-century romanticization of the early log house. In the cabin, the logs are left unhewn, not squared off, and the corner notches are more than likely to be simple V-shaped indentations rather than the more intricate dove-tail notches common in northern Georgia in the nineteenth century. The corner overhangs are also likely to be much longer in the cabin form. Lastly, cabins have served as vacation, retreat or resort housing as opposed to that of permanent, primary dwelling places.

The Powers-Jackson Cabin, a log house with frame additions.

A one-room log house to which an entire house has been attached, a common evolution for Cobb County log structures.

A very rare, untouched single-pen (one-room) structure which probably is built of hewn logs, now covered with tar paper siding.

An elevation and basic floor plan, below, of a single-entry saddlebag house.

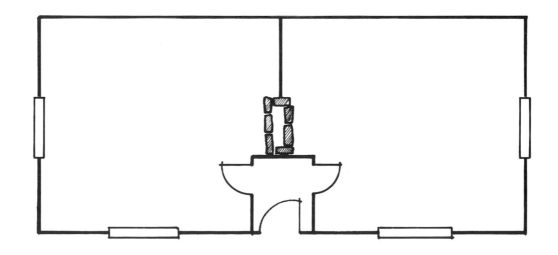

An elevation and basic floor plan, below, of a double-entry saddlebag house. A full front porch is a common addition.

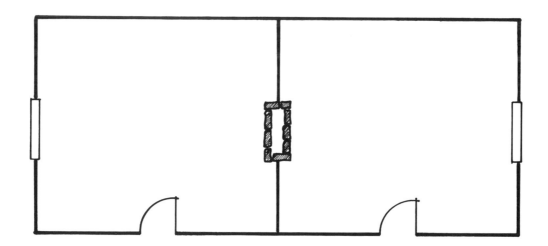

Log houses of one-room sized units, called pens, which contained more than one room, have been referred to as "double-pen" houses. There are a number of plans for double-pen houses, several of which are found in Cobb County. A floor plan incorporating two rooms off one central chimney is called a "saddlebag" house. These come with either single or double entries: with one door going to the middle of the house and interior doors leading to the two main rooms or with two doors leading inside, one per room. A two-room house with one chimney at the end of the house is simply called a "double-pen" house or sometimes a hall and parlor house after its medieval English ancestor (here, such houses are called simply double-pens). Two-room houses, where the rooms are separated by a central opening or breezeway, are called "dogtrots".

Originally, these styles were built of logs, later often covered with weatherboarding or board-and-batten covering. As frame construction replaced log construction, the house forms were retained and simply built of milled lumber, often pre-cut to size. Saddlebags and double-pens were still being built as share-cropper cabins in the first three decades of the twentieth century. Due to their consistent design features over time, these folk housing forms are almost ageless. Thus, they are difficult to date from just their appearance. Chimneys are one clue to their age. Originally, the chimneys were composed of clay and small logs; later fieldstone was used, often dry mounted. Sometimes, the lower portion of the chimney was fieldstone and the upper portion brick. Finally, the chimneys would be made completely of brick. Only rarely were chimneys stuccoed over. In this century, chimney replacements might be made of concrete block or similar materials. It is more customary for the chimney to disappear altogether in favor of a stovepipe, usually placed on the interior roof line rather than at the end of the gable. For Cobb County, fieldstone chimneys are a good clue to age, especially in combination with other factors such as foundations, roof pitch and wood clapboarding.

The custom in rural southeastern housing has been to raise the house on piers made of brick or fieldstone. Fieldstones, especially unworked ones, and handmade bricks are another indication of house age. In the twentieth century, it became common for the foundation to be filled-in between the brick or stone piers with concrete block, latticework, siding or cement. The continued presence of these foundation piers, however, indicates that the structure is likely to be fifty years old or older.

Roof pitch has also been altered over time; as a rule of thumb, the higher the pitch, the older the house. Accordingly, saddlebag or double pen houses with interior stove pipes instead of chimneys and low pitched roofs are definite twentieth century productions; they may still predate 1940. Houses with higher roof pitch and end chimneys are much older; these may be a century or more old depending on framing and finish, both items that cannot usually be seen from the outside of the structure. It has become a common practice in the Southeast to cover the woodframe of the house with some kind of cladding over the weatherboarding such as asbestos shingles, asphalt composition shingles, metal composition sheeting, shingles, plastic strips and fiberboard. Consequently, it is difficult to ascertain the age of a covered house without removing some of the siding, or even some of the original board. Generally speaking, straight-edged, evenly planed, but rough-cut boards predate finished boarding with beveled or beaded edges.

Because of the popularity of both saddlebag and double-pen houses (or variants thereof) for rural tenant houses, these two house forms have lasted a long time in Cobb County as well as in other parts of the Georgia Piedmont. There are, however, not many good examples of either in Cobb County in their original state; if found, they are generally in a dilapidated condition. Altered structures are sometimes modernized beyond easy recognition. Double entry saddlebags are rare as are early double-pens without rear or side additions. Three-room variants of the double-pen house, commonly constructed from the early 1900s through the Depression, are more numerous; however, good examples are scarce. These particular houses are not generally considered to be valuable housing stock today, and they are disappearing rapidly in the face of newer, larger, and more fashionable dwellings.

A decrepit double-entry saddlebag with board-and-batten finish.

A dilapidated double-entry saddlebag of indeterminate age.

A clapboarded saddlebag with rear addition

A 20th century saddlebag house with rear and side additions and modernized porch.

A typical double-pen house with a rear (usually a kitchen) addition. Early examples have an end wall chimney of fieldstone and brick.

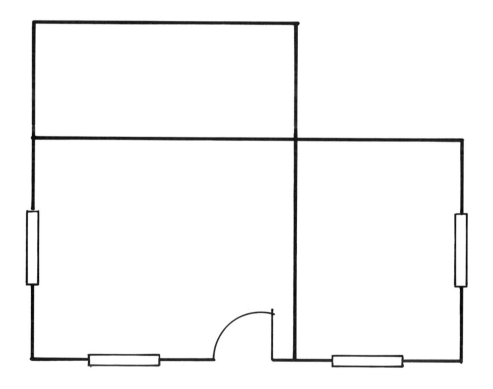

The Davis-Cook House, a very early double-pen house with rear additions. The house was subsequently covered with siding.

A mixed board and batten and clapboarded double-pen house with a fieldstone and brick end chimney, and rear additions.

A circa 1910 double-pen variant where the rear kitchen room was built as part of the original house.

A 20th century double-pen house with front porch but no rear additions. Note the low roof pitch.

HALL AND PARLOR HOUSES
1840s to c. 1890

Elevation and typical floor plan, below, of a hall and parlor house.

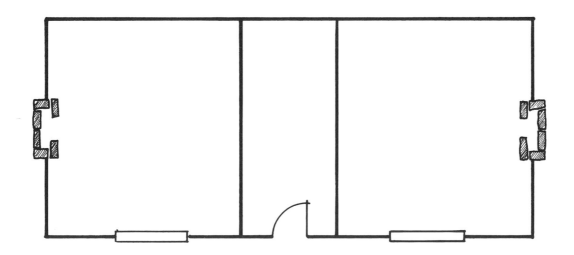

There are no known remaining examples of log-constructed dogtrot houses in Cobb County; however, there are probably two hundred examples of a similarly styled house, the central hall plan "hall and parlor" house. While the floorplan for the latter looks much like that of the dogtrot house, there are important differences in construction and derivation.

The hall and parlor house is a traditional British folk house form, two rooms wide and one room deep, which expanded with time to include a central hall with a room to either side, a front porch of either full or partial width, and rear additions (usually a long kitchen set perpendicular to the main part of the house). The central hall plan appeared along the Tidewater coast of the southeastern United States in the seventeenth century, built primarily of clay bricks and tabby. Wood was also used but few of these have survived today on the coast from the seventeenth and eighteenth century; a few examples may be seen in Savannah, Georgia. In Cobb County, this form seems to have been extremely popular throughout the nineteenth century as many examples have survived. At first, heavy timber framing was probably used to be subsequently replaced by light framing and shaped clapboard wallboards. The earliest examples in Cobb County incorporated some Greek Revival details on what was essentially a Georgian house form in the form of narrow lines of sidelights around the front door, occasionally topped by a transom, cornerboards or small pilasters at the corners. Additionally, there were accents at the cornice line of the roof including a wide band of boarding beneath the cornice. As a rule, these houses were one story or one-and-one-half stories tall. Second story windows might be cut through the gable ends of the house or dormers added later to let more light in under the eaves. Porches and pedimented entryways were common.

Brick hall and parlor, rare in Cobb County, with fieldstone chimneys.

A hall and parlor house in excellent condition with Victorian detailing on the porch brackets and supports.

There are many examples of this house style still standing in Cobb County in every state of repair from dilapidated to completely refurbished ones in modern style. Most of these houses have the front facades still intact and many additions in the rear; occasionally, there are also side additions but the latter ruin the symmetry of the basic house form. There are hall and parlor houses with every form of siding on them from asphalt to vinyl, stuccoed versions and shingled versions. Some have Victorian bric-a-brac scrollwork porches, some have no porches at all. Many are still surrounded by the marker trees planted when the house was first erected; these are now tall, mature specimens. Some of the oldest trees in the county are found in these locations.

An outstanding characteristic of these houses is their tenacity as part of the housing stock. With additions and modernizations, they have remained preferential residences, at times even show-pieces. Together, they constitute the oldest collection of historic housing in Cobb County and an exemplary model of evolution of a style through history.

A hall and parlor house with replacement chimneys, siding, and more contemporary scrollwork porch supports and balustrade. Note the shutters, instead of sidelights, on either side of the front door.

A hall and parlor house "modernized" with stucco , a shingle roof and shutters.

A classic hall and parlor house with later additions, now undergoing rehabilitation.

A hall and parlor house with elements of its original setting. Note the trees and the rear addition.

I-HOUSE

The I-house is simply a two-story hall and parlor, often referred to, along with the hall and parlor houses, as "Plantation Plain" style in the Georgia Piedmont. I-houses are rare in Cobb County. Of the few remaining ones, however, there are some good examples. They are distinguishable from the story-and-half hall and parlor houses by the height of the building which rises above the first story line and by the occasional presence of windows above the first story line on the front of the house (below the eaves). Hall and parlor houses incorporate windows on the first story only on the front facade. Like the hall and parlor houses, the I-houses have end chimneys, usually two, one on either end of the house. The silhouette for the hall and parlor house is somewhat tall and narrow; the I-house is even taller and, therefore, looks even narrower. Both forms are one room deep and three rooms wide (counting the central hall as the third room).

Of the properties listed on the National Register of Historic Places within Cobb County, three are of this style. They are the Braswell-Carnes House, the Israel Causey House, and the Marble House. Furthermore, one of the houses within the Concord Covered Bridge Historic District is of the same design.

A particularly fine example of an I-house in west Cobb County.

An I-style house designed by Atlanta architect Henry Toombs in 1940. The porch was added in the 1960s.

MASSED-PLAN HALL AND PARLOR HOUSES
LATE 19TH CENTURY to 1920s

A number of these houses remain standing in Cobb County. While they are similar in appearance to the original hall and parlor form, they are two rooms deep (usually given away by the window pattern on the gable sides of the house). In addition, they frequently have dormer windows and interior roofline chimneys. Massed plan hall and parlor houses date from the late nineteenth century up to the 1920s. Some have Classical Revival transom and sidelight windows, like their two earlier (and smaller) predecessors, but they are not to be confused with the Greek Revival elements on the older forms.

A massed-plan hall and parlor house with fieldstone and brick chimneys and "modernizations"--dormers, porch railings, and wide aluminum siding.

Massed-plan hall and parlor with side addition and interior chimneys. Note the sidelights on either side of the doorway and corner boards.

A massed-plan hall and parlor with small rear addition, interior chimneys, and single dormer. Note the prominent cornice returns on the gable wall.

A nicely representative massed-plan hall and parlor. Note the lowered roof pitch, the rear addition, and the wide cornice board trim under the eaves.

FOLK VICTORIAN AND RAILROAD HOUSES
1870s to 1940s

With the extension of the railroads across the entire continental United States after the Civil War, many cultural patterns became standardized because of the easier transfer of goods and communication. Housing styles and construction methods were no exceptions to this. After about 1870, the same house forms, built in standardized sizes and patterns, were to be found all over the country. Some regional folk house traditions persisted, but the housing stock in the Southeast, by and large, gradually changed from the earlier forms to these later, more economical, more contemporary, and also roomier shapes. "Prefab" housing became not only available but the norm, as pattern books and house-building kits were assembled by various manufacturers around the nation and shipped to individual owners and builders. A new home owner could order an entire house including everything but the paint and furnishings from catalogs; the latter could be ordered on separate orders from the same company. Thus, many older houses, even "fancy" ones, look very similar from Rockport, Maine to San Diego, California. Cobb County is no exception in this regard; from the 1870s through the 1940s, the housing stock resembles mainstream patterns of design and construction more than regional or local patterns of style and preference, as was true for the single and double-pen forms of housing. Following the mail order period of packaged housing, styles remained universal until today, due to the advanced communication skills as well as mass production technology. These later houses are of historical interest to the county as a measure of the degree to which the rural sections participated in national cultural patterns and consumed popularly marketed goods and styles; however, as individual specimens, these houses are probably less compelling than the earlier house types.

Pyramidal Hip-Roofed Houses
c. 1870 to 1910

These have quite distinctive forms because of the shape of the roof. Basically, this house is a pyramid supported by a box; the latter form is square and usually built with four rooms to a floor. In Cobb County, most of the examples are one-story structures, though elsewhere in the Atlanta metropolitan area, two-story versions dominate. Smyrna and Marietta also have some two-story versions, usually called "American Foursquare" houses.

The pyramidal hip-roofed houses come with simple and elaborate detailing. In Cobb County, the most common embellishments include a front porch or wraparound porches with simple supports and/or Victorian bric-a-brac finishing; a single central gable is often added to the front of the house on the roof along with shutters or other window decorations. The simple, smaller versions of this house type also contain a central chimney or several interior chimneys. This style of house continued to be constructed into the 1940s in the Southeast and elsewhere in the nation, but with important differences over the pre-1920 examples; the roof pitch was lowered with time, the porches became integral to the house (inside rather than outside the roof line), and the materials reverted from wood to stucco, concrete block, and brick.

A deteriorating pyramidal hip-roofed house with no additions to the basic form.

There are abundant examples of the pyramidal hip-roofed houses in Cobb County ranging from large to small as well as from simple to elaborate. Most were built as individual farmstead houses while many others were erected in what would appear to be a "suburban" relationship to the small towns within Cobb County (turn-of-the-century Acworth, Powder Springs, and Kennesaw). Still others were built as worker housing for local factories (such as the older mill village attached to the Coats and Clark Thread Mill near Austell).

The most intricately styled examples of rural housing in Cobb County occur as a variation of the pyramidal hip-roofed house form. These are large Queen Anne derivatives with a basic pyramidal hip roof shape to which front and sometimes side gables were added along with decorative trims and surface details. These Queen Anne houses are the most fashionably styled as well as the most pretentiously accomplished, in a positive sense, of all the historic rural housing stock in Georgia.

A classic example of pyramidal hip-roofed house with added front gable and full-facade porch.

The basic pyramidal hip-roofed house with porch and interior chimneys, without front gable. Note rear addition.

A fine example of a pyramidal hip-roofed house at the Macland crossroads.

An uncommon duplex in pyramidal hip-roofed form with central chimney.

A pyramidal hip-roofed house, with side entrance and wraparound porch.

A very large late pryamidal hip-roofed form (c. 1920s), with a three-sided wrap porch.

A pyramidal hip-roofed house with a single gable on the front side

A Queen Anne style pyramidal hip-roofed design with gable and dormer, added front porch and shingle textured surface on the gable.

A Queen Anne pyramidal hip-roofed house with crossing gables, front "dormer" gable and wrap porch.

An elaborate Queen Anne style pyramidal hip-roofed house with decorative barge boards on the gables, turned porch supports and lattice work foundation, with intersecting gables on the front and sides.

Victorian "L" or "Bent" House
1870s to 1940s

The Victorian "L" is so called because of the perpendicular axis of its shape. This is an extremely common form of house emanating from the Victorian era, with a facade composed of a long or short wing jutting out from a gable wall facing the front. It is common for the wing portion to contain a porch with spindlework or jigsaw cut detailing which is the "wedding cake" decorations of the Victorian period.

There are two types of Victorian "L" houses in Cobb County: (1) those which began life as linear forms (double-pen houses) to which a gable has been added, or sometimes a whole house, and (2) those which were fully constructed at one time. Most of these were built as farm houses; others appear within community settings within the unincorporated towns at crossroads, on major highways, and along streets in places like Mableton. These houses have remained, along with many of the altered hall and parlor houses, as part of the continuously usable housing stock in the county. Their chances for preservation lie primarily in their appeal as roomy, well-planned, and often well-built places as opposed to such factors as their individual age and history.

A classic example of the Victorian "L" house.

An "L" house created from a saddlebag with additions.

A Victorian "L" house added to a tiny double pen house.

A Victorian "L" house with turned porch supports, decorative barge boards and carved brackets.

A completely rehabilitated Victorian "L" with an unusually long wing portion

A 20th century version of the Victorian "L" house.

Early Twentieth Century Houses
1910s to 1940s

A typical bungalow house.

A typical temple-form house.

Bungalows and "temple form" houses are probably the most common and most familiar historic house forms in the county. The bungalow is a rectangular-shaped house with the gable end fronting on the street; it appears with or without porches, which may be add-ons or integral to the roof line. Bungalows appear with decorative fenestrations (multi-paned window strips over single panes, for example) and with craftsman detailing such as intricate brick work, turned and styled porch columns, exposed roof beams, caps and hoods on the gables, dormers, beveled and beaded boarding, eave brackets and latticework trim.

In Cobb County, these houses were constructed both as individual farm houses as well as the housing stock in the first planned subdivisions in the County. As collections of this particular house type, therefore, they have historic significance within those early subdivisions. The very best examples, that is the most highly fashioned, are located in Smyrna and along the route of the old Interurban Trolley Line (along Log Cabin Road, lower Atlanta Road and Oakdale Road especially). There are also very good collections of more modest bungalows along Cooper Lake Road

The basic bungalow.

as well as on Bankhead Highway at Leland. Like the folk Victorian styles, the bungalows have remained as part of the usable housing stock in the county; preservation on this basis is anticipated unless redevelopment is introduced. The isolated farm house bungalows might be viewed by some as "disposable", as they are a ubiquitous national house form; however, for Cobb County, bungalow farm houses were the last farm houses to be built new in any numbers. Since their time (roughly after World War II), the pattern of farming and farm living in the county has been altered extensively; accordingly, residential structures erected on farm properties after 1940 represent a wholly different demographic and economic pattern. There are examples of new (1950s - 1980s) houses on old farmsteads in Cobb County; the sight of a brick ranch style house in front of old barns is not a rarity in the county. However, in these instances, the house is a replacement for an older structure and does not represent a newly created home and farmsite.

The basic bungalow with an extended front porch and "matching" bungalow form garage.

A bungalow with a double gable, the front one of which covers the porch.

A temple form house with integral porch and "hooded" or capped gable. Variations of this form, with four posts or supports for the porch, are very common in Cobb.

A double-gabled bungalow with craftsman detailing. Note the eaves brackets and the multi-paned windows.

FARMSITES, BARNS AND OUTBUILDINGS

While the main house is a primary component of any farm site, it is not the only component; the setting and the outbuildings are also integral to the farm's identity. As indicated in the historical narrative, the size of Cobb County farm holdings has varied through time, as has the relationship of the fields to the farm house (especially the main house) under periods of tenancy. As resources for preservation, farms are problematical since the size and definition of the actual farm property, the unit which constituted it, was so changeable over time. There is some agreement over certain recognizable features, without which no farm could be a farm and these elements would have to be part of the preservation. One of these elements is the farm house; another is the setting immediately surrounding the farm house, which usually contained some kitchen gardens and monumental "marker" trees (which today are aged and very tall), and the necessary outbuildings which serviced the work on the farm. In the South, including Cobb County, these later buildings were usually makeshift, impermanent storage structures, built with minimum concern for their fashionability. They were built as the need arose for such concerns as cribs, sheds, smokehouses, pig sties, animal pens, fenced yards and other assorted animal "houses". The variety of outbuildings on a typical southern farm over the last century is impressive. On one nineteenth century farm in Cobb County, there stands a wellhouse, a privy, a blacksmith shop, a woodshed, a combination henhouse/garage, a hothouse, fenced hogpens, and two larger barns, one with a loft and one without. Other "structures" include a grape arbor and a gourd trellis. Most Cobb County barns are unpainted wooden structures, small or moderate in size, and rather carelessly erected. While finished and painted barns such as those found in Pennsylvania or New England are uncommon in the county, the variety of structures is greater here.

A Queen Anne style pyramidal hip-roofed house with turn of the century barn to the left and 1940s garage in the middle. Mixed aged buildings are common to Cobb County farm sites.

The classic English barn form, with the main entrance in the middle of the widest side.

Many design styles of barns are found in Cobb County. The English barn predominates with its opening on the long side. There are few crib barns built in the Midland (Appalachian) style and even fewer bi-level barns. The ancient barn at the Powers-Jackson Cabin site is a bi-level barn on a German plan, with an upper side entrance and a lower main entrance. Two-story barns exist but they are the exception. Lake Erie Shore or Kentucky style barns are also rare and usually fairly recent creations. Plank finishing covers most barn structures and the planking runs vertically in most instances. Horizontal planking, however, is not unknown. Dairy farming, truck farming, and poultry farming brought different outbuilding styles to Cobb County in the early decades of the twentieth century.

Barns and other outbuildings are expendable features on properties no longer used for agricultural purposes. For that reason, they are probably in greater potential jeopardy than are farm houses. While the cost of land in the county grows rapidly, the farm site itself is at risk of being lost as a comprehensive single resource. Some limited number of historic farm sites may lend themselves to passive park use but the majority of the Cobb County agricultural heritage and open land cannot be thus preserved.

20th century dairy farm barns and sheds.

A gambrel roofed "Erie Shore" style barn, not indigenous to Cobb County.

A mix of barns with horizontal and vertical planking, entrance at wide and narrow sides.

RURAL INSTITUTIONS

The structures classified as rural institutions serving Cobb County's historic past include school houses and churches. The churches have survived better than the schools; however, neither class of building has been untouched by change.

At the turn of the century, there were probably three dozen remaining country school houses in the county; of these, not more than a half dozen are known to have survived intact, several of which have been added to and altered beyond recognition in order to serve other purposes. Rural school houses, in Cobb County as elsewhere, were private matters, the materials and personnel for which were the responsibility of the local school districts within the militia districts. In the 1890s there were 13 separate school districts in the county in place of the county-wide system in existence today. When the county-wide system was created, it superseded the authority of the older, local systems including control of the one-room school buildings; the latter were easily replaced by campuses and more progressive facilities. Where the old school houses are being used as community centers, such as Red Rock and Nickajack, the twin challenge exists to save the school building and at the same time avoid destroying its architectural integrity with subsequent "improvements" needed to accommodate the adaptive re-use.

The classic temple-form church with vestibule, but without a tower.

According to the 1985 Cobb Data Book, there are 302 churches in Cobb County; not all of these are located on Church Street in Marietta. The rural church buildings are almost uniformly of one style, a basic temple form structure with or without a tower, a vestibule, the ornate glass in the windows and an associated graveyard. They are usually sided with aluminum, vinyl or asphalt siding. Few can be documented to have retained their original building fabric as the walls, roofs, ceilings, floors, doorways and entrances have been updated, repaired, replaced or improved over time. Mt. Bethel is a good example of a "redone" church. The cornice returns and the pulpit may be the only "original" material remaining, though the old sanctuary has retained its original shape; it was, however, enlarged and even moved. In conclusion, the churches are refreshing landmarks on the landscape of Cobb County, but because of their manifold alterations, they are limited in value as a historic resource.

The Red Rock School house, now the Mars Hill Community Center, which has been altered but is still recognizable.

The classic temple-form church with vestibule and tower.

A much altered church form with siding, louvered windows and reformed cement foundation.

A much altered church form with siding, new vestibule, steps, windows, and foundation.

COBB COUNTY SITES LISTED ON THE NATIONAL REGISTER OF HISTORIC PLACES
AND
THE COBB REGISTER OF HISTORIC PLACES

The Congress finds and declares that the spirit and direction of the Nation are founded upon and reflected in its historic heritage; [and] the historical and cultural foundations of the Nation should be preserved as a living part of our community life and development in order to give a sense of orientation to the American people.

National Historic Preservation Act of 1966,
as amended
16 U. S. C. 470

INTRODUCTION

In 1906, the United States Congress passed the Antiquities Act which provided a process by which the President could designate national monuments. The Act was valuable in that it did ultimately provide protection to major archaeological sites, but its intent was basically directed to protection of land already owned by the federal government. In 1935, the Historic Sites Act was passed into law. This law authorized the Department of the Interior to begin surveying and identifying historic sites throughout the country. Thirty years later, under the National Historic Preservation Act of 1966, the survey program begun in 1935 under the auspices of the Historic Sites Act became the basis of the National Register of Historic Places. To date, the National Register contains some 46,500 sites nationwide and approximately 1,300 sites in Georgia.

The Cobb Register of Historic Places was created by the 1984 ordinance which created the Cobb County Historic Preservation Commission. The ordinance provides the legal basis for preservation action in the county and qualifies Cobb as the only county government in Georgia which meets National Park Service criteria for protecting historic resources. Modeled after the National Register of Historic Places, the Cobb Register contains sites which have been documented as to their history, historic context and value to the county. To date, the Cobb Register only lists sites which meet the National Register criteria for evaluation. The criteria, quoted from the Code of Federal Regulations, are as follows:

> The quality of significance in American history, architecture, archaeology, engineering and culture is present in districts, sites, buildings, structures, and objects that possess integrity of location, design, setting, materials, workmanship, feeling, and association, and
>
> (a) that are associated with events that have made a significant contribution to the broad patterns of our history; or
>
> (b) that are associated with the lives of persons significant in our past; or
>
> (c) that embody the distinctive characteristics of a type, period, or method of construction, or that represent the work of a master, or that possess high artistic values, or that represent a significant and distinguishable entity whose components may lack individual distinction; or
>
> (d) that have yielded, or may be likely to yield, information important in prehistory or history.

Sites considered for listing on the National Register of Historic Places are generally documented by private researchers and are submitted to the State of Georgia National Register Review Board for their consideration, after being reviewed by the Historic Preservation Section of the Georgia Department of Natural Resources. Once recommended by the Review Board, the application is sent to the Keeper of the National Register, National Park Service in Washington, D.C., where a final determination is made as to the level of significance of a site (local, state, or national) and whether or not the site will be added to the National Register.

Sites considered for listing on the Cobb Register of Historic Places are generally documented by private researchers using criteria and research methods consistent with National Register listing and are submitted to the Cobb County Historic Preservation Commission for consideration. The Commission holds a public hearing to receive comments from citizens concerning the proposed

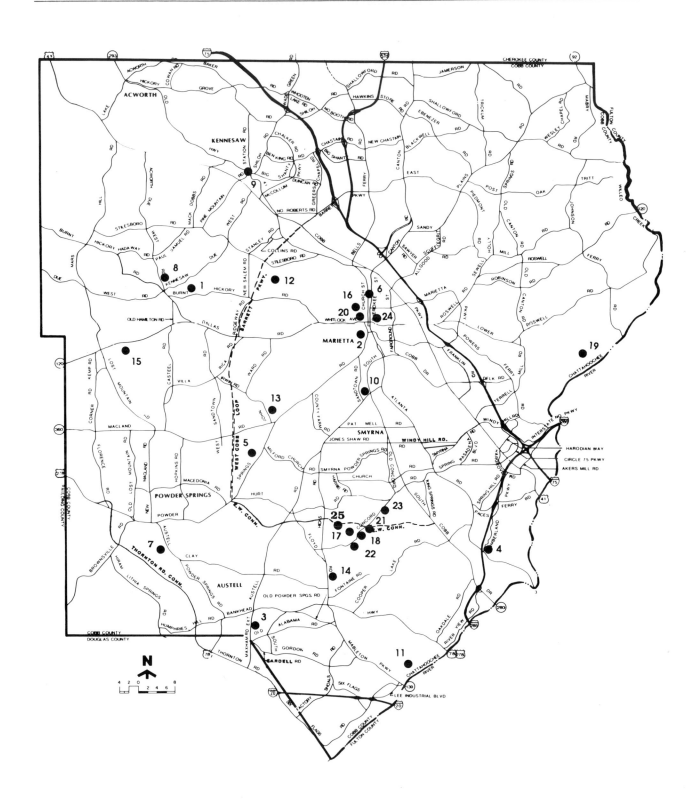

NATIONAL REGISTER AND COBB REGISTER SITES

Map Location	Site Name

Sites listed on the National Register of Historic Places:

1	Braswell-Carnes House
2	Brumby-Little House (Marietta)
3	Israel Causey-Maxham House
4	J. H. Carmichael Farm and General Store
5	Andrew J. Cheney-Newcomer House
6	Church Street/Cherokee Street Historic District (Marietta)
7	Clarkdale Mill and Village
8	Gilgal Church Battlefield
9	Kennesaw Multiple Resource Area and the General (Kennesaw), includes: Camp McDonald
	Cherokee Street Historic District
	John S. Gibson Farmhouse
	North Main Street Historic District
	Summers Street Historic District
10	Glover-McLeod-Garrison House
11	Johnston's River Line
12	Kennesaw Mountain National Battlefield
13	William Gibbs McAdoo House
14	Robert Mable House and Cemetery
15	Midway Presbyterian Church
16	Northwest Marietta Historic District (Marietta)
17	Rock House (John W. Rice Summer Cottage)
18	Concord Covered Bridge and Ruff's Mill
19	Sope Creek Ruins
20	Whitlock Avenue Historic District (Marietta; nomination in process)
24	Washington Avenue Historic District (Marietta; nomination in process)

Sites listed on the Cobb County Register of Historic Places:

11	Johnston's River Line
	Concord Covered Bridge Historic District which includes:
17	Rock House (John W. Rice Summer Cottage)
18	Concord Covered Bridge and Ruff's Mill
21	Concord Woolen Mill Ruins
22	Gann House
23	Ruff Homeplace and Cemetery
25	Railroad Trestle Bridge

nomination, and then makes their recommendation to the Board of Commissioners as to whether or not a site should be added to the Cobb Register. In addition, the State of Georgia Historic Preservation Section has the opportunity to offer their advice to the Commission and to the Board. Ultimately, the Board of Commissioners decides which sites are added to the Cobb Register.

Much misinformation exists about the relative value of being listed in the National Register and the Cobb Register. In brief, listing on the National Register is largely honorary, carrying little or no substantial protection for any property so listed. A project which impacts a National Register site (or a property which is eligible for such designation but has not yet been listed) is subject to a variety of procedural reviews if and only if there is federal government involvement in the project. National Register properties are also eligible for tax credits if rehabilitation of the income-producing property is carried out within guidelines established by the Secretary of the Interior. The Georgia Historic Preservation Section can assist interested property owners with any questions or concerns about National Register, or National Register-eligible, sites. They can be reached at (404) 656-2840.

In contrast, listing a property on the Cobb Register of Historic Places provides substantial protection from insensitive or inappropriate redevelopment. Under the authority of Cobb County's historic preservation ordinance, "no material change in the appearance of such historic property, or of a structure, site or work of art within such historic district, shall be made or permitted to be made by the owner or occupant thereof unless or until application for a certificate of appropriateness has been submitted to and approved by the [Historic Preservation] Commission." In considering applications for certificates of appropriateness, the Commission is instructed by the ordinance to approve such applications "if it finds that the proposed material change(s) in the appearance would not have a substantial adverse effect on the aesthetic, historic or architectural significance and value of the historic property or the historic district." Such review of alterations to historic sites and districts allows the Historic Preservation Commission to ensure that sites and districts listed on the Cobb Register of Historic Places retain their integrity and value to all the citizens of Cobb County.

The map on page 110 shows all the National Register and Cobb Register sites presently listed in Cobb County. This list does not contain all of the eligible sites in the county. Generally, only the most visible sites and districts have been listed on either Register in that sites which have the interest or backing of individuals who are willing to complete the necessary research are the sites which become listed. Other eligible districts certainly exist -- Vinings, Mableton, areas surrounding Kennesaw Mountain, and various crossroad communities such as Lost Mountain to name just a few -- and many individual sites have yet to be documented. Sites such as the Tritt Farm or the Hyde Farm are outstanding examples, as are many individual vernacular and high-style structures. In addition, the rural landscape is a new focus of the National Register and the Cobb Register and, indeed, is worthy of preservation. Much of the rural landscape is still found in Cobb and should be listed and protected.

The following information presented below is drawn mainly from the National Register nomination for each site and from other secondary sources. It is only a summary of the historic documentation available for each site and, of course, additional documentation is always welcome. Unless otherwise noted, the site is listed on the National Register; Cobb Register designation is in process. If you know of a site which you feel should be added to the Cobb Register, please contact the Cobb County Historic Preservation Planner. Sites which might be considered for the National Register should be discussed with the Georgia Department of Natural Resources, Historic Preservation Section.

BRASWELL-CARNES HOUSE

The Braswell-Carnes House is located at 2430 Burnt Hickory Road, District 20, Land Lot 291, on about 13 acres of land. It is a one-story frame structure with six rooms, a large central hall and a shallow wraparound porch. There is a wellhouse on the site, but other outbuildings have been destroyed. The house was constructed in 1865 and the original materials are still in the house. For example, it sits on rock piers of native stone in a natural setting with many trees, flowers, and shrubs which help it to blend with nearby woods and a lake.

The air of authenticity is enhanced by the absence of a lawn or formal landscaping elements. The Braswell-Carnes house retains its appearance as an early settler farm site. It is a good example of vernacular architecture existing immediately after the Civil War and is of a revised Plantation Plain style, reflecting the use of local materials. The house was the home of Ephraim Braswell, a returning Civil War veteran. It was bought by James Davis Carnes in 1898. He was a farmer who arranged sharecropping for most of his holdings. The house remains in the Carnes family today.

Braswell - Carnes House. Note the wraparound porch, the finely detailed porch supports, and the original stone foundation element.

J. H. CARMICHAEL FARM AND GENERAL STORE

The J. H. Carmichael Farm and General Store are located at 501 Log Cabin Road in the 17th District, Land Lot 821, near the intersection of I-285 and Route 3 (Atlanta Road.) It consists of a Victorian farmhouse, a twentieth-century commercial building, several agricultural outbuildings, Civil War breastworks, (part of Johnston's River Line), cleared fields, and a wooded ravine. The property originally included 38 acres, but the family no longer owns all of this acreage. The Carmichael house was built in 1884 as a one-story Victorian cottage. It was enlarged in 1908 to its present size and appearance, with a square, windowed tower located on the front facade. The rear of the house has been altered to allow a bathroom and other modernization. The interior of the house is otherwise nearly original.

The Carmichael Building was built in 1914-15 to serve as a store. It originally had a shed roof that has been removed. There are also several agricultural outbuildings, such as a large barn, and other structures. A rock spring house is found in the deep ravine behind the house, and the Civil War breastworks are located northeast of the Carmichael house. Mr. J. H. Carmichael operated the general store, and under his management it functioned as a community center as well. There was also a cotton gin and a wagon yard which provided overnight parking for travelers on the Dixie Highway. The Atlanta-Marietta Interurban Trolley Line was in the vicinity of the Carmichael Store. There was a trolley stop known as Carmichael's.

Local and state historians find the site significant because it was the birthplace of James Vinson (Jimmy) Carmichael. Mr. Carmichael was a successful attorney who was instrumental in bringing the Bell Bomber Plant to Marietta to build B-29s during World War II. Bell closed at the end of the war, but was replaced by Lockheed-Georgia in 1950. He ran for governor in 1946 and while he did not win the election, he is credited with bringing forth the demise of the county unit system of voting in the state of Georgia. Attorney Carmichael was opposed by Eugene Talmadge, and E. D. Rivers. Carmichael was endorsed by incumbent governor Ellis Arnall and received 46 percent of the popular vote. Talmadge received 44 percent and Rivers received 10 percent. However due to the county unit system of voting, Talmadge was elected. This event created a furor in state politics and helped set the stage for the end of the unit system of voting. It was declared unconstitutional in 1962.

The Carmichael House and properties are under great pressure due to surrounding development and transportation infrastructure concerns. It is among the most endangered of Cobb's National Register sites.

J. H. Carmichael House. Originally built in 1884 as a one-story cottage, the house was enlarged in 1908 to its present appearance.

Located immediately west of the Carmichael House, the Carmichael Building was built in 1914 - 15 and served as a general store and community center.

This building, just west of the Carmichael Building is an example of an early frame commercial building.

ISRAEL CAUSEY-MAXHAM HOUSE

The Israel Causey House, or the Causey-Maxham House, is located at 5909 Maxham Road near Austell, in District 18, Land Lot 88. It was built in 1840 and is a frame, one and a half story, plain style dwelling with a four room central hall plan. The house has a pitched roof which extends into a shed porch on the front facade and shed additions and porch on the rear. Two of the original chimneys are still standing. Inside the house are original flooring, fireplaces, and some mantlepieces. Boards over a foot wide are visible in the attic space. Two outbuildings and orchards also remain, although they are not on the National Register nomination.

The Causey family was among Cobb County's pioneer settlers. This house, like many others in the county, has a Civil War history of Union soldiers quartering there during the Atlanta campaign. Two of the Causey sons died in the Civil War and are buried in the Causey/Shady Grove Cemetery. Family legend says that at the approach of the Union troops, Israel Causey took what food and supplies that he could, loaded them on a wagon, and went to Villa Rica, leaving his wife and daughters at home alone. The Union troops under Colonel McPherson occupied the house and confined the Causey ladies to the attic for the duration of their stay. When one soldier attempted to force his way into the attic, Mrs. Margaret Foyle Causey, (born in Scotland), hit him over the head with a board from the attic, knocking him backwards and causing him to die of a broken neck.

A daughter of Causey's first marriage inherited the house and sold it to Herbert Maxham in 1887. The present owners, Maxham descendants, are at home in the house while they continue the traditional occupation of farming on the old homestead.

Israel Causey-Maxham House. Note the simple shed roof extending over the porch, and the dormer window.

Israel Causey-Maxham House, south face. Note the brick chimney with string courses, the 9-over-9 windows, and the extension of the roof line which covers a porch on the north and east side (not visible here).

Israel Causey-Maxham House outbuilding. Located on the east side of the house, this barn/equipment shed may or may not be original to the site, although it almost certainly dates from the early 20th century.

ANDREW J. CHENEY-NEWCOMER HOUSE

The Andrew J. Cheney or Cheney-Newcomer House is located at 2760 Bankstone Road, facing Powder Springs Road at Bankstone Road, on nine acres of land in District 19, Land Lot 621. It is a Greek Revival plantation structure. Fluted Doric columns define the house which was built about 1856 by Andrew Jackson Cheney. The front door is shaded by a two-story portico supported by four columns which rest on tall plinths paired on each side of an entrance porch. The columns are replacements of the originals.

The house, like most antebellum structures in Cobb County, survived the Civil War because of its use by Federal troops as a headquarters building. The house was favorably situated as a 19th century rural site on a working farm. The original well was still in use in 1979, and the house lot contains fine landmark specimen trees. It is at the crossing of two important early roads, Old Sandtown Road, now Bankstone Road, and the Old Tennessee Wagon Road, which parallels Powder Springs Road.

Cheney-Newcomer House, front view. Fluted Doric columns are paired at the entrance of this c. 1856 Greek Revival plantation structure.

COATS AND CLARK THREAD MILL AND VILLAGE (CLARKDALE)

The Coats and Clark Thread Mill and Village located on roughly 50 acres in the southeast quadrant of Cobb County between Austell and Powder Springs on Highway 278, is in the 19th District, Land Lots 1163, 1164, 1165, 1204, and 1205. The mill is a privately owned industrial complex now renovated and open to use as a shopping/office center. Its history reflects Cobb County's 20th century march to industrial/commercial significance in the metropolitan Atlanta region. It is a mixed use site, with the millworkers' and managers' houses now in individual owners' hands. The Thread Mill itself was restored in such a manner as to take advantage of the Federal tax incentive program available to owners who restore historic properties for commercial use.

The Clarkdale district is an intact planned industrial community developed in 1931. The three-story brick mill building measures 125 x 500 feet and is located on a knoll, said to be the highest elevation in a 30 mile circumference. To the west of the mill building there are several industrial structures including a water processing plant and a brick and frame warehouse. A small one-story brick office is located north of the mill building. Situated at the base of the knoll, east of the industrial complex, is the densely developed residential area, consisting of 138 small dwellings located along curvilinear tree-lined streets. The district consists of recreational facilities, open green spaces, industrial buildings, and residences.

Coats and Clark Thread Mill. This photograph shows the stair tower on the south end of the building.

The Clark Thread Company, a Scottish firm, moved their American operation from New Jersey to the South in 1931, with the construction of the Clarkdale plant in Georgia. Sewing thread was the only product of the Clarkdale mill, and its success may well have been aided by the economic distress of the Depression, since many people made their own clothing at home rather than buying manufactured items. Another possible cause for the building of the Clarkdale plant was labor unrest at the Newark, New Jersey factory. Certainly, the mill management enjoyed 50 years of non-union labor at its Cobb county site before closing in 1983.

The Clarkdale community represents the efforts to design modern industrial communities. The J. E. Sirrine Company Engineers from Greenville, South Carolina and the Fisk Carter Construction Company from South Carolina were the designers and builders of the 50 acre mill village site. Sirrine also designed the mill itself. Later years saw the addition of various recreational amenities. In 1933 the Clarkdale Civic Club was formed by the mill. Each employee was automatically a member of the Club and dues of 50¢ per year per family were deducted from their paychecks. Mill managers served as the Board of Directors of the Civic Club, which acted as conduit for Clarkdale's recreational, social and educational improvements. Under the auspices of the Civic association, the following improvements were made: 1933, local post office; 1934, community center (with a ballpark next to it), hospitalization plan created; 1934, frame multi-family garages; 1936, swimming pool created south of the plant (now filled in), and tennis court; 1947, $5000 given to build a Baptist and Methodist church on the north side of Highway 278, (not included in the National Register nomination because of its age); 1950, Pineview Lake created and stocked with fish, (not included in the National Register nomination because of its age) and federal credit union formed. The Civic Club also served food and beverages to the workers on mobile lunch carts. In the mid-60s Coats and Clark began to sell the houses to residents at a reasonable price. Thus, the uniform appearance of the village maintained by the mill owners has begun to change. The mill building was purchased in 1985 by Landmark Technology Corporation.

Coats and Clark Thread Mill. Originally, there were large expanses of windows, which were later replaced with brick. This photograph shows the appearance of the building and the lawn following rehabilitation.

Clarkdale Mill Village. Workers' duplex in nearly original condition.

Clarkdale Mill Village. Typical streetscape in the workers' section.

Clarkdale Mill Village. Example of housing provided for management.

Clarkdale Mill Village. Street scene in the management section.

GILGAL CHURCH BATTLEFIELD

The Gilgal Church Battlefield lies nine miles west of Marietta and about one fourth of a mile from the Due West crossroads on Kennesaw Due West Road in District 20, Land Lot 275. The site is virtually unchanged from its appearance in 1864, consisting today of approximately twenty acres of hardwood forest. The front of the Union line runs 175 yards from Kennesaw Due West Road to the edge of the deep ravine leading to a creek branch. Another perpendicular line runs along the branch for about 125 yards. Several other lines are evident on the site; shorter lines leading from the trenches to the creek branch are water procurement lines. A series of seven rifle pits about 50 feet long lie near Acworth Due West Road. There are also such features as command posts, officers' pits and scattered grave sites. Bodies buried on the site were removed to Marietta after the Civil War and the original gravesites are marked with small crosses.

The Battle of Gilgal Church was one of an almost continuous series of skirmishes and major actions lasting from June 10 to July 3, 1864, between General William T. Sherman's Federal troops and General Joseph E. Johnston's Confederate troops. It was part of the fierce fighting for the approach to Atlanta which took place in that summer. Among the participants in the general fighting around Gilgal Church was Benjamin Harrison, who later became President of the United States. Harrison served with the 70th Indiana under Lieutenant General Daniel Butterfield. Also participating in the Gilgal fighting was Arthur MacArthur, 24th Wisconsin Regiment, the father of one the most famous American generals of this century -- Douglas MacArthur.

Gilgal Church itself burned in the military action. It was located at the intersection of present-day Kennesaw Due West and Acworth Due West Roads. The battlefield named for the church is owned by the estate of Sydney C. Kerksis, who bought and preserved the site. There is an endowed trust for the preservation of the battlefield that is administered by several individuals, including members of the Atlanta Historical Society's Board of Trustees. Gilgal Church Battlefield became a National Register site in 1973. Work is currently underway to create a passive history park on the site.

Gilgal Church Battlefield, Federal trench line. Note the Union trenchwork in the center foreground.

Gilgal Church Battlefield. Bodies buried on the site were removed to Marietta after the war. Crosses mark the original site of battlefield burials.

Gilgal Church Battlefield. Note the Union trenchwork which begins in the right foreground.

GLOVER- McLEOD-GARRISON HOUSE

The Glover-McLeod-Garrison House is also known as "Bushy Park" or "Rocking Chair Hill." Today it is the site of The Planters' Restaurant. It is located just outside the Marietta City limits at 250 Garrison Rd. in District 17, Land Lot 291 on about nine acres of land.

The house is a raised two and one-half story temple form structure with a monumental pedimented four column Doric portico. It was originally built as a country house. The interior has a ten foot central stair hall, four original 20' X 20' rooms, and additions dating from c. 1939. The third floor was used as a boys' dormitory and it also has a rear stair for private access to the upper levels. There were originally extensive outbuildings and slave quarters, although only one of the original outbuildings is standing today.

The land was purchased by John Heyward Glover in 1847 and the next year he began to build his house. Glover was one of Marietta's leading businessmen. He built a tannery north of the house, founded a bank in Marietta, and organized the first telegraph company. He served as mayor of Marietta in 1852. The house was sold in 1851 by Glover who moved to another residence in the city. It was bought by Francis H. McLeod as a part-time residence. His daughter married William King, son of Roswell King, and they lived in the house, particularly in the summer of 1864. The King family told of surviving the battle which raged around "Bushy Park" by hiding in the basement. The house miraculously survived the shelling and general skirmishing around it . The house was subsequently owned by the Thomas W. Garrison family who used it as a rental property in the 1930s. It was restored by a Garrison grandson, Robert T. Garrison. Today the house is used as a restaurant serving gourmet food with a decidedly southern flavor.

Glover-McLeod-Garrison House. A classic example of a Greek Revival temple-form house with a monumental pediment supported by four Doric columns.

Glover-McLeod-Garrison House. The stone outbuilding is undoubtedly original; the wellhouse and the barn are of more recent construction.

JOHNSTON'S RIVER LINE

These Union and Confederate earthen fortifications lie on both sides of Nickajack Creek where it enters the Chattahoochee River, between Bankhead Highway and Mableton Parkway near Mableton in the 18th District, Land Lots 397 through 401. They are segments of the unique Confederate defensive line, the only one engineered in advance, used in the summer of 1864 in the battle for Atlanta. The trench lines were a seven-mile defensive line stretching from Vinings to Mableton in Cobb County. While the land around these trenches was cultivated in later years, the trenches themselves were left untouched for the most part. Generally speaking, the entrenchments east of the Nickajack Creek are Confederate and the western lines were Union. The Confederate line was constructed of materials at hand in June, 1864, with General Johnston's engineers, units of the Georgia militia and about a thousand impressed black laborers working on it.

This site is comprised of one remaining section of General J. E. Johnston's "river lines", which were engineered to oppose Sherman's approach to Atlanta in June of 1864. The remaining lines are well-preserved. They exhibit breastworks, cannon forts, and traverse lines. It was listed on both the National Register in 1972 at the national level of significance and the Cobb Register of Historic Places in 1988.

A segment of Johnston's River Line. General J. E. Johnston, C. S. A. and his engineers constructed extensive entrenchments in the summer of 1864 to fortify Atlanta against the Union armies.

General William Sherman wrote of the fighting which accompanied his approach to the Chattahoochee River and of the battle for Atlanta in the second volume of his memoirs. He described how the trenches at the river generally were constructed and of their invulnerability, calling them "one of the strongest pieces of field fortifications I ever saw".

> The enemy and ourselves used the same form of rifle trench, varied according to the nature of the ground, viz: the trees and bushes were cut away for a hundred yards or more in front, serving as an abatis or entanglement. The parapets varied from four to six feet high, the dirt taken from a ditch outside and from a covered way inside, and this parapet was surmounted by a "head-log", composed of the trunk of a tree from twelve to twenty inches at the butt, lying along the interior crests of the parapet and resting in notches cut in other trunks which extended back forming an inclined plane, in case the head-log should be knocked inward by a cannon-shot. The men of both armies became extremely skillful in the construction of these works, because each man realized their value and importance to himself, so that it required no orders for their construction.

Johnston's River Line. Photograph shows a borrow pit from which dirt was thrown up to form a seven-gun fort which is located at the extreme southern end of the Line.

Johnston's River Line. Photograph shows one of the gun emplacements at the seven-gun fort.

KENNESAW MOUNTAIN NATIONAL BATTLEFIELD PARK

Kennesaw Mountain and Little Kennesaw Mountain.

Kennesaw Mountain National Battlefield Park was established to commemorate the 1864 Atlanta Campaign. It contains 2,884 acres of meadowland, forests and landscape features such as Kennesaw and Little Kennesaw Mountains, Pigeon and Cheatham Hills and Kolb Farm. There are well-marked driving and walking trails through the Park which describe local flora, location, and descriptions of the progress of the battles which occurred in the area. The Park is located three miles north and west of Marietta (see map on page 130) and is administered by the National Park Service, U.S. Department of the Interior.

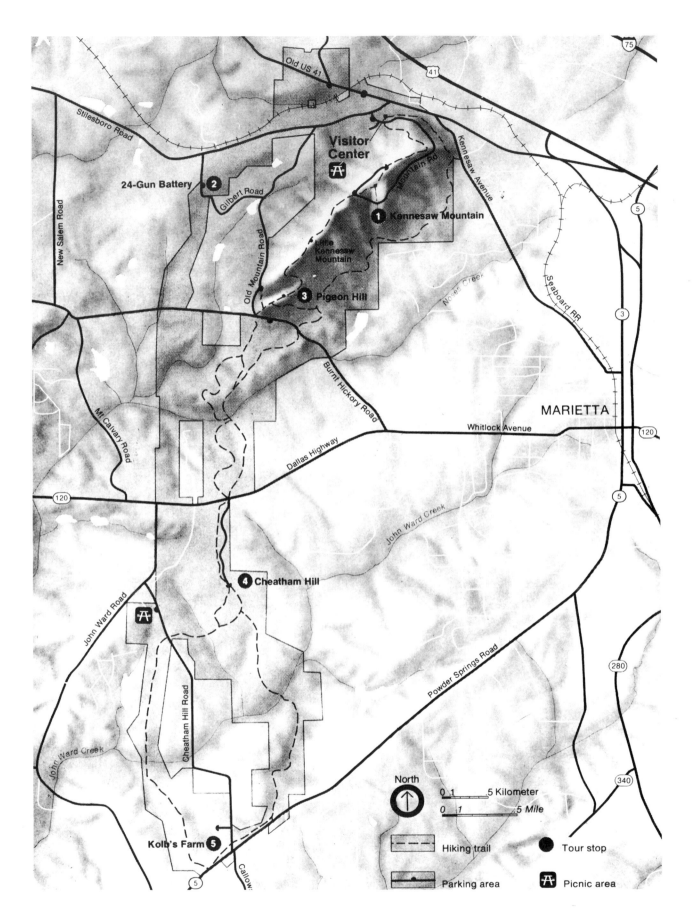

Kennesaw Mountain

Visitor Center

24-Gun Battery **2**

1 Kennesaw Mountain

Little Kennesaw Mountain

3 Pigeon Hill

4 Cheatham Hill

5 Kolb's Farm

MARIETTA

Stilesboro Road

Old US 41

Gilbert Road

New Salem Road

Old Mountain Road

Mountain Rd

Kennesaw Avenue

Noses Creek

Seaboard RR

Burnt Hickory Road

Whitlock Avenue

Dallas Highway

Mt Calvary Road

John Ward Creek

John Ward Road

Cheatham Hill Road

Powder Springs Road

Calloway

North

0 1   5 Kilometer

0 1   5 Mile

- - - - Hiking trail   ● Tour stop

───── Parking area   Picnic area

41 75 5 3 120 5 280 340

In May, 1864, U.S. General Ulysses S. Grant ordered General William T. Sherman, then at Chattanooga, to attack the Confederate army in Georgia, "break it up, and go into the interior of the enemy's country as far as you can, inflicting all the damage you can upon their war resources." Sherman's 100,000 men and 254 pieces of artillery headed south, encountering General Joseph E. Johnston's Confederate forces of 65,000 with 187 cannon. The march south by the Union became a contest for Atlanta, a railroad hub and war manufacturing and storage facility for the Confederacy.

After numerous battles, Sherman's troops forced Johnston's forces to retreat yet again to a prepared defensive position anchored on Kennesaw Mountain. On June 22, fierce fighting between Sherman's forces and General John Bell Hood's Confederates occurred at Kolb's Farm; although the Union was not driven back, their southward movement was halted. On June 27, the fighting raged at Pigeon Hill where Confederates on nearby Little Kennesaw rolled huge rocks downhill and broke up the fighting; again, the Union forces withdrew. Brutal fighting occurred almost simultaneously at today's Cheatham Hill; both sides nicknamed this place "Dead Angle" due to the ferocity of the battle which included hand-to-hand fighting for a time. In total, the Union lost 3,000 men, the Confederates 500. Sherman resumed his successful flanking strategy and the Confederates abandoned the Kennesaw lines during the night of July 2, retreating to Johnston's River Line at the Chattahoochee River. The mountain was never captured during combat. Sherman crossed the river near Roswell on July 9 and Atlanta fell on September 2.

Kennesaw Mountain National Battlefield Park. Confederate soldiers manning cannon atop Kennesaw Mountain commanded a particularly imposing position.

Kennesaw Mountain National Battlefield Park. Cannon used during the battle were returned to the battlefield from storage after the war.

After the war, veterans created and joined a large number of veteran organizations. Through these associations, Congress was lobbied to set aside battlefields to honor the deceased and, in 1890, they began to do so. In 1917, Kennesaw Mountain National Battlefield Park was established by law as a national battlefield. Once established, battlefields were mandated to establish commissions composed of one retired Union officer, one retired Confederate officer, and one serving U.S. Army officer. The commission was responsible for surveying the battlefields, researching extant records, interviewing veterans, marking the fields where various corps served, and returning cannons, which had been stored in Armories, to battlefield locations where artillery batteries had served during the war.

Veterans organizations also lobbied state governments to mark sites with monuments. During the hostilities surrounding Kennesaw Mountain, many soldiers from Illinois and Ohio served. Some veterans from these states formed the Colonel Dan McCook Brigade Association which, in 1899, bought 60 acres over which they had fought. By 1914, they had raised the $19,240 necessary to construct and dedicate the Illinois monument at Cheatham Hill.

Under the management of the War Department, the battlefield sites were maintained for the purpose of military and historical study, particularly for serving officers who used the battlefields for the study of military strategy. More property was gradually added to the park through the late 1930s. In 1932, through an executive order issued by President Franklin Roosevelt, certain government departments were reorganized and the battlefields were brought under the auspices of the National Park Service. When the National Historic Preservation Act was signed into law on October 15, 1966, Kennesaw Mountain National Battlefield Park became Cobb's first National Register site by order of the Secretary of the Interior, and is listed at the national level of significance.

WILLIAM GIBBS McADOO HOUSE

The William Gibbs McAdoo House is located on the north side of US Highway 5, at its intersection with Macland Road in the 19th District, Land Lot 402. The house is a one and one-half story Greek Revival plantation house on a full daylight basement. The main body of the house is three bays wide and four deep under a gable roof. The raised foundation is built of coursed fieldstone. The window sash is nine over nine throughout.

The front has a full-width pedimented portico which serves as a front porch with Doric columns supporting the massively-scaled entablature. The portico stands on four square stuccoed brick piers which rise to the height of the raised foundation. Access to the front porch over the portico seems to have been made via spiral stairs, the stone foundations of which can be seen at either end of the porch.

The William Gibbs McAdoo House is one of the few antebellum houses to survive the Civil War devastation in the area. In 1863, William Gibbs McAdoo was born in the house that his parents called "Melora." They had bought the house while fleeing from the Union advance through Tennessee. McAdoo was the Secretary of the Treasury during Woodrow Wilson's presidency, and he was a senator from California later in his life. His second wife was Eleanor Wilson, daughter of the president.

The house was used as a school for young ladies for a short period of time. It was sold to Reverend Isaac M. Springer along with 76 acres for less than five dollars an acre. In the 1930s the house and property were acquired by the Johnny Walker estate, which uses it today as rental property. It is in the shadow of the Kennesaw National Battlefield Park and is one of the most endangered of the few antebellum houses in Cobb County.

William Gibbs McAdoo House. A one and one-half story Greek Revival plantation house on a full daylight basement, the house has a full width pedimented portico with Doric columns.

William Gibbs McAdoo House. From the back of the house, the foundation of coursed fieldstone can be readily seen as well as the 9 over 9 windows.

ROBERT MABLE HOUSE AND CEMETERY

The Mable House is located at 5239 Floyd Road near the Mableton community, District 17, Land Lot 40. The most recent addition to the National Register, it is a 16 acre tract of land with a two story frame antebellum house, a one-story frame smokehouse, a one-story frame free-standing remodeled kitchen, a family cemetery and a large wooded tract. Other suitable buildings may be moved to the site when they are located. The building is currently leased by the South Cobb Development Authority and work on the nomination has been spearheaded by that group.

The house dates from 1843 and has been a farm complex for over 100 years. It was the scene of a Federal encampment on July 3, 1864, during the Civil War. The Mable House was actually used as a field hospital by both Union and Confederate troops which helped to save it from destruction during the war. It has been well kept for use by a family or by tenants. It has its original heartpine flooring which was a typical building material in a large but plain farmhouse such as the Mable House. There are also hand-hewn beams, rough sawed lumber and wooden pegs used in the construction. Early settlement and continuous ownership (for the Mable House is still in the Mable family estate) make this a highly significant local historical property.

Robert Mable House. Built in 1843, the Mable House has remained in the same family for over a century.

The owner/builder was Robert Mable who was a native of Scotland. He acquired the property from Denson C. Melton who got the land in the 1832 land lottery. Mr. Mable contributed to the early industrialization/commercialization of the county by giving a right-of-way for the laying of a rail line through his property. The town of Mableton grew up around the railroad and by 1883-84 it had such town fixtures as a railroad station, a post office, a Baptist church, a school, a mill and a factory as well as a number of professional people.

MIDWAY PRESBYTERIAN CHURCH AND CEMETERY

The Midway Presbyterian Church and its cemetery are located at 4635 Dallas Highway (GA 120) in the 19th District, Land Lots 13 and 16. This rural congregation dates from about 1850. The historic church was constructed of concrete blocks in 1904-05. It is said to be the only known example of the use of this material in a rural church in the early 20th century. Behind the church is its graveyard, dating from the 1850s and containing about 850 graves.

Midway has recently been painted to a color more nearly like its 1905 dark shading. Originally the church had a slate-roof which proved to be so heavy that support bars had to be put in to hold the building up. The tongue and groove ceiling is still intact, although it is now hidden by a modern, lowered ceiling. The wainscoting is modern, but the pews are original as are the stained glass windows. The windows are said to have been made in Marietta, although no one knows the identity of the craftsmen.

The most remarkable feature of Midway Presbyterian Church is its heavy Norman arched front entrance tower supported by five columns. The short, squat tower has a steeple topped with its original finial. Since placing the church on the National Register, a modern sanctuary has been constructed immediately west of the historic church. Such churches with their cemeteries are highly visible reminders of the heritage of a changing rural landscape.

It is interesting to note that this community of Presbyterians existed in a region where the Presbyterian faith was that of a minority of the citizenry. The history of the church begins September 8, 1849, when the Cherokee Presbytery was petitioned by 31 people to allow a church to be organized in the Oregon militia district of Cobb County "midway" between the established town of Marietta and the newly emerging town of Dallas. Five acres were given by Alexander McCoy for a burial ground. The present building was preceded by at least two frame structures. The well-tended cemetery is the result of the formation of the Midway Memorial Association in 1913. The group meets each May, and they have incorporated in order to establish perpetual care for the cemetery.

Midway Presbyterian Church c. 1904. The photograph shows the Norman arched front entrance tower and the concrete block construction.

Midway Presbyterian Church Cemetery. Such churches with their cemeteries are highly visible reminders of the heritage of the rural landscape and early settler history.

SOPE CREEK MILL RUINS
(CHATTAHOOCHEE RIVER NATIONAL RECREATION AREA)

The Sope Creek Ruins consist of a number of structures now in ruins which once comprised the Marietta Paper Mills and other mills. The ruins are located in the 17th District, Land Lot 1078, near Paper Mill Road at Sope Creek.

The mills were incorporated on December 19, 1859. The Marietta Paper Mills and the Edward Denmead Flour Mills were burned by General Kenner Garrard's Cavalry, USA, during the Civil War and were rebuilt during post-Civil War times. In 1888 a wood pulp mill was added to the complex, and a twine factory was built in 1889. The mills ceased operating in 1902. An electrical power dam (c. 1922) and its outbuildings add to the late 19th century and early 20th century industrial complex present today at the site. The ruins are located in a scenic landscape which is reported to be one of the few remaining undisturbed rock gorges of a Chattahoochee River tributary.

Indications of aboriginal American people abound in the area, although only preliminary archaeological studies have been made. It is said that the name Sope is taken from the name of an old Cherokee Indian who somehow stayed in the area after the Trail of Tears removal. "Old Sope" is listed in the 1836 evaluation of Cherokee property as having a cabin and peach and apple trees near Sharp Mountain Creek.

Sope Creek, one of the few remaining undisturbed rock gorges of a Chattahoochee River tributary.

Sope Creek Mill ruins. Closed in 1902, the Marietta Paper Mills, and other mills in the area, were an important part of Cobb County's early industrial history.

CONCORD COVERED BRIDGE HISTORIC DISTRICT

The Concord Covered Bridge Historic District is located in the 17th District of Cobb County, Land Lots 170, 171, 172, 189, 190, 191. It is listed on both the National and Cobb Register of Historic Places, although the boundaries of the Cobb district include more sites than those of the National Register. Historic structures or sites within the Cobb district include the Martin L. Ruff homeplace and cemetery, the Miller's House, the Grist Mill, the Concord Covered Bridge, Concord Woolen Mills and Millworkers Village (both in ruins), the Gann-Love-Hill House, the Rock House (John W. Rice Summer Cottage) and a railroad trestle bridge.

The early significance of the area plus the possibilities of archaeological exploration makes this area one of the most interesting of all of Cobb county's historic resources. The important natural features within the area include Nickajack Creek and the wooded, hilly topography. Nickajack Creek flows into the Chattahoochee River and forms one of the 12 major drainage basins in Cobb County. The creek is approximately 30 feet wide and is a picturesque element in the historic district. The creek is full of large rocks, and in several places there are shoals. In the area of the Miller's House and the Grist Mill (Ruff's Mill), the creek follows a double horseshoe loop, leaving the house and mill on a peninsula of land. The loop makes a sharp drop, which provided a natural place for a millpond, remnants of which can be seen.

The history of the area is closely related to Martin L. Ruff, Sr. and Robert Daniell. They owned and developed this area as a manufacturing center in the early 1850s. The relative isolation caused by the closing of the factories and the railroad siding has resulted in the preservation of the terrain and infrastructure much as Mr. Ruff and Mr. Daniell knew it.

Robert Daniell, a great-grandson of Robert Daniell, a colonial governor of Charleston, South Carolina, moved from Clarke County, Georgia, to Cobb County in 1850. Martin L. Ruff, Sr. moved to this area from Henry County, Georgia. They were early settlers taking advantage of the land lottery of Georgia which made the Cherokee lands available to white settlers. In the 1851 tax digest, Ruff is listed as a landowner, and in 1850 the two joined their holdings to operate several enterprises including a grist mill, woolen mill, and sawmill.

The Daniell homeplace does not stand today. It was located in the Smyrna city limits where the present-day subdivision known as Bennett Woods now stands. The family burying ground was located in the Maloney Springs Cemetery in Fair Oaks, although some family members were buried near their homesite following an outbreak of smallpox in the area.

Concord Covered Bridge

Central to the entire district is the Concord Covered Bridge itself. While the current bridge is largely a reconstruction and repair of the older structure, a bridge has stood on this site since the 1850s. Only the central pier of the present bridge is part of the early construction. That bridge was burned in the Civil War actions in 1864 and was replaced by a covered bridge in 1872. Subsequent use has required reinforcement and reconstruction of the bridge to strengthen its load-bearing capacity. It belongs to Cobb County and is maintained by the county Department of Transportation. It is 133 feet long, 16 feet wide, and 13 feet high, with less than an eight foot clearance. The stonemasonry supports are original. The concrete piers were added in 1965. The structure consists of Queenpost trusses. It is one of the 17 covered bridges remaining in Georgia and is one of just two that embody the Queenpost truss. This bridge was included in the *World Guide to Covered Bridges* (1972), published by the National Society for Preservation of Covered Bridges. The bridge is included on both the National and Cobb Register of Historic Places.

Although this bridge is largely a reconstruction and repair of an older structure, a bridge has stood on this site since the 1850s.

Ruff's Mill

Ruff's Mill, which was a grist mill, is located off Concord Road on the same peninsula containing the Miller's House. It was built around 1850. It was later operated by Asbury Martin and was known as Martin Feed and Grain. There are no millworks left within the structure. It is included in both the National and Cobb Register of Historic Places.

Originally a grist mill built around 1850, Ruff's Mill no longer contains the original millworks.

Miller's House

The Miller's House is also listed on both the National and Cobb Registers. It is located centrally on the peninsula of land which also contains the grist mill. This two-story frame structure of simple design with Victorian alterations was built around 1850. This structure appears to predate Ruff's ownership of the property. Original portions of the house can be seen in the heavy timber frame of hand-hewn beam resting on fieldstone foundations. The two end chimneys are constructed with fieldstone bases and brick stacks. The grounds feature terraces, walks, fieldstone retaining walls, a concrete swimming pool and other formal landscape elements. These improvements were added in the 1930s by the owner of the property, Dr. Clinton Reed. The landscaping plan was designed by William C. Pauley, a noted landscape architect. The house was listed on the National Register by more recent owners, Gordon and Alice Ruckart.

The Miller's House. Built about 1850, the house is of simple design with later Victorian alterations. The rear yard features formal landscaping elements and originally overlooked a mill pond.

The Rock House (John W. Rice Summer Cottage)

The Rice Cottage, c. 1900, is a turn of the century residence built entirely of fieldstone held in place by thick mortar joints. Listed on the National Register in 1983 and standing above the Nickajack Creek, the Rice cottage oversees the ruins of the dam that once served the Ruff-Daniell industrial site on the opposite side of Concord Road. The Rock House was probably built as a summer residence for the Rice family who were a prominent Atlanta family, according to newspaper accounts of the day. When the cottage was constructed, no two windows were made alike. The builder was an inventor and held patents for many innovations, including an adjustable shaving stand. He owned the Concord Woolen Mills where an early mill village was constructed. The Seaboard Railroad built tracks just north of the mills where there was a stop named Rice's Station or Rice, evidently named for the Rice family.

Rice sold the property, including mills and the house, to Mrs. Annie E. Gillespie Johnson, whose bachelor son (Gillespie Johnson) lived in the house. Mrs. Johnson owned the house and mills until they closed about 1910. With the mill closed and the millpond breached, no further effort was made to maintain the industrial character of the area. The mill workers moved on, the railroad abandoned Rice's Station and today only the Rock House attests to John W. Rice's presence in the area.

The Rock House. Note that the windows in the south wall are of a variety of shapes and sizes.

Rock House (John W. Rice Summer Cottage) north side. Note stonework and chimneys amid recent alterations.

Rock House. Back of house overlooking Nickajack Creek.

Concord Woolen Mills and Millworkers Village

The Concord Woolen Mills and Millworkers Village ruins consist of a three-story shell of fieldstone with framed window and door openings. The facades of the structure are in various stages of deterioration and in some places the building is only one story tall. There is no roof, and trees grow in the interior spaces. The antebellum factory built by Robert Daniell and Martin Ruff, Sr., was burned during the Civil War. It was rebuilt by 1869 and burned again in 1889. A third structure was completed in the 1890s and operated until about 1912 when new technology rendered the mills obsolete and the mills closed. There has been little effort at preservation of the site since then. Just north of the mill there are ruins of an accessory building and also a small mill village, said to be one of the earliest in the state. Local residents describe a number of old well sites, springs, and former building sites in this area. There was a superintendent's house and there may have been a railroad siding as well.

According to Sarah Gober Temple's book, *The First Hundred Years*, Martin L. Ruff and Robert Daniell erected and operated the Concord Woolen Mills on Nickajack Creek, and they rebuilt them

Concord Woolen Mills. Chimney from millworker's cottage.

after the war. The mill was sold in 1872 to a group of Atlanta businessmen: Zachary A. Rice, James H. Porter, and S. B. Love. It is from Zachary A. Rice that John W. Rice came into ownership of the woolen mills.

The last owner of the working mills was Annie E. Gillespie Johnson. She also owned the Rock House, and her son lived there. She was from New York and was married in 1876 to J. Lindsay Johnson, a native Georgian who was a lawyer in Rome, a planter, a state legislator in the 1880s, and after 1903, publisher of the *Rome Tribune.* He was U. S. Census Bureau Chief in the Philippines in 1914. After his death, Mrs. Johnson ran the newspaper. In 1910, she attempted to make arrangements for establishing a colony for Russian Jews in the mill village. This unsuccessful effort made her one of the few Georgians to evidence an interest in immigrant problems of the era. She was associated with efforts to disperse immigrants by using various ports of entry, especially New Orleans, Louisiana and Galveston, Texas. She was a founder of the Georgia Federation of Women's Clubs and from 1897 to 1901 she served as the Federation's second statewide president. The mill ruins and the mill village are not listed on the National Register, but are included in the Cobb Register.

Concord Woolen Mills. A view of the three-story shell of fieldstone showing an intact plinth, the sills having been removed by vandals in recent times.

Concord Woolen Mills. A facade of the structure shows the need for stabilization of the ruins. Note the framing of the window in the upper center of the picture.

Concord Woolen Mills. Accessory storage facility at the mill site.

Gann-Love-Hill House

The Gann-Love-Hill House is located to the west of the Concord Covered Bridge complex on Concord Road. It is an antebellum structure dating from the 1840s. It was built by State Senator John Gann on land awarded in the land lottery of 1832. There is a family story that the house was spared during the Civil War battle because a Yankee general saw the Masonic flag flying from an upstairs window. Be that as it may, the house survived and today is known as Surrey Hills Farm. It is on a fairly large tract of land with several frame outbuildings complementing the frame construction of the dwelling.

The house was owned by S. B. Love, one of the proprietors of the Concord Woolen Mills in the last quarter of the 19th century. In the 1930s, it was the childhood home of Agnes Louise Bradford Barnes. (One of Mrs. Barnes' sons is State Senator Roy Barnes of Mableton.) At that time, it was a working dairy farm. The house and property was purchased by the present owners in 1947. Like the mill ruins and the mill village, the Gann-Love-Hill house is included in the Cobb Register, but is not listed on the National Register.

Gann- Love - Hill house. An antebellum structure dating from the 1840s, the house is a simple farmhouse with added Victorian features.

Gann-Love-Hill house. Large barn located near the house, with an attached shed. A small storage building also with vertical timbers, is nearest the driveway.

Martin Ruff Homeplace and Cemetery

The Martin Ruff Homeplace contains a residence (parts of which may be antebellum), a barn, and a cemetery. The residence is about 500 feet from Concord Road and is accessible by a long dirt driveway. The structure is a simple, frame, neoclassical farm house rebuilt around the turn of the century by John Wesley Ruff, one of Martin Ruff's sons, following a fire. The property remained in the Ruff family until 1943. The current owners have done extensive restoration and repair work to the house and property in general. It is included in the Cobb Register, but is not listed on the National Register.

Martin Ruff homeplace. The house is a simple, frame, neoclassical farm house in extremely good condition, and is located amid several acres of pasture and woodlot.

The Martin Ruff Family Cemetery. The cemetery has been well-maintained unlike many family burying grounds in Cobb County.

Railroad Trestle Bridge

Of undetermined age, although certainly dating from the late 19th or early 20th century, the railroad trestle bridge is included in the Cobb Register as a fine example of engineering technology. Additional research into the parameters of railroad trestle construction statewide should be undertaken to determine the contribution of this bridge to an important facet of the history of the state and Cobb County. It is not listed on the National Register.

Railroad Trestle Bridge in the Concord Covered Bridge County Historic District. The bridge is a fine example of engineering technology in the late 19th or early 20th century.

THE GEORGIA HISTORICAL MARKER PROGRAM IN COBB COUNTY

A great deal of the force of the preservation movement comes from contemporary architecture's failure to build well, its failure to build in a style that satisfies the needs of our cities and the needs of our senses. A lot of our belief in preservation comes from our fear of what will replace buildings that are not preserved; all too often we fight to save not because what we want to save is so good but because we know that what will replace it will be no better.

Paul Goldberger
Preservation: Toward an Ethic in the 1980s (1980)

The Georgia Historical Marker Program was begun in 1951 by the Georgia Historical Commission. The first markers erected commemorated the Civil War, but the program soon began marking the entire scope of Georgia history as it was intended. In the years since its inception the marker program has recognized over 1900 sites and events in Georgia history.

Today the Parks and Historic Sites Division of the Georgia Department of Natural Resources administers the Historical Marker Program. A marker maintenance shop at Panola Mountain State Park repairs and refurbishes over 170 markers each year with the assistance of Georgia's State Parks and Historic Sites Division.

Historical Markers are often targets of vandals, out of control motor vehicles and road maintenance crews. The public's assistance is always welcome. To report a missing or damaged marker or to inquire about the program contact the Parks and Historic Sites Division at (404) 656-7092 or the Historic Marker Shop at (404) 474-8813.

The text of the markers was supplied by the Parks and Historic Sites Division, and is copied directly from their records. No assumption of the validity or accuracy of this information should be implied by its inclusion in this book; the editors have not visited each marker to verify a correlation between the actual marker and this text. The abbreviations used on the markers are used here without further interpretation. The only material alteration to this material was the insertion of the correct spelling of Sope Creek, where appropriate.

A typical historical marker location on Paces Ferry Road near the Chattahoochee River in Vinings.

Davis' Cross Roads

Site of house of Rev. Gary Davis (1799-1875). June, 1864, this was an outpost of operations on Johnston's left flank, C by rt. wing of Sherman's forces F moving from New Hope Ch. toward the State R.R.

Hardee's Corps C occupied a line at Gilgal Church, 1.5 mi. S.E.

June 10, Strickland's (3d) Brigade, Hascall's (2d) Div., 23d A.C., F assaulted Cleburne's sharpshooters C at the Davis house & on the adjacent hill. After a sharp contest, the Confederates withdrew to Gilgal Church.

Due West Community

Site of Gilgal Primitive Baptist Church, a log structure and prominent landmark during military operations, June 5-17, 1864, in which church was destroyed.

Cleburne's Div. (C), was posted at the church - the left of Johnston's line (C) after the withdrawal of Polk's Corps (C) from Lost Mt., June 9. Confronting Cleburne were the 23d A.C. and Butterfield's (3d) Div., 20th A.C. (F).

Due to pressure on his extended front, Johnston swung Hardee's Corps (C), back to the Mud Creek line E. of Sandtown Road, June 16.

(In front of the Church at Due West.)

Lost Mountain Cross Roads

On May 23-24, 1864, Lt. Gen. Leonidas Polk's Corps marched from Allatoona, Bartow Co., to Dallas, Paulding Co., passing Lost Mountain P.O.

June 4-5, Polk withdrew from the Dallas-New Hope front to Lost Mtn., this position being the left on the 1st. Kennesaw Line.

June 9th, the Corps was shifted eastward to the vicinity of New Salem Ch., N. of Burnt Hickory Rd., where it formed the center.

This shift was a necessary move in the extension of Johnston's line eastward of the State R.R. because of the arrival of the 17th Corps (F) on his right flank.

(At Lost Mountain Community on Ga. 76.)

Old Sandtown Road

1.5 miles N.W. is the site of old Gilgal Primitive Baptist Ch. (at Due West), a landmark of military operations.

June 5-17,1864

S.E. along this road, Cleburne's Div. of Hardee's Corps (C) withdrew from Gilgal to Old Marietta

Rd. S. of the Darby house, turning E. to ridge beyond Mud Cr.

June 16.

Schofield's 23rd Corps marched S. on this Rd. from Gilgal to the Moss house (Floyd Station) June 17 - July 2, -at which time it was the right flank of Sherman's forces on Kennesaw front.

(On Ga 120 at the fork leading to Due West.)

Green Plantation

Polk's Corps (C) having held the sector centering on Lost Mountain, June 5-9, was withdrawn E., leaving Gen. W. H. Jackson's Cav. Div. (C) to hold the vacated line.

On the 17th, Johnston (C) shifted his left flank E. to Mud Creek; during this withdrawal, Ross' Brigade (C) of Jackson's Cav. fought a spirited action from the hill W. of the Widow (Piety M.) Green house, which was used as a hospital.

Ross' Texas Brigade held the position until forced to retreat by Hascall's (2d) Div., 23d Corps (F), which had seized Lost Mountain that morning.

(Ga 120 near the micro-wave relay tower.)

Mud Creek Line

Hardee's entrenched line crossed the Rd. at this point - position held June 17-19, 1864 by Cleburne's Div., after withdrawal of Johnston's left flank from Gilgal Ch.

A sharp artillery duel & severe rain marked the 48 hrs. here - the opposition being the 20th & 23d Corps batteries at Darby's, W. of the creek.

Brig. Gen. Lucius E. Polk (nephew of Lt. Gen. Polk) was severely wounded & the regiments of his brigade were assigned to other commends in Cleburne's Division.

(Location: Ga 120, east of Mud Creek.)

Darby Plantation

The old Marietta Rd. joined the Sandtown Road here - 1864.

June 17-19, Geary's (2) Div., 20th A.C., (F) supporting 13th N.Y. & Pa. E. batteries were N. of Rd. & Cox's (3d) Div., 23d A.C., (F) supporting 1st Ohio Bat. D. were S. of Rd. - in area from Darby house to Mud. Cr.

The artillery duel with Cleburne (C) on high ridge E. of creek & Geary's rain-soaked infantry in flooded area next to stream, are a part of the record.

On 19th, Cleburne (C) moved E. followed by 20th A.C. (F) 23d A.C. (F) moved S. - a march that broke the Kennesaw stalemate.

Manning's Mill

June 19, 1864 - 23d A.C. (F), finding Noses's Cr. flooded and only the string-pieces of bridge in place, camped at night, W side.

June 20 - Cameron's (2d) Brigade, Cox's (3d) (F) Div. seized and repaired bridge - forcing back Jackson's Cavalry (C) and occupied high ground E, June 21, a section of 1st Ohio Battery and 12th Kentucky (F) moved S to the Cheney House.

June 22-23d - A.C. crossed cr. Cox's Division moved S on Sandtown Road to Cheney's and Hascall's (2d) Div. moved E to Kolb's school-house where it joined the 20th A.C. (F) in the Battle of Kolb's Farm.

Schofield's Headquarters
Home of Andrew J. Cheney (1815-1886)
Built about 1856

Headquarters of Maj. Gen. John M. Schofield commanding Army of the Ohio (F) - right wing of Sherman's forces on the Kennesaw front, June 22-30, 1864, while directing the flanking march of 23d A.C. (F) S on the Sandtown Road.

Cox's (3d) Div. camped here and supported Hascall's (2d) Div. (F) near the McAdoo house during Battle of Kolb's Farm. Sherman inspected the right of Kennesaw line (F) here, June 23 and 25.

(Powder Springs Road at Sandtown Road.)

Wm. G. McAdoo's Birthplace

The house atop hill is one of few battlefield houses surviving military operations of the Kennesaw Campaign.

McAdoo ownership was Jan. 6, 1863 - Feb. 3, 1864. Here, Oct. 31, 1863 was born the Hon. Wm. G. McAdoo, Secy. Treasury. 1913 - 1918. Candidate Dem. presidential nomination 1924, 1928, U.S. Senator, California, 1933-1939.

Place was name MELORA during McAdoo occupancy. S.B. Oatman owned it at time of Battle of Kolb's Farm.

(Powder Springs Road near Mt. Zion Church.)

Battle of Kolb's Farm
June 22, 1864

Hascall's (2d) Div., 23d A.C., Union, via Manning's Mill, reached Kolb's schoolhouse (site of Mt. Zion Ch.) 2 p.m. and joined its left to right of William's (1st) Div., 20th A.C. (F) at the McAdoo-Oatman house on the Powder Springs Rd.

Hascall placed 3 brigades on high ground S.E. of the road. Skirmishers, supported by the 14th Ky. (F) seized a ridge E. of the Valentine Kolb house and stubbornly held it until forced to withdraw.

The left of Stevenson's Div. (C), after dislodging 14th Ky., advanced toward Hascall's line but were driven back.

(Powder Springs Road (Ga 5) at Mt. Zion Church.)

Battle of Kolb's Farm
June 22, 1864

The 14th Ky. (2d Div., 23d A.C.,) together with the 123d N.Y. (1st Div., 20th A.C.,) (F) were posted as skirmishers E. of the Kolb farmstead.

The stubborn resistance by the 14th Ky., and 123d N.Y., disrupted the concerted assault by Stevenson's Div. (C) upon the main line (F) astride the Powder Springs Rd. W. of this point.

This delaying action, together with Federal artillery fire halted Stevenson's attempt to win his objective.

(Powder Springs Road (Ga 5) at the John Ward (Cheatham Hill) Road.)

Battle of Kolb's Farm
June 22, 1864

The extension of the right wing of Federal forces S. of the Dallas Rd., threatening to outflank him, Johnston sent Hood's Corps (C) from the right, (E. of Kennesaw) to this, the extreme left, with directions to stop further Federal advances.

Hood sent Stevenson's 4 brigades (C)-2, astride the road, and 2 N. of it, against 20th and 23d Corps troops (F) posted astride the road to the W.

This, and later attempts failed to check the Federal extensions Southward.

(Powder Springs Road (Ga 5)

Battle of Kolb's Farm
June 22, 1864

The 3 brigades of William's (1st) Div., 20th A.C. (F) were posted on the high ground W. of the road between this point and the Powder Springs road.

Geary's (2d) Div. (F) right joined Williams at the ravine W. of the Greer house, his artillery sweeping the low ground.

Brown's and Reynold's brigades of Stevenson's Div. (C), assaulted the low ground.
Brown's and Reynold's brigades of Stevenson's Div. (C), assaulted the left of William's line by way of the ravine - trying to turn his left, but the 20th A.C. artillery broke up the assault and Stevenson's two brigades (C) withdrew.

(John Ward (Cheatham Hill) Road about 0.7 mile north of the Powder Springs Road at a fork of Noses Cr.)

Gen George H. Thomas' Headquarters (In Field)
Army of the Cumberland (F)
June 24 - July 3, 1864

In field west of road, where right of 14th joined left of 20th Corps (F).

From this point, June 27, Gen. Thomas (F) directed the assault of 5 brigades of 4th & 14th Corps, against Hardee's Corps (C) posted on Cheatham's Hill, E., across valley of Nose's Cr.

This attempt to penetrate Johnston's (C) Kennesaw line was void of results.

(John Ward (Cheatham Hill) road between Powder Springs Road (Ga 5) and the Dallas Road (Ga 120).)

Gen. J. E. Johnston's Headquarters

Cyrus York housesite: June 10-19, 1864. Johnston's forces (C) moved from Paulding Co. to Kennesaw area, June 5, and occupied lines from Lost to Brushy Mtns. June 16, the left was withdrawn E. of Mud Creek. June 19, all forces shifted to mountain line.

June 19. Headquarters moved to the Kirkpatrick house south of the mountain.

The advanced Fed. line crossed the road several hundred ft. W. Between June 19 and 27, the two-story York house, used by Fed. sharpshooters, was destroyed by Confederate artillery fire from the mountain.

(Burnt Hickory Road west of Old Mountain Rd.)

Logan's 15th A. C. Line

June 25, 26, 1864. These troops, being designated to assault Confederate forces on Kennesaw Spur, moved to this sector and were aligned astride the Burnt Hickory road at this point.

June 27. Walcutt's brigade (Harrow's Div.) N. of road, G. A. Smith's astride the road and Lightbourn's S. of it (M. L. Smith's Div.) moved E toward Kennesaw Spur where the attack fell upon Gen. S. G. French's div., (Loring's A.C.) (C), and the right of Hardee's A.C. (C) just S. of it.
This assault failed to break the Confederate line; a similar one, at Cheatham Hill, 2.5 mi. S. was also devoid of results - the 2 engagements known as the Battle of Kennesaw Mtn.

(Burnt Hickory Road wet of Old Mountain Rd.)

Gen. Leonidas Polk's Headquarters

G. W. Hardage house; June 10-14, 1864. After withdrawing his corps from Lost Mtn. June 9, Polk's Headquarters (C) were at the John Kirk house 1 mile W. on this road. June 10, headquarters were moved to Hardage house.

Sun. June 12. The Bishop-General read the church service (Episcopal) for his staff, escort, and the Hardage family.

June 14. Polk rode with Johnston, Hardee and others to Pine Mtn. to inspect Bate's (C) line at that advanced outpost. While there, Polk was killed by a Federal shell.

(Burnt Hickory Road west of Old Mountain Rd.)

Gen. O. O. Howard's Headquarters

Wallis house; June 19, 22, 1864. Following the withdrawal of Johnston's forces, from the Mud Creek - Brushy Mtn. line, June 19, to the final one, which included Kennesaw Mtn., Howard's 4th A.C. (F) moved E. from Hardee's salient. (C)
Astride this, the Burnt Hickory Rd., the corps (F) advanced toward Kennesaw until halted by a counter-attack from the mtn. (C)

An entrenched position (F) was established at the York House one mile E. which line was later occupied by the 15th Corps of the Army of the Tennessee. (F)

(Burnt Hickory Rd. west of Old Mountain Road near Mt. Cavalry Church.)

Hardee's Salient

June 16, 1864. From this point as a pivot, the Confederate line W. to Gilgal Church and Lost Mtn. was swung back to a N. and S. line E. of Mud Creek, thereby making a salient angle - Hardee's A.C. on the left or S. Polk's & Hood's Corps on the right, or E. (C).

This shift of Hardee's line was due to pressure on his front by the 20th & 23rd Corps (F), from June 9 to 15.

Further pressure by the 4th, 14th & 20th Corps (F) upon Hardee's salient, June 17, 18, forced Johnston to abandon his entire line, June 19, for a final position which included Kennesaw Mountain.

(New Salem Road south of Stilesboro Road near New Salem Church.)

Lt. Gen. Leonidas Polk
Killed at Pine Mtn.

The wooded knob W. was a fortified outpost, 1.25 mi. N. of Johnston's (C) entrenched line from Lost to Brushy Mtns., June 5-15, 1864. Pine Mtn. was held by Bate's Div. of Hardee's A.C., 5th Co. Washington Artillery of New Orleans and Lt. R. T. Beauregard's S. Carolina Battery (C).

June 14, while observing Fed. lines with Generals Johnston and Hardee, Gen. Polk was killed by a shell from a Federal battery - identity of which is not certain.

The outpost was abandoned the next day and withdrawn to the main line (C).

(Stilesboro Road at Hamilton Road near Pine Mountain.)

Pine Mountain

June 10, 1864. The 4th A.C. (F) moved from Mars Hill Ch. to position along this road, facing S. toward Pine Mtn. - highest point between Lost & Kennesaw Mtns. The 14th A.C. was on the left; the 20th on the right (F).

Pine Mtn. was fortified & held as an outpost of the main Confederate line 1.25 miles S. - the line that extended from Lost Mtn. to Brushy Mtn. - June 5-15.

June 14. Generals Johnston, Hardee & Polk (C) while observing Federal lines from Pine Mtn., were fired on by 4th & 20th Corps batteries (F); Gen. Leonidas Polk was killed by a shell.

(Stilesboro Road at Pine Mountain Road.)

Stilesboro-Sandtown Crossroads

From this vicinity was launched the 1st attacks by Sherman's forces (F) on Johnston's Kennesaw lines (C), after withdrawal of both armies from Paulding County.

June 6, 1864. 20th A.C. (F) occupied E-W line on Stilesboro Road (facing S.) extending 1 mi. E. Old Mt. Olivet Ch. stood .25 mi. E; it was burned the same day.

June 9. Cox's Div. (23d A.C. (F) took position W. along Stilesboro Road, connecting with Hascall's Div. (F) astride Burnt Hickory Road. The objective of Federal forces was Hardee's A.C. (C) from Gilgal Ch. to Pine Mtn.

(Stilesboro Road at the Acworth-Due West Rd.)

Route of Polk's Corps

May 23d, 1864, Lt. Gen. Leonidas Polk's Corps (C), marching S. from Allatoona, camped at night in this vicinity enroute to Dallas in Paulding County via Lost Mountain.

This was the left wing of Johnston's army (C) which had crossed the Etowah River May 20, and remained at Allatoona until the 23rd.

Learning that Sherman's forces (F) had left Cassville & Kingston for Dallas, Johnston moved S. on parallel roads to checkmate the Federal flanking march - Hood's & Hardee's Corps (C) marched by the New Hope road four miles west.

(Acworth-Due West (Old Sandtown Road) near Mt. Olivet Baptist Church.)

Durham House

Headquarters of Brig. Gen. Absalom Baird, commanding 3d Div. 14th A.C., Army of the Cumberland (F), June 6-10, 1864.

Baird's, together with 1st & 2nd divisions, were camped along Proctor's Cr., E - a part of the concerted drive on Johnston's forces (C) near Kennesaw. Heavy rains halted military movements for several days in this area.

Oct. 9 Baird revisited Durham house enroute to Gaylesville, Ala., in pursuit of Hood's forces (C) withdrawing to Tennessee.

(Acworth-Due West (Old Sandtown Road) 0.3 mile north of Mt. Olivet Baptist Church.)

Gen. George H. Thomas' Headquarters

Near Mars Hill Ch., June 6-10, 1864. Headquarters Army of the Cumberland (F), which had crossed Allatoona Cr., 1.25 mi. S.W. June 6 - its objectives: Allatoona, the State R.R., & the Confederate front at Kennesaw Mtn.

The 4th Corps (Howard), camped near the church - headquarters at Dr. James Peter's house (Davenport place); the 14th (Palmer), at Durham & Pritchard farms N. of new Mt. Olivet Ch.; the 20th (Hooker), at Stilesboro and Sandtown crossroads.
Excessive rain & mud halted troop movements for four days.

(Mars Hill Road south of US 41 near Mars Hill Church.)

Site - Mason's Bridge

June 4, 1864. Ireland's (3d) Brigade, Geary's (2d) Div., 20th A.C. (F), seized, repaired & held Mason's Bridge, which had been wrecked by Confederate forces retreating eastward.

June 6, the Army of the Cumberland (F), commanded by Maj. Gen. George H. Thomas crossed Allatoona Creek here, enroute from Dallas-New Hope front in Paulding County to the Kennesaw Mtn. environs.

The Cumberland Army consisted of three Corps: 4th, 14th & 20th, which formed the center during the twenty-nine days of conflict - June 5, July 3 - in Cobb County.

(County Line (Old Stilesboro) Road at Allatoona Creek.)

Site of Old Allatoona Church

Extreme left of Federal line on the Dallas-New Hope front where Johnston's & Sherman's forces had been in daily conflict since May 25, 1864.
June 3. Hovey's (1st) Div., 23d A.C. (F), drove Armstrong's cavalry (C) from this road, thereby uncovering right of Confederate line - Walker's Div., Hardee's Corp - near the Foster house 1 mile, S.W.

Seizure of this road broke the 10-day stalemate & the opposing lines shifted East to the Kennesaw front.

(County Line Road near McLain Road west of Allatoona Creek.)

Dallas-Acworth Road

June 2, 1864. The rt. of Johnston's Dallas-New Hope line - a short distance E. of road, was held by Bate's Div. of Hardee's Corps (C), after being pressed back by Fed. 23rd A.C.

June 3. Walker's Div., of Hardee, prolonged Bate's line N.E., endeavoring to hold the position, but seizure of road 1.5 mi. N.E. by Hovey's (1st) Div., 23d A.C. (F), forced Johnston to abandoned his Dallas-New Hope line & withdraw E. toward the State R.R.

Johnston maintained the Dallas-New Hope line during ten days of constant battle in a rugged wilderness.

(County Line (Old Stilesboro) Road at the Burnt Hickory Road.)

James Foster House
Old Burnt Hickory Road

Pressure on right of Johnston's line (C) by 23d A.C. (F), forced the rt. of Hardee's Corps (C) E. of the Dallas-Acworth road, enabling Schofield (F) to gain a position near the Foster house. June 2, 1864.

Failing to get promised support from the 20th A.C. (F), Schofield was unable to pursue his advantage & night found Hardee's forces still holding the rt. of the line.

This movement was in line with the Fed. drive to outflank Johnston & force his withdrawal E. to the R.R. heavy rains began & continued until June 19.

(Burnt Hickory Road at the County Line Rd.)

Hood & Hardee
Withdraw E. to R.R.

June 2-4, 1864. Hood's A.C. was posted 1 mi. W. & Hardee's A.C. was aligned along Dallas-Acworth Rd., N. 1.5 mi. to Burnt Hickory Rd. - Confederate center & rt.

These Corps withdrew, along with the rest of Johnston's forces (c), when the Federal 23d A.C. seized the Dallas-Acworth Rd. near old Allatoona Ch., 2.5 mi. N.E. June 3.

Hood & Hardee retreated E. along this road June 4, to positions between Lost Mountain & the State R.R.

(Due West Road near the Paulding County Line.)

The Wm. Nickols House

Hardee's Corps (C) marched by this road to points S. of New Hope Ch., from Stegall's Station (Emerson) May 23, 24, 1864.

Hood's Corps (C) followed Hardee's, May 24, 25, from Etowah River (at R.R. Bridge), reaching New

Hope Ch. in time to check 20th A.C. (F) at that point.

Hood's Corps was rear guard of Johnston's march to checkmate Sherman's forces (F) moving toward Dallas, on roads westward to outflank Johnston's position in the Allatoona mountains. Stewart's Div. of Hood's Corps camped at the Nickols farm, night of May 24.

(Ga 92, 0.6 mile southwest of US 41.)

Residence of Alice McLellan Birney
(1872 - 1884)

This house was the residence of Alice McLellan Birney, co-founder of the National Congress of Parents and Teachers during the post-war era.

The home was probably built by Miss Mary Ann Nesbit prior to 1869, in which year it was purchased by William R. Gignilliatt.

In 1887 it was bought by St. James Episcopal Church for use as a Rectory.

(Church Street at Kennesaw Avenue in Marietta.)

Camp McDonald

To the east were the parade grounds and tents of Camp McDonald, established by Governor Joseph E. Brown, June 1861, to train citizens for the defense of the Confederacy. Here Phillips legion, and other Georgia units trained, that rendered valiant service to the Southern cause.

The camp closed in the late fall of 1861 but reopened in 1862 and 1863 to train more troops for the Confederacy. Sham battles and parades here attracted large and appreciative audiences.

(US 41 in Kennesaw)

Sope Creek Industries

By 1854 Edward Denmead was operating a large flour mill upstream from the covered bridge.

By 1859 a paper mill was operating downstream, making writing, printing, and wrapping paper. Both industries were built here to utilize water power.

Burned by the Federals, the paper mill was rebuilt and operated until the early 1900s. A unit of the paper mill operated in Marietta until 1918.

The wartime bridge was probably similar to this one, built about 1880. [Paper Mill at Sope Cr.]

[Ed. note: The covered bridge was burned by vandals in 1964.]

Cobb County

Created December 3, 1832, and named for Judge Thomas W. Cobb, a former U.S. Senator. Marietta was named for his wife.

Fertile lands gave impetus to farming; ample water power encouraged industries. People from further south sought Marietta as a summer resort due to delightful climate and society.

Cobb County sacrificed much for the Southern Confederacy; ravaged by war, it fought slowly upward through reconstruction. In recent years industry has brought wealth and growth to the area.

(Mounted on the front wall of the Courthouse in Marietta.)

Hardee's Corps at Powder Springs

May 23, 1864. Lt. Gen. Wm. J. Hardee's A.C. (C) marched from Stegall's Station (Emerson), & Etowah River, via New Hope Ch., reaching Powder Springs afternoon of the 24th.

The Corps made this march in advance of Johnston's forces (C) to find the rt. flank of Sherman's army (F) ascertained to be approaching Dallas, Paulding Co., from the W.

Marking time, Hardee moved S.E. to Powder Springs for water. May 25, 3 a.m. the Corps counter-marched toward Dallas, there to await orders placing it on the embattled Dallas-New Hope Church line.

(Ga 6 west of Powder Springs at bridge over Powder Springs Creek.)

Big Shanty

In 1838-41, a construction camp of laborers, grading & building the State R.R. was located at the spring approximately 250 yds. W. of here, where temporary structures (shanties) housed the workmen.

Track level here, being some 345 ft. above the level at Cartersville, 19 mi. N., the grade was 18 ft. per mi. at time of construction.

In railroad parlance, this was known as "the big grade to the shanties" - later shortened to "big shanty grade", finally to "Big Shanty", which was changed to Kennesaw about 1870. In June, 1864, Federal Forces on the Kennesaw Mtn. front, drew supplies at this point.

(In Kennesaw at intersection of Cherokee and Old U.S. 41.)

Site - Lacy Hotel

Eastward across R.R. stood the 2-story frame hotel, leased by George M. Lacy in 1859 - an eating house for passengers on the state-owned railway until June 9, 1864, at which time the Federal forces occupied Big Shanty.

April 12, 1862, the Andrews' Raiders (F) seized the locomotive "General" while train crew & passengers were breakfasting at the hotel.

Fortified by a stockade, it housed a Federal garrison from June 9 to Oct. 3, 1864, when it was captured by Confederate forces. Reoccupied by Federal troops it was maintained as a R.R. blockhouse until abandoned & burned by them, Nov. 14.

(Old US 41 in Kennesaw.)

The Andrews Raid

About 6 a.m., April 12, 1862, a Federal spy & contraband merchant, James J. Andrews, of Ky., together with 18 soldiers & 1 civilian of Ohio, seized the locomotive "General", & three box cars while train-crew & passengers were breakfasting at the Lacy Hotel.

Intending to sabotage the State R.R. between Atlanta & Chattanooga, the raiders steamed N. to destroy track & burn bridges.

They were foiled in this attempt by the persistent pursuit of Capt. W. A. Fuller, conductor of the train; Jeff Cain, fireman; & Anthony Murphy, of the Atlanta R.R. Shops, after a chase of eighty-seven miles.

(Old US 41 in Kennesaw.)

Federal Occupation of Big Shanty

After the wide flanking movement W. & S. of Allatoona Mtns., Sherman's forces (F) regained the State R.R., at Acworth, June 6, 1864.

June 9, Minty's & Wilder's brigades, Garrard's Cav., with Bennett's section, Chicago Board of Trade Battery (F), moved S. from Acworth. At Morgan's Hill, they encountered Martin's div. of Wheeler's cav. & Benton's brigade, Hood's A.C. (C).

Benton & Martin withdrew S.E. to Johnston's 1st defense line (C) on the Kennesaw Mtn. front. Big Shanty was occupied & Sherman maintained h'dq'rs. here, June 10-24. The 17th A.C. joined McPherson's forces at Acworth, June 6.

(Old US 41 in Kennesaw.)

Stewart's Corps at Big Shanty

During the march of Lt. Gen. Hood's army N. from Palmetto, Stewart's A.C., & Armstrong's cav. (C) were sent from Lost Mtn., Oct. 3, 1864 to destroy the State R.R. at Big Shanty.

Featherston's brigade, Loring's Div. (C), captured the Federal garrison (detachments, 14th & 15th Ill., 4th Div., 17th A.C.) posted in the stockaded Lacy Hotel Walthall's & Loring's divs. were sent to seize the stockade at Moon's Station & Acworth, 2 & 6 mi. N.

French's div. (C), was sent North eleven miles to engage in one of the most noted battles along the State R.R. - Allatoona, Oct. 5, 1864.

(Old US 41 in Kennesaw.)

Site Moon's Station

A wood-shed, water-tank, siding & log house. Here, April 12, 1862, the pursuers of the Andrews Raiders (F) - Fuller Cain & Murphy (C), acquired a push-car from section foreman Jackson Bond, which carried them 14 mi. down grade to the Etowah River.

Oct. 3, 1864. A Federal stockade, garrisoned by 84 officers & men from the 14th & 15th Ill., was located on the high ground 50 yds. E. of the track.

The stockade was attached & captured by Reynold's brigade, Walthall's div., Stewart's A.C. (C) Loring's div. captured the Acworth garrison (F), 4 mi N., Oct. 4th.

(Where the Moon Station crosses the railroad two miles north of Kennesaw.)

Summer's House

Antebellum res. of Thomas F. Summers (1812-1883), a land-mark of the advance of the left wing of Federal forces upon Confederate positions on & near Kennesaw Mtn. - June 1864.

June 9. Garrard's cav (F) (dismounted), forced withdrawal of Benton's Mississippi Brigade from (C) positions N. of Big Shanty, to a line at the Summers' house - later, to one several hundred yds. S. at the Roberts' farm.

This latter line became the 1st position of McPherson's 15th, 16th & 17th Corps which were later shifted S. to the Brushy Mtn. line. From June 9 to July 2, 25 days, Federal & Confederate forces battled on a ten-mile front.

(Old US 41 about 1 mile south of Kennesaw.)

Brushy Mountain Line

June 19, 1864. McPherson's Army of the Tenn., left wing of Sherman's army (F), moved into this sector - the rugged terrain of Brushy Mtn. - on the Kennesaw Mountain front.

The 17th A.C. & Garrard's Cav. were N.E. of this point; 15th & 16th S.W. (F) Hood's A.C. & Wheeler's Cav. (C) (E. of Kennesaw mtn.) were opp. the 17th A.C.; Polk's A.C. (Loring), on the mtn.; Hardee's A.C. on Loring's left (C), S. of the mtn. June 21, Hood was shifted to Hardee's left - prolonging the line S. to the Powder Springs Road, leaving Wheeler's cav. to hold the Confederate right.

For two weeks, Kennesaw Mountain was the strategic point of the Confederate position.

(US 41 south of Greer's Chapel Road.)

Robert McAfee House

After the seizure of Big Shanty (Kennesaw) by Sherman's forces. June 9, 1864, Brig. Gen. Kenner Garrard's cav. div. (F), was posted on the left flank during operations on the Kennesaw Mountain front.

Garrard's cav. guarded Noonday Creek valley from Woodstock to the left of the 17th A.C. (in the rugged Brushy Mtn. area), with patrols on the Canton, Bell's Ferry & Alabama roads. Daily conflict with his opponent - Maj. Gen. Joseph Wheeler's cavalry (C) - marked the period from June 11 to July 3.

The Robert McAfee house was Garrard's h'dq'rs. during a portion of this period.

(Bell's Ferry Road at Roberts Road east of US 41.)

Federal 15th Corps

June 19, 1864. Maj. Gen. John A. Logan's 15th A.C. (F) was deployed astride this, the old Marietta road; Smith's 2d div., N.E. of it; Osterhaus' 1st, S.W.; Harrow's 4th, in reserve. This was the 2d & final sector held by Sherman's left wing on the Kennesaw Mountain front.

Heavy fire from the Confederate artillery on the mountain, was countered, June 23, by 2 batteries of Rodman & Parrott guns, erected by Osterhaus on the hill just W. - the excavations being still visible.

June 25, 27. Logan's troops, shifted S.W. to the Burnt Hickory Rd., relieved the 14th A.C., & assaulted the lower end of the mountain.

(Old US 41 near north limits of Kennesaw Mtn. Na'l Park.)

"Oakton"
Ante-Bellum Residence of John R. Wilder

June 19, 1864. Johnston's Army of Tennessee (C) withdrew to its Kennesaw line - Polk's A.C. (under Loring), posted on the mountain; Hardee's extending S. from Loring's left, prolonged the line beyond Cheatham Hill; Hood's corps on Loring's right, prolonged the line E. to the Canton road, where it was supported by Wheeler's cav. - the extreme right of the army.

June 21, Hood's A.C. was shifted to the left, of Hardee's line (C) - prolonging it to & S. of Powder Springs Rd., leaving Wheeler to guard the rt. flank. Maj. Gen. W. W. Loring had his headquarters at "Oakton", the Wilder house.

(Kennesaw Avenue in the northeast edge of Marietta.)

Johnston's Line East of Kennesaw

A point on the entrenched line of Loring's (formerly Polk's) A.C. (C), which extended from the mtn. down its E. slope to the Bell's Ferry Rd.

This sector was held by Featherston's div. - the rt. of the corps. Hood's A.C. (C) prolonged the line E. beyond the Canton Rd., where Wheeler's cav. (C) was posted. June 21, Featherston extended E. to occupy the line vacated by Hood's A.C. when it was shifted to the left of the line below Kennesaw, on Powder Springs road.

June 27. Featherston's & Wheeler withstood a spirited attack by the 17th A.C., which advanced S. from the Brushy Mountain area.

(Old US 41 at Elizabeth.)

Kennesaw Battlefield

One of the two abortive attempts to break Johnston's line (C), June 27, 1864, was made in this area by 3 Federal brigades. Deployed on the ridge W. of the stream & astride Burnt Hickory road, they moved E. toward the Spur of the mountain, which was the center of the attack.

The left of the charging line entered the gorge between the Spur & little Kennesaw; the right swung around the point where the Spur impinges on the road.

During the battle, Federal regiments from Missouri battled Cockrell's Missouri brigade (French's div., Loring's Corps. Confederate), posted on Kennesaw Spur.

(Burnt Hickory Road at Old Mountain Road.)

Kennesaw Spur

June 19, 1864. When Johnston's forces (C) moved to a third position on the Kennesaw front, the defense works included the mountain. Bearing N.E. & E., the line ran to the Canton Rd.; southward, it reached below the Dallas Rd.

The left of French's div. (Loring's A.C. (C), posted on the mtn.) rested on this road, where the right of Hardee's A.C. (Walker's div.) joined.

June 27. The left of French & the right of Walker withstood the assaults of 3 Federal brigades - moving E. astride this, the Burnt Hickory Rd. - in a vain endeavor to break the line here coincident with a like attempt at Cheatham Hill 2.5 mi. southward.

(Burnt Hickory Road at Old Mountain Road.)

Federal Troops Occupy Marietta, 1864

The 23d A.C. (F) seized a position at Moss' house (at Floyd Station), lower Sandtown Rd., July 1, nearer Chattahoochee River than Johnston's Kennesaw line (C), whereupon he withdrew his army, via Marietta, to his Smyrna-Ruff's Mill line, 6 mi. S., during the night, July 2-3.

Pursuit followed: two divs. of Logan's 15th A.C. (F) (Osterhaus & Harrow) were sent via Burnt Hickory & Dallas rds. to occupy Marietta.

Being replaced, they marched, 9 a.m. July 4 via Powder Springs Rd. & the Cheney house to the lower Sandtown Rd. where they joined the rest of McPherson's Army of the Tennessee (F).

(Dallas Road (Ga 120) just south of junction with Burnt Hickory Road.)

Cheatham Hill

The entrenched line of the Confederate Army of Tenn. as of July 19 - July 3, 1864, crossed the road here. This sector was held by Lt. Gen. Wm. J. Hardee's A.C. - the right of his line at Kennesaw Mtn., the left, from 1 to 2 miles southward of this point.

June 27. Cheatham's & Cleburne's divs. withstood an assault by 5 Federal brigades - the spearhead of the attack directed toward a salient angle 3/4 mi. S., held by Vaughan's & Maney's brigades of Cheatham's division.

The Illinois monument to McCook's brigade, (F) erected in 1914, stands at the so-called "Dead Angle" of Cheatham's entrenched line.

(Dallas Road (Ga 120) opposite the park road to Cheatham Hill.)

Federal, Confederate Lines
June 22, 27, 1864

One-half mi. S., at the road-fork, is SIGNAL HILL, where Sherman observed the assault on Cheatham Hill by troops of the 4th & 14th Corps (F), June 27.

The John Ward Road - left turn at the fork leads to Thomas' Headquarters, June 27, & the battlefield of Kolb's Farm, on & near Powder Springs road, 2.5 mi. S., where Hood (C) attacked the right of the 20th & the left of the 23d Corps (F), June 22.

The road W. leads to Dallas & New Hope Ch., in Paulding County, where Federal & Confederate forces were in daily conflict 10 days.

(Dallas Road (Ga 120) at the John Ward (Cheatham Hill) Road.)

McCook's Brigade

E. on the ridge beyond the valley is the Illinois memorial to Col. Dan McCook's brigade, Davis' div., 14th A.C. (F). It stands at an angle in breastworks of Cheatham's div., Hardee's A.C. (C).

McCook's was 1 of 5 brigades designated to attempt a break-through, June 27. Its 5 regiments formed on the then wooded slope this side of the stream-four in column, of regimental fronts, one advanced as skirmishers.

The assault was toward the angle; down the hill - across the stream - up the cleared slope beyond, to the objective - the only brigade of 5 to reach it, where a close-up line was held until Cheatham withdrew July 3.

(John Ward (Cheatham Hill) Road between the Powder Springs Road (Ga 5 and the Dallas Road (Ga 120).)

Five Federal Brigades

June 27, 1864. At 8 a.m., five brigades assaulted the Confederates of Hardee's Corps, posted on the wooded ridge across the valley eastward.

From left to right they were: Kimball's, Wagner's & Harker's brigades, Newton's div., 4th A.C.; McCook's & Mitchell's brigades, Davis' div., 14th A.C. - all army of the Cumberland troops. (F)

Kimball & Wagner struck Cleburne's left; Harker, McCook & Mitchell centered on the salient angle at the right of Cheatham's div. The assaults were in parallel regimental columns. These & similar ones, at the same time, by 3 brigades at Kennesaw Mtn., 2.5 mi. N., failed to break Johnston's line. (C)

(John Ward (Cheatham Hill) Road between the Powder Springs Road (Ga 5) and the Dallas Road (Ga 120).)

Powder Springs Road
June-July, 1864

Old Zion Church stood 150 ft. E. Confederate trenches crossed Rd. in N.S. direction - the left of Johnston's Kennesaw line, occupied by Hood's A.C. (C), June 21, when it was shifted to this sector from E. of Kennesaw Mtn. Hood's corps deployed here & moved S.W. to the battle field of Kolb's Farm, June 22.

July 3. Line evacuated by Confederate forces, withdrawing S.E. across Olley's Creek to the Nickajack. Federal 14th & 20th A.C. marched from John Ward Road toward Marietta where they joined the 4th, which had moved there via the Dallas Rd. from 3.5 mi. W. of the town.

(Ga 5 about one mile northeast of the John Ward (Cheatham Hill) Road.)

16th A.C. to Roswell

When the 23d A.C. (F) crossed the Chattahoochee at Sope Creek, above the State R.R., July 8, 1864, Johnston's River Line (C) (Oakdale Rd.) was evacuated to the Fulton County side, July 9.

There being no further need of McPherson's Army of the Tenn. (F) on the lower Sandtown Rd., it was sent up river to Roswell. The 16th was the first corps to be shifted; it began its 27 mi. march from Mitchell's, 10 a.m. June 9, & camped that night 1 mi. E. of Marietta.

Its line of march included Powder Springs Rd. from the Cheney house to the Marietta Public Square, traversing, enroute the battlefield of Kolb's Farm.

(Powder Springs Road (Ga 5) at the Sandtown Road.)

Ross' Headquarters

Brig. Gen. L. S. Ross, commanding the Texas brigade of Brig. Gen. Wm. H. Jackson's cavalry (C), had fought delaying actions with Schofield's 23d A.C. (F), the rt. of Sherman's forces since both armies moved from Paulding Co. Ross had h'dq'rs. at the Shaw house, June 22, 27, 1864.

June 22, Schofield's troops reached Cheney's house. Hascall's div. supported the 20th A.C. (F) at Kolb's Farm, while Cox's div. at Cheney's held the extreme Federal right.

June 26, 27. The 23d A.C. continued the flanking movement S. from Cheney's, crossed Olley's Cr. & pushed down the Sandtown Rd. - forcing Ross to withdraw his cav. at the Shaw house.

(Old Sandtown Road, 1 mile south of Powder Springs Road, opposite Old Shaw house on east side of Sandtown Rd. which is on a high bluff.)

"The Only Advantage of the Day"

June 27, 1864. While 8 Federal brigades at Kennesaw Mtn. & at Cheatham Hill made futile attempts to break Johnston's line (C), Schofield's 23d A.C. moved S. from Powder Springs road.

This flanking move was opposed by Hood's A.C. (extended below Kolb's Farm), & Ross' cav. (C) on this the old Sandtown road.

Schofield reached & fortified these crossroads - a strategic position that posed more of a threat to Johnston's Kennesaw line than the assaults by 8 brigades further N. - a fact noted in Sherman's dispatch to Thomas as "the only advantage of the day". (38-IV-610)

(Intersection of old Sandtown Road and Floyd Road.)

Site - Wm. Moss House

The stalemate on the Kennesaw Mtn. front was broken when the rt. wing of Sherman's forces was extended S. on the old Sandtown road to this point.

This eventuated July 1, 1864, when Brig. Gen. Milo S. Hascall's (2d) div., 23d A.C. (F) moved to this strategic position which threatened Johnston's lines (C) of communication & retreat - the State R.R. & highways E. of here & S. of Kennesaw Mountain.

McPherson's Army of the Tennessee joined the 23d A.C. here, July 2d & 3d. The 15th & 16th A.C. moved E. to Nickajack Creek & the 17th moved S. toward the Chattahoochee River.

(Concord Road east of Concord Church.)

The Extended Right

July 3, 1864. Concurrent with Johnston's evacuation of his Kennesaw Mtn. line (C), McPherson's Army of the Tenn. (F), was shifted to the rt. of Sherman's forces & via Sandtown Rd. Schofield's 23d A.C. reached this vicinity - joining Hascall's div., 23d. A.C.

These troops operated as a threat to Johnston's lines of communication & retreat from Kennesaw to the Chattahoochee River.

Detachments from the 4 Federal corps began aggressive moves from here on Johnston's left & rear as he withdrew from Kennesaw; a column was sent E. to Ruff's Mill on Nickajack Creek & one S. via Mableton & the Mitchell house, toward the river crossings.

(Concord Road at Hick's Road.)

The Mable House

Ante-bellum res. of Robert Mable (1803-1885). July 3, 1864. Maj. Gen. R. P. Blair's 17th A.C., of McPherson's Army of the Tenn., having marched from Kennesaw Mtn., via Sandtown Rd., reached Moss' house (near Floyd Station), 1.2 mi. N.

2 p.m. Gresham's 4th div., 17th A.C., moved with the 15th A.C. troops to points S. of the Mitchell house (below Mableton), to threaten river crossings at left-rear of Johnston's Smyrna line (C).

At dark, Gresham's troops withdrew N. to the Mable plantation, which afforded an ample supply of water, & camped here for the night. Walter W. Gresham was Secretary of State in President Cleveland's Cabinet, 1893-1895.

(Floyd Drive north of Mableton.)

Turner's, Howell's, Baker's & Sandtown Ferries

This, the old Sandtown Road was the route of McPherson's Army of the Tennessee (F), south to the Mitchell house, July 5, 1864.

From Mitchell's, an old road ran east to the Chattahoochee River at Turner's Ferry, most of its course being U.S. Highway 78. South of Mitchell's, the E. fork (State Highway 139) leads to Howell's Ferry; the W. fork to Baker's & Sandtown Ferries.

From Mitchell's, McPherson sent detachments to these crossings to threaten the left & rear of Johnston's forces (C) at the River Line.

(Mableton where old Sandtown Road (Ga 139) leaves southward from US 78 (Ga 6).)

The Mitchell House

Ante-bellum res. of Wiley Martin Mitchell, 1800-1857.

Cited in Official Records of the Atlanta Campaign, 1864, as the "Widow Mitchell's" house. A key position of the Federal right wing in military operations on the Sandtown Rd. during the retreat of Johnston's forces S. from Kennesaw to the Chattahoochee River.

McPherson's Army of the Tennessee (F) occupied this intersection of the Sandtown & Turner's Ferry roads, July 5-9. From this strategic position, demonstrations made toward crossings at & below Turner's Ferry, signified an intention to outflank Johnston's River Line (C).

(Ga 139 southeast of Mableton.)

Toward the River

During the 5 days when Army of the Tennessee headquarters were here, the troops of the 15th & 17th A.C. (F), were posted on a ridge just W. of Nickajack Creek, facing the left of Johnston's River Line. (July 5-9, 1864).

16th A.C. troops (F), were sent to Howell's, Baker's & Sandtown ferries, below Nickajack Cr., where demonstrations were made as if crossings at these points were intended.

Johnston's formidable River Line (C) forbade a frontal attack by the outnumbering Federals; only by feinting on the right & thrusting on the left (up river at Sope Creek), were the Federals able to pass the Chattahoochee.

(Ga 139 southeast of Mableton. Near Mitchell house.)

Advance of the 17th A.C. Toward the River

July 4, 1864. Maj. Gen. F. P. Blair's 17th A.C. of McPherson's Army of the Tennessee & Stoneman's cavalry (F), moved from Sandtown Rd. E. on this, the old Turner's Ferry Rd. to outflank Johnston's Smyrna-Ruff's Mill line.

Encountering the Georgia Militia, under Maj. Gen. Gustavus Smith & Gen. L. S. Ross' cavalry, the Federals drove them eastward 1.25 miles/Blair's troops entrenched here for the night.

This action was coincident with 4th & 16th A.C. assaults on Johnston's line at Smyrna & at Ruff's Mill, some four miles N.E. on the old Concord Road.

(US 78 at Lee Road east of Leland).

Georgia Militia on Turner's Ferry Road

Gen. Gustavus W. Smith's. Georgia Militia & Gen. L. S. Ross' cav. driven E. to this point, from Sandtown Rd. (at Mableton), July 4, 1864, was again assailed by the 17th A.C. (F) July 5.

Gresham's 4th div., astride the road, together with Leggett's 3d, & Stoneman's cav. S. of it on Howell's Fy. Rd., forced the Georgia Militia & cavalry E. to Johnston's line at the river, to which he had withdrawn, night of the 4th from his Smyrna-Ruff's Mill line.

Johnston stated he left the Smyrna-Ruff's Mill line because of Smith's & Ross' failure to hold his left flank on Turner's Ferry Rd.

(US 78 at Mt. Harmony Church about two miles west of the Chattahoochee River.)

Federals Halted by Johnston's River Line

July 5, 1864. Gresham's 4th div., on this Rd. & Leggett's 3d (17th A.C.), with Stoneman's ca. (F), on Howell's Fy. Rd. S. of it, drove the Ga. Militia & Ross' cav. E. across Nickajack Cr. where they occupied the left of Johnston's River Line.

Gresham's div., astride this rd & Leggett's div. on the right cast up a line on this ridge, facing Johnston's line across Nickajack Cr.

July 7. Logan's 15th A.C. was brought up & prolonged Gresham's line N. on high ridge. These & 16th A.C. (F), troops down river, threatened to cross while actual crossings were made above the State R.R. bridge.

(US 78 (Ga 6) where it passes through the high ridge west of Nickajack Creek.)

Johnston's River Line

July, 1864, a heavy entrenched line of field works, from the mouth of Nickajack Cr. (.8 mi. S.W.) extended N.E. to a point 1 mi. above State R.R. bridge. This line prepared in advance, was occupied by Johnston's forces (C), when they withdrew from the Smyrna-Ruff's Mill line, July 5.

Ga. Militia held the ferries below Nickajack. In sequence, N.E., were Hood's, Hardee's & Loring's corps. The line was evacuated July 9, after the Federals crossed above State R.R. bridge.

This line is said to have been the heaviest field works of the Atlanta campaign. In 1935 their formidable character was still visible along Oakdale Rd., & just above the State R.R.

(US 78 at Oakdale Road.)

The March to Sope Creek

Schofield's 23d A.C. (F), marked time in this vicinity while McPherson's Army of the Tenn. (F) made demonstrations at Chattahoochee ferries below Johnston's River Line (C) - indicating, falsely, that crossings would be made there while actual passages upstream were planned.

July 6, 1864. The 23d A.C. began its march to upper reaches of the river by moving E. on this, the Old Concord Road via the battlefields of Ruff's Mill & Smyrna, to the mouth of Sope Creek, 11 miles N.E.

Passage of the river there, July 8, forced Johnston to evacuate his River Line, July 9.

(Concord Road at Hick's Road.)

Battle of Ruff's Mill

July 4, 1864. Early a.m., Brig. Gen. John Fuller's brigade, 4th div. 16th A.C. (F), moved 1 mi. from Nickajack Cr. bridge, Concord Rd., to ascertain the strength of Hood's A.C. (C). Finding it strongly posted, Fuller returned to the Ruff's Mill.

Late p.m., Fuller's men again advance, supported by Sweeny's 2d div. & after a bitter struggle seized the first line of works on Hood's rt. near the present Gann Cemetery.

This Federal assault on Johnston's (C), left & the one at Smyrna, on his rt., were incidental to his retreat from Kennesaw to the river. Col. Edward Noyes, 39th O.V.V.I. (Governor of Ohio 1872-1874), lost a leg in this battle.

(Concord Road on the east side of Nickajack Creek.)

Hood's Corps at Battle of Ruff's Mill

When Johnston's forces (C) withdrew from Kennesaw Mtn., July 3, 1864, they occupied a double line of field works extending from Smyrna S.W. to Nickajack Creek at Dodgen's Mill, more or less along this, the old Concord Road.

Hood's Corps held the left, (S.W.) sector of the line which crossed the road at this point.

July 4. Federal forces moved up, investing the entire Confederate position. Dodge's 16th A.C. (F), crossed Nickajack at Ruff's Mill & late P.M., Fuller's brigade (4th div.) moved up this Rd., the attack falling upon Stevenson's div. (C), driving it from the first line of works.

(Concord Road 0.1 mile west of junction with Hurt Road.)

Smyrna-Ruff's Mill Confederate Line

July 3, 1864. Johnston's army, retreating from Kennesaw, took position in a double line of breastworks, prepared in advance, along this Rd. - the right, E. of the State R.R.; the left at Nickajack Cr., S. of Ruff's Mill. From right to left were: Loring's, Hardee's & Hood's corps (C).

July 4, Federal forces attacked both ends of line: at Smyrna & near Ruff's Mill. Johnston withdrew S. to the Chattahoochee that night.

July 6, Schofield's 23d A.C. (F), marched from Sandtown Rd. via this Rd., to the mouth of Sope Cr., where his passage of the river there, caused Johnston's retreat to the Fulton County side.

(Junction of Concord Road and Old Concord Road in the west edge of the Nickajack Community.)

Battle of Smyrna

July 3, 1864. Gen. J. E. Johnston's army (C) withdrew from Kennesaw Mtn. & occupied a double line of field-works which crossed the R.R. at old Smyrna Camp Ground, facing N.W. Loring's A.C. was on the rt. (N.E. of R.R.); Hardee's, at center; Hood's on left, near Ruff's mill, Nickajack Cr.

July 4. The 4th A.C. (F), E. of R.R., attacked the Confederate right to ascertain strength of the position; it was found impregnable. A similar attack on the left near Ruff's Mill was alike ineffective. Being outflanked, Johnston withdrew to his River Line that night.

July 6. The 23d A.C. (F), moving from Ruff's Mill to Sope Creek, camped just E. of the R.R.

(Old US 41 north of the business district in Smyrna.)

The Alexander Eaton House; Hood's Headquarters

S. on this Rd., .8 mi. stands the ante-bellum residence of Alexander Eaton (1809-1905). July 3, 4, 5, 1864, the entrenched lines of Gen. John B. Hood's A.C. (C), extended along the Rd. from the Gann. Cem. to site of Cooper's Lake. The Eaton housed, being but 1 mi. E. of these lines, was used by Gen. Hood as headquarters.

From Eaton's house, Hood directed his troops in the Battle of Ruff's Mill, July 4 - the A.C. being the left flank of Johnston's Smyrna - Ruff's Mill Line (C), after his retreat from Kennesaw. Rufus Eaton, age 6, son of Alex. said he saw Johnston at the house during the battle.

(South Cobb Drive (Ga. 280) south of King's Spring Road near Smyrna.)

Here Johnston's River Line Crossed the Road

July 5, 1864. Gen. J. E. Johnston's Army of Tenn. (C), withdrew from the Smyrna-Ruff's Mill line to formidable field-works which crossed the Rd. at this point. The left of the line was at Nickajack Cr., 4.5 mi. S.W.; the rt. curved to the Chattahoochee, 1 mi. N. of State R.R. bridge. Loring's (Stewart's) A.C. was on the rt.; Hardee's at center, & Hood's on left.

The R.R. & highway bridges, together with 3 pontoons, spanned the river 1.5 mi. to the rear of this line. The 23d A.C. (F), crossing at the mouth of Sope Cr., 7 mi. N., July 8, forced Johnston's retreat across the river, July 9.

(Old US 41, 1.5 miles north of bridge at Bolton at Log Cabin Road.)

The Cumberland Army to Powers' & Pace's Ferries

July 5, 1864. The entrenched line of the 4th, 14th, & 20th A.C. (F), facing Johnston's River Line (C), crossed Rd. at this point; the 4th at Vining's Station, N.E.; the 14th, astride both the R.R. & this Rd.; the 20th, S.W. to Nickajack Creek.

These troops marked time while the 23d A.C. (F), crossed the Chattahoochee at Sope Cr., July 8, & Johnston evacuated his River Line, July 9.

This alignment was maintained, awaiting R.R. repairs, arrival of supplies at Vining's depot, & general preparations for the shift across the river. By July 17, Thomas' army (F), was over the Chattahoochee at Powers' & Pace's Ferries.

(New section of old US 41, 2.5 mi. northwest of the river crossing at Bolton, at site of old Interurban Car stop at Carmichael's station.)

The March of McPherson's Army of the Tennessee to Roswell

Maj. Gen. James V. McPherson's troops, the right flank of Sherman's forces (F) operating at Chattahoochee River crossings S. of Kennesaw Mtn., were shifted to up-river crossings at Roswell, after Johnston's (C) withdrawal to the Fulton County side, at the State R.R. bridge.

The 15th, 16th, & 17th A.C. made this march from the lower Sandtown Rd., via Marietta between July 9 & 17, 1864. These troops were across at Roswell by the 17th, & enroute to Decatur & Stone Mountain - the left wing of the Federal forces E. of Atlanta.

(0.7 mile northeast of junction of the Roswell Road (Ga 120) and the Lower Roswell Road.)

23d Army Corps to Sope Creek

July 6, 1864. Schofield's Federal 23d A.C. having been shifted N.E. from Sandtown Rd. (at Floyd Station), camped at Smyrna. Resuming the march, July 7, it traversed only 2 mi. to this point where it camped. July 8, 4 a.m. the march continued to Sope Creek- four miles N.E.

This was a strategic maneuver to effect a river crossing at Sope Cr., N. of Johnston's defense line (C), on Cobb County side (at & S. of the State R.R. bridge). The move was designed to render the Confederate line untenable.

Being thus outflanked July 8, Johnston withdrew his army to the Fulton Co. side, July 9.

(US 41 north of Terrell Mill Road.)

The 4th Corps at Vining's Station

July 5, 1864. When Johnston's army (C) withdrew from Smyrna to the river, Howard's 4th A.C., & Baird's div. (14th A.C.) (F), via highway 7 R.R. occupied Vining's Station. Baird's troops kept on down the R.R. until halted by Johnston's River Line.

4th A.C. troops pursued the Confederate wagon trains, escorted by Wheeler's Cav., toward the pontoon bridge at Pace's Ferry where they crossed the river. Morgan's 7th Ind. Battery (F), shelled the column from Vining's Hill.

Also, from this eminence, Generals Sherman, Thomas & Baird, had their first view of Atlanta, across the Chattahoochee, 9.5 mi. S.E.

(At Vining's Station on road from Pace's Ferry some 100 to 200 feet east of the railroad.)

Site: Hardy Pace's Residence
Howard's Headquarters

Hardy Pace (1785-1864), operated the Chattahoochee River ferry at site of bridge where Pace's Ferry Rd. crosses. Federal forces occupied Vining's Station, July 5-17, 1864, while preparing to cross at Pace's & Power's for the move on Atlanta. Gen. O. O. Howard, 4th A.C. had headquarters at the Pace res., July 5-10.

Vining's temporary terminal of the R.R., was the subsistence & ammunition dump of the Federal army during the siege & capture of Atlanta. Wounded from the Atlanta front were sent to Vining's where the Pace house was used as a hospital - later, destroyed by fire.

(East edge of Vining's, just west of US 41, in front of the old Solomon K. Pace house.)

The Errant Pontoon Bridge: Pace's Ferry

July 5, 1864. During Johnston's retreat from Smyrna, a portion of his wagon-train detoured from the Atlanta-Marietta Rd, via Vining's Station to a pontoon bridge at Pace's Ferry.

Wheeler's Cav. escorted the trains; when all were across, the bridge was cut loose so as to swing down stream to the Fulton Co. side.

Federal gun-fire, preventing its removal, the bridge was cut loose by the Confederates, but instead of floating down to shelter within Johnston's River Line at Bolton, it lodged on this side where it was seized by troops of Hazen's 4th A.C. brigade, July 8.

(Cobb County end of Steel one-way bridge on Pace's Ferry Road, about 100 or 150 feet west of bridge.)

The 14th & 20th A.C. Cross at Pace's Ferry

July 17, 1864. Palmer's 14th & Hooker's 20th A.C. crossed to the Fulton Co. side of the river on two pontoon bridges. This passage was covered by Wood's 4th A.C. div., which marched down Mt. Paran Rd. from Power's Ferry, 3 mi. N.

To divert attention of Johnston's forces (C) to crossings below, Stoneman's cav. was sent S. (July 13) to threaten the A. & W.P.R.R. When it returned (July 16), Blair's 17th A.C. began its 29 mi. march from Turner's Fy. to Roswell where it crossed the 17th. This & the passage of the 14th & 20th Corps at Pace's, completed the crossings of the Federal infantry.

(Cobb County end of steel one-way bridge on Pace's Ferry Road.)

The 4th Corps Posted Along the River

When the 4th A.C. reached the Chattahoochee July 5, attempts to cross were found impractical because of Confederate opposition on the other side. Pending the crossing of the 23d A.C. at Sope Cr., July 8, the 4th A.C. marked time in trenches between Rottenwood Cr. (N), & the R.R. below Vining's Station (S).

July 9: Newton's (2d) div. moved N. to Roswell to support Garrard's cav. July 10: Stanley's (1st) & Wood's (3d) moved N. to Sope Cr. to join the 23d A.C. Stoneman's cav., returned from a raid below Atlanta, the 14th & 20th Corps crossed at Pace's Ferry, one-half mi. S.

(US 41 at north end of bridge over the Chattahoochee River.)

The Hargrove House

Ante-bellum residence of Asbury Hargrove - 1809-1879.

Headquarters of Brig. Gen. Edward M. McCook - July 6-15, 1864.

McCook's (1st) div. (Dorr's & Lamson's brigades), Elliott's cav. Corps (Army of the Cumberland) (F), was posted here to patrol the Chattahoochee - between Rottenwood Cr. (S) & Roswell (N).

McCook's horsemen served as a screen, behind which the 23d & 4th Corps moved to crossings at the mouth of Sope Cr. & at Power's Fy.

July 15. McCook's cav. left Hargrove's to patrol the river, on the Cobb Co. side, above & below the State R.R. (at Bolton) until the 22d.

(Winding Mill Road between US 41 and the Power's Ferry Road.)

The River Patrol & Cochran's Ford

Pending Federal crossings of the Chattahoochee, Gen. E. M. McCook's cav. div. (F), screened 4th & 23d Corps movements to fords & ferries in this vicinity, July 6, 15, 1864.

July 7, Brownlow's 1st Tennessee reg't., Dorr's brigade (McCook's cav.) seized the upper island near Power's Ferry, as an observation point.

July 9, Col. Dorr, with a detachment, crossed at the mouth of Sope Cr., 3 mi. N. (Schofield's crossing, July 8), to scout the country below. Another detachment crossed at Cochran's Ford, 1.25 mi. S. of Sope Cr., as a support. Dismounted, carrying guns & cartridges aloft, they waded the deep stream, wearing nothing but hats.

(Power's Ferry Road at the bridge.)

Power's Ferry

Established 1835 by James Power, (1790-1870).

Maj. Gen. O. O. Howard's 4th A.C. (Army of the Cumberland) (F), moved from Vining's Station to this vicinity July 9, 10, 1864. Newton's (2d) div. was diverted to Roswell to support Garrard's cav. Stanley's (1st) & Wood's (3d) camped 3 mi. N. near Sope Creek, July 10.

Stanley crossed the Chattahoochee on Schofield's pontoon bridge at mouth of Sope Cr. & moved S. on the other side to cover Power's Ferry where Wood crossed on a pontoon bridge July 12. Newton, back from Roswell, crossed July 13. Stanley's & Newton's men built a trestle bridge at the upper island, July 14-16.

(Power's Ferry Road at a safe distance from the bridge.)

Sope Creek Paper Mills

The original structure which housed the Marietta Paper Mills - incorporated in 1859 - stood one-fourth mile down stream. This industry manufactured newsprint, wrapping paper & stationery - a pioneer enterprise in this section of the state.

July 5, 1864. The mills were burned by a detachment of Gen. Kenner Garrard's cavalry division while guarding the left flank of Federal forces preparing to cross the Chattahoochee River at the mouth of Sope Creek.

Rebuilt after the war, the mills burned in 1870. Restored, 1871, they operated until 1902.

(Paper Mill Road near Marietta end of bridge over Sope Creek.)

The 23d Corps at Sope Creek

July 8, 1864. The first passage of the Chattahoochee River by Federal forces was made at mouth of Sope Cr. by Cox's div. 23d, A.C. Cameron's brigade crossed cr. at the dam & passing the blackened ruins of the Paper mills, scaled the high ridge E. wading the river at a fish-dam, Cameron moved S. to support a contingent crossing in pontoons at mouth of cr.

A Confederate cav. outpost & field-piece were captured. This Federal crossing forced Johnston to abandon his River Line at & below Bolton; he withdrew to the Fulton Co. side of the Chattahoochee River, July 9.

(Paper Mill Road near end of bridge over Sope Creek.)

Garrard & Newton Move on Roswell

300 ft. W. stood the res. of Wm. Johnston who operated the ferry in the 1850s, where Johnston's Fy. Rd. crossed the Chattahoochee River.

July 5, 1864. Gen. Kenner Garrard's ca. (F), div. enroute from Marietta to Roswell via this road, camped on Willeo Cr., from which point he sent a regiment S. to burn the Paper Mills on Sope Creek.

July 9. Newton's 4th A.C. div. (F), moving from Vining's Station, traversed this road to Roswell to support Garrard's passage of the river at Shallow Ford - retracing July 12 & crossing the river at Power's Ferry, July 13.

(Johnson Ferry Road at Columns Drive just south of one-way steel bridge.)

[Ed. note: Steel bridge is now gone.]

Garrard's Cavalry at Roswell

With the occupation of Marietta by Federal forces July 3, 1864, Garrard's cav. was sent to Roswell to secure a Chattahoochee River crossing for the passage of McPherson's Army of the Tennessee, which was later shifted from the Federal right to the extreme left.

July 5. Garrard reached this point on Willeo Creek, where he camped. From here a regiment was sent to burn the Sope Creek Paper Mills. On the same day a detachment moved to Roswell & while the 7th Pa. Cav. drove the Confederate defenders across the bridge, the cotton & woolen factories were burned.

(Lower (South) Roswell Road, about 1.5 miles east of junction with Ga 120 where road crosses Willeo Creek.)

Army of the Tennessee at Roswell

July 3, 16, 1864, McPherson's Army of the Tenn. formed the right of the Federal forces operating south of Kennesaw Mountain.

After Johnston's forces (C) withdrew S. of the Chattahoochee, July 9, Sherman shifted his forces to river crossings N. of the State R.R. bridge. In this move, McPherson's three corps were marched to the left some 30 miles to cross the river at Roswell.

Dodge's 16th A.C. reached Roswell July 10, relieving Garrard's cav. & Newton's div. S. of the river & building two bridges. Logan's 15th A.C. joined July 15; Blair's 17th A.C., July 17.

(Upper Roswell Road (Ga 120) just where it crosses Willeo Creek.)

Confederate Cemetery

3,000 Confederate dead from every southern state are buried in this cemetery. First established for (C) soldiers killed in a railroad collision in 1863, it became the resting place for dead from nearby battlefields. In 1866, under the direction of Miss Mary J. Green and Mrs. Charles J. Williams of the Ga. Mem. Assn., bodies were moved here from the Chickamauga area. Land for the cemetery was given by Mrs. Jane Glover, Miss Ann Moyer and other citizens of Marietta. A cannon, which served Ga. Military Inst. from 1852 to 1864, was used by the Confederate army, captured by Sherman's forces, held as a trophy of war until 1910 and then placed in this cemetery.

(By the Confederate monument in the Confederate Cemetery in Marietta.)

Confederate Cemetery

Burial of Confederates killed in a railroad collision, September, 1863, on land given by Mrs. Jane Glover, established this cemetery. Later more land was given by Ann Moyer and others, and the (C) dead from Marietta hospitals and the Kennesaw battlefield were interred here. In 1866 Georgia provided funds to move her dead here from Chickamauga area, under the direction of Miss Mary J. Green and Mrs. Charles J. Williams of the Georgia Memorial Association. Soldiers from every southern state rest here, and annual Memorial Day exercises are a custom of long standing.

(Powder Spring Street in Marietta by the Confederate Cemetery.)

Kennesaw House

In ante-bellum days, this hotel was a summer resort for planters attracted by the gay social activities of the town. In 1862, J. J. Andrews and his Federal raiders met here to begin the daring Locomotive Chase. Confederate wounded were fed and treated here after many battles, and civilian refugees from overrun Tennessee and Kentucky stayed here, moving south as Federals drew near. July 3, 1864, Sherman had his headquarters in the hotel, while directing pursuit of the Confederates retiring into Atlanta. After the War, numerous northern visitors wintered in Marietta, many stopping at the Kennesaw House.

(Mounted on east wall of Kennesaw House in Marietta.)

UDC and Kennesaw House

The Kennesaw Chapter United Daughters of the Confederacy was organized July 29, 1898, in the parlors of the Kennesaw House on the second floor corner nearest the railroad station. Mrs. R. L. Nesbitt was elected the first president. There were forty women at the meeting. The nucleus of this chapter was the Ladies Memorial Association, formed soon after the close of the war. The nucleus of that association was the Ladies Aid, who had served the armies and soldiers of the Confederacy in field and in camp.

(Mounted on east wall of Kennesaw House in Marietta.)

The Archibald Howell Home

Here, in the spring of 1865, Gen. Henry M. Judah had his headquarters and saw evidence which helped him make a decision of much importance to local people. Since no crops had been grown here on the battlefields in 1864 and, as the surrender had paralyzed economy and government, local people lacked food, funds and employment. Judah, seeing that aid was needed to prevent suffering, proposed to issue corn and bacon to the needy until a crop could be made. The issue, approved, was made and these rations did much to put Georgians and their economy on a sound basis.

(Kennesaw Avenue at Holland Street in Marietta.)

Peachtree Trail

The Indians knew this trail as the route from the heart of the Cherokee Nation to Standing Peachtree, Creek village that grew into a trading post and fort just south of the Chattahoochee. Pioneers who used Montgomery's Ferry at Standing Peachtree called this the Peachtree or Montgomery Ferry Road. Confederate and Federal troops fought along this route in 1864. Advent of automobiles and tourist travel made this road the Dixie Highway, later known as U.S. Highway 41. The Indians planned well; this trail straightened and widened is now a busy four-lane road, a key national highway.

(Old US 41, 200 to 300 yards north of entrance to Kennesaw Mountain National Battlefield Museum.)

The final resting place of Hardy Pace on Vinings Mountain. Hardy Pace was one of the early settlers of Cobb County.

COBB COUNTY
HISTORIC SITES INVENTORY

The concept of the public welfare is broad and inclusive . . . . The values it represents are spiritual as well as physical, aesthetic as well as monetary. It is within the power of the legislature to determine that the community should be beautiful as well as healthy, spacious as well as clean, well-balanced as well as carefully patrolled.

United States Supreme Court
Berman v. Parker
348 U.S. 26, 33 (1954)

INTRODUCTION

The historic sites inventory prepared and maintained by the Cobb County Historic Preservation Commission lists buildings, structures, and other sites of historical, architectural, archaeological, and artifactual interest by District and Land Lot number for unincorporated Cobb County. The listings include cemeteries, areas of known archaeological sensitivity, sites with probable but as yet untested archaeological value, historical markers, paths of two primary native American trails which run through Cobb County (The Peachtree Trail and the Sandtown Trail), areas of Civil War activity, structures (such as bridges and towers) of architectural and/or historical interest, and commercial, residential, and industrial buildings of architectural and/or historical value.

The Commission has assigned a letter "grade" to each building and structure on the list, which grade reflects the relative estimated value of each structure and building to the County. This value is actually stated as a degree of potential eligibility for listing in the National Register of Historic Places. The grades are as follows:

A: This structure has already been listed in the National Register of Historic Places, has been determined eligible for listing in the National Register of Historic Places through an environmental impact assessment or investment tax credit certification, or is in the process of nomination for listing in the Register (i.e., a nomination has been prepared by a local citizen's group, and is being reviewed by the State Historic Preservation Officer). All National Register sites in unincorporated Cobb County will be considered to be certified as Cobb County historic sites to come under the jurisdiction of the Cobb County Historic Preservation Commission as a Certified Local Government recognized by the National Park Service.

B: This structure appears to meet the criteria for the National Register of Historic Places from information already known about it; it may be under consideration for listing in the National Register as an individual building or as a contributing structure to a proposed historic district. Generally speaking, "B" sites are those which are presently under consideration by the Cobb County Historic Preservation Commission to become certified Cobb County historic sites.

C: This structure contributes to the architectural and historical legacy of Cobb County, but more information is needed about its specific history. Given sufficient information "C" sites may become "B" sites and then "A" sites.

D: This structure contributes to the architectural and historical legacy of Cobb County but does not meet the full set of criteria for listing in the National Register. Sites which are less than 50 years old and which therefore do not meet the age criterion for the Register at this time have all been given a "D" classification.

E: This structure contributes to the historical legacy of Cobb County, but because of additions and alterations, decay or demolition, it no longer retains its architectural integrity. Ruins and recent demolitions of known historic properties are included in this designation.

Buildings are identified by street address; where there is no street address, the property parcel number may be given. In addition, the Cobb County Historic Preservation Commission maintains a set of 1985 United States Geological Survey maps of Cobb County on which the building locations may be located. An identical set of maps is held by the Historic Preservation Section of the Georgia Department of Natural Resources. The CCHPC also maintains the photograph and information files of surveyed properties. These are available for reference by Cobb County citizens and others. Questions about historic sites in Cobb County should be referred to the County historic preservation planner.

The commission's consultant compiled the inventory information from numerous sources, which sources are implied in the listings. The Cobb County Genealogical Society provided the location and names of cemeteries. The county archaeologist supplied information on archaeologically sensitive areas, on old mining and manufacturing locations, on 1830s settlements, and Indian landscapes. The historical markers are cited from either the book called *Georgia Historical Markers* or the Bicentennial Survey of Cobb County conducted by Dr. Phil Secrist. Architectural sites are identified in the lists by number, which number refers to one of architectural and historical field surveys which have been conducted of the County. A "ps" number refers to a site identified in the Phil Secrist Bicentennial survey conducted in 1975. A "dnr" number refers to a site identified in the architectural survey sponsored by the Historic Preservation Section of the Department of Natural Resources in 1974. And a "dr" number refers to photographs taken during the field survey conducted during 1985-86 by the Cobb County Historic Preservation Commission, coordinated by Dr. Darlene Roth. These photographs are on file with the county historic preservation planner.

The land lot listings also include, by way of reference points, the names of local communities and municipalities. Users may refer to separate historic resource listings for Marietta, Acworth, Austell, Smyrna, and Powder Springs. Information on historic sites in the municipalities is drawn from the Secrist and the DNR surveys but is not confirmed, and no guarantee is given of its accuracy. Park sites, landforms, (e.g., Blackjack Mountain, Chattahoochee Recreation Area) are also included as points of reference.

The following abbreviations have been used in the listings:

ar	Allatoona Reservoir
chat rec	Chattahoochee River National Recreation Area
cw	Civil War. Indicates known Civil War activity occurred in this land lot.
dnr	Department of National Resources. Used to indicate a site identified in their 1974 survey.
dr	Darlene Roth. Used to indicate a site identified in the CCHPC 1985-86 survey.
ghm	Georgia Historical Marker. Indicates presence of a marker or markers in the land lot. Followed by the title identifying the marker.
HD	Historic District. Indicates presence of a marker or markers in the land lot. Followed by the title identifying the marker.
hs	House.
kmnbp	Kennesaw Mountain National Battlefield Park Recreation area.
larp	Lake Acworth Regional Park.
mmp	Mines and mineral prospects. Indicates past mining activity area.

| **MRA** | Multiple Resource Area. Another name for a proposed potential historic district, one which contains more than one kind of resource. |

mrb Military Reservation Boundary.

N.R. National Register. Used to identify sites already listed in the National Register of Historic Places.

opt Old Peachtree Trail. Used to identify the land lots through which the Peachtree Trail is known to have passed.

osr Old Sandtown Trail. Used to identify the land lots through which the old Sandtown Trail is known to have passed.

ps Phil Secrist. Used to indicate a site identified in the 1975 Bicentennial Survey of Cobb County.

*** Indicates that skipped land lots are not located in Cobb County.

** Indicates archaeological sensitivity. When ** occurs alone, it indicates that archaeological sites have been identified in this land lot. When followed by the name of a site, it indicates that a particular site may have archaeological potential.

+ "and." Used to separate individual site listings under each land lot. Indicates a different site identification each time it appears.

A-E: The grade given each architectural site, as explained above. The letters A, B, C, D, and E, are followed by a colon and then by the street address or the parcel number of the site being identified.

Dist. District number

LL Land lot number

NOTE: The Cobb County Historic Preservation Commission does not assert that the following inventory is complete in every detail. This inventory is presented as an aid to development planning, those interested in local history, and others who may find this information useful. The Cobb County Historic Preservation Commission assumes no responsibility or liability for the inclusion or exclusion of any site from this inventory.

COBB COUNTY DISTRICT INDEX MAP

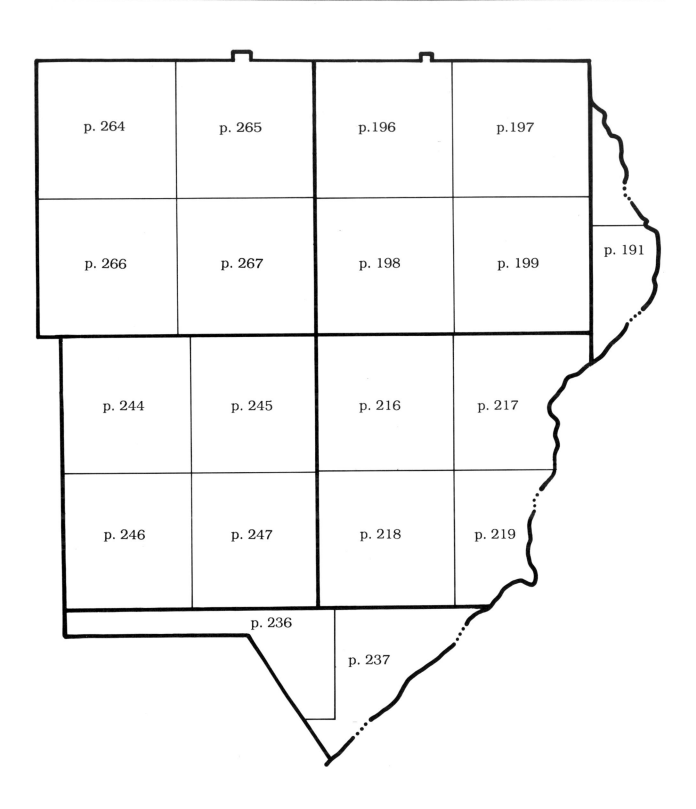

p. 264

p. 265

p.196

p.197

p. 266

p. 267

p. 198

p. 199

p. 191

p. 244

p. 245

p. 216

p. 217

p. 246

p. 247

p. 218

p. 219

p. 236

p. 237

1st DISTRICT

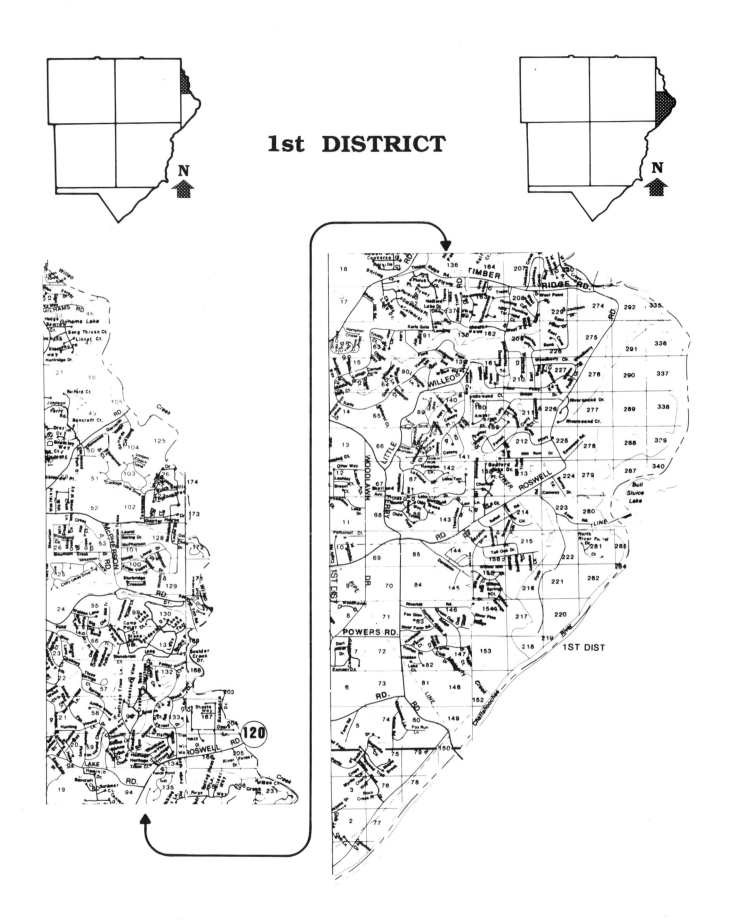

DISTRICT 1

District 1 occupies the easternmost section of Cobb County and shares qualities of heavy suburbanization with the 16th district. The Chattahoochee River edge, which serves as the eastern boundary, is not fully developed; some lands lie in the Chattahoochee Recreation Area, some are owned by Georgia Power Company, and others are retained in private hands. District 1 is the smallest district in Cobb County and contains the smallest number of known historic resources.

1.   The most valuable site in District 1 in terms of its potential as an informative source for rural life in the County from the 1830s to the 1980s is the complex of buildings comprising the Hyde farm. This complex represents a working farm over 130 years old, and the buildings and land configurations illustrate the long pattern of use. In combination with the Powers family cabin on an adjacent lot, the Hyde Brothers property is linked to rural county traditions and the pioneering Powers family.

2.   The Power-Jackson Cabin, reputedly the oldest extant building in Cobb County, sits on Post-Oak Tritt Road just west of its intersection with McPherson Road. The cabin is well marked, though privately owned.

3.   Bishop Lake Subdivision. This weekend resort was platted in 1936 on land owned by the Bishop family and developed slowly. It contains small lots and cottages, many of them sited directly on the lake with docks and boat slips. Most of the subdivision dates are too late to meet National Register criteria yet, but there is potential for a historic district here in the future.

4.   A number of land lots contained farms in 1832, which are noted on the land lot listings. None of the farm houses associated with these farms are known to be still standing, but there would be some archaeological potential in the land lots so designated in this district as well as in the others.

5.   Remnants of the old Mt. Bethel community are still to be found in District 1, but they are scattered, altered, and intruded upon to such an extent that there is no truly cohesive center. The community center is a severely altered building, as is the church, which has been relocated from its original site. The main part of the Mt. Bethel cemetery now rests next to a gas station. There is no potential for listing individual sites.

6.   Some folk and vernacular style farm and country houses are scattered through District 1, none of individual significance except a 1940s I-house designed by architect Henry Toombs in the exact local vernacular pattern as an overseers house to the Spalding bean farm. A front porch was added in the 1960s, but otherwise the house is an interesting adaptation of an old, endemic house style and may have future potential for National Register listing, especially considering the professional reputation of Henry Toombs.

Land Lot	Description	Land Lot	Description
1	** + Roswell Presbyterian Cemetery	56	
2	Founder's Cemetery	57	
3	Roswell Methodist Cemetery	58	
4	D: 4620 Paper Mill (dr3-1)	59	
5		60	
6		61	
7		62	
8		63	
9	C: 503 Woodlawn Rd (dr20-11)	64	
10		65	
11		66	
12		67	
13		68	Mt. Bethel Cemetery
14		69	C: Mt. Bethel Comm. Ctr. (dr12-3) +
15			C: 746 Woodlawn Rd (dr20-10) +
16			cemetery + Mt. Bethel Park + E: Mt.
17			Bethel Methodist Church 4385 Lower
18			Roswell Rd. (dr11-12)
19	D: Bishop Lake Subdivision (dr23/3-14)	70	Chattahoochee Baptist Cemetery
20		71	
21		72	** 1832 farm site
22		73	ghm Garrard & Newton Move on Roswell + ** 1832 farm site
23		74	
24	Hardman Cemetery	75	
25		76	
26		77	**
27		78	**
28		79	**
29		80	chat rec
30		81	ghm Garrard & Newton Move on Roswell + ** 1832 farm site
31		82	** 1832 farm site
32		83	
33		84	
34		85	cemetery
***		86	cemetery
46	E: at end of Gilham's Rd (dr15-32A)	87	
47		88	
48		89	
49		90	
50		91	
51		92	
52		93	
53		94	
54	B: ps131(dnr210; dr22-13+) Power-Jackson Cabin Post Oak-Tritt Rd, just west of intersection with McPherson Rd	95	** 1832 farm site
		96	** 1832 farm site
55		97	

Land Lot	Description	Land Lot	Description
98		157	
99		158	Haney/Old Mt. Bethel Cemetery
100		159	
101		160	
102		161	
103		162	
104		163	
105		164	
***		165	
125		166	
126		167	
127	** 1832 farm site	168	E: ** ps119 Ruins: King's Mill, on Willeo Creek, west side, about 300 yds south of Willeo Rd
128	** 1832 farm site		
129			
130	** 1832 farm site	169	E: ** ps119 Ruins: King's Mill, on Willeo Creek, west side, about 300 yds south of Willeo Rd
131	E: ** ps119 Ruins: King's Mill, on Willeo Creek, west side, about 300 yds south of Willeo Rd + ** 1832 farm site		
132	E: ** ps119 Ruins: King's Mill, on Willeo Creek, west side, about 300 yds south of Willeo Rd	170	C: parcel 1, Willeo Rd across frm Long Lake Dr (dr22-26) + ** 1832 farm site
		171	
		172	
133	** 1832 farm site	173	** 1832 farm site
134	** 1832 farm site + Willeo Baptist Church Cemetery	174	
		***	
135		203	
136		204	
137		205	ghm Army of the Tennessee at Roswell + ** 1832 farm site
138			
139		206	** 1832 farm site
140		207	
141		208	
142		209	
143		210	
144		211	
145		212	
146		213	
147		214	Power Family Cemetery
148	** 1832 farm site + chat rec	215	
149	** ps7 Johnson's Ferry Site, Johnson's Ferry Rd at Chattahoochee River + chat rec + ** 1832 farm site	216	B: Hyde Farm (dr 11/20-32)
		217	** + B: Hyde Farm (dr 11/20-32)
		218	**
150		219	**
151	** 1832 farm site + chat rec	220	
152	** 1832 farm site + chat rec	221	B: Hyde Farm (dr 11/20-32)
153	** 1832 farm site + chat rec	222	
154		223	**
155		224	** 1832 farm site + chat rec
156			

Land Lot	Description	Land Lot	Description
225	** 1832 farm site + chat rec	281	**
226	E: Miegle-Johnson hs 5625 Lower Roswell (dr 12-10) + chat rec	282	** + B: Hyde Farm (dr 11/20-32)
		283	
227	C: 5545 Lower Roswell (dr 12-12) + chat rec	284	**
		285	**
228		286	
229		287	chat rec
230		288	chat rec
231	** 1832 farm site	289	chat rec
***		290	chat rec
274	chat rec + ghm: Garrard's Cavalry at Roswell	291	** + chat rec
		292	chat rec
275	C: 5524 Lower Roswell (dr 12-14) + chat rec	***	
		335	
276	chat rec	336	
277	chat rec	337	
278	** 1832 farm site + chat rec	338	
279	** 1832 farm site + chat rec	339	
280	** 1832 farm site + chat rec	340	

Sope Creek mill ruins

16th DISTRICT

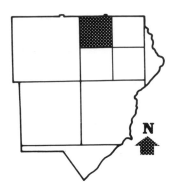

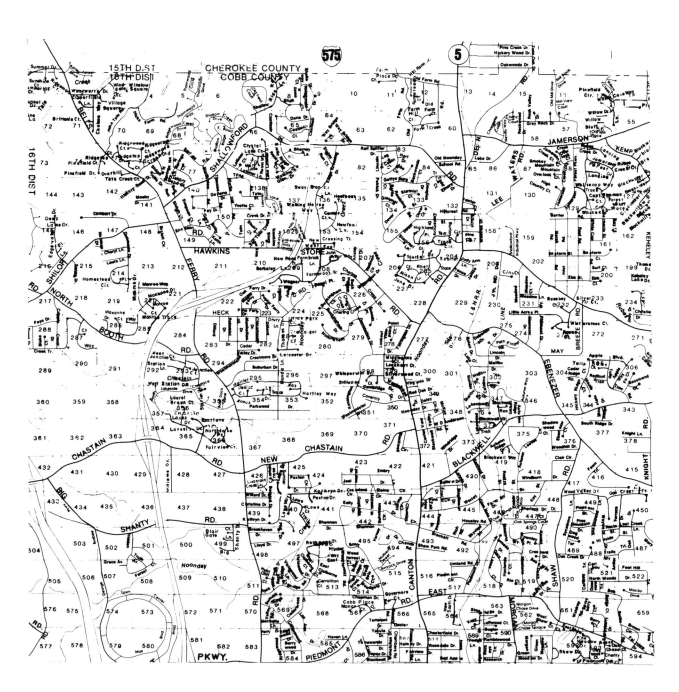

16th DISTRICT

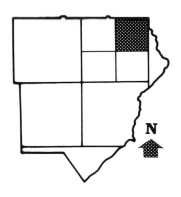

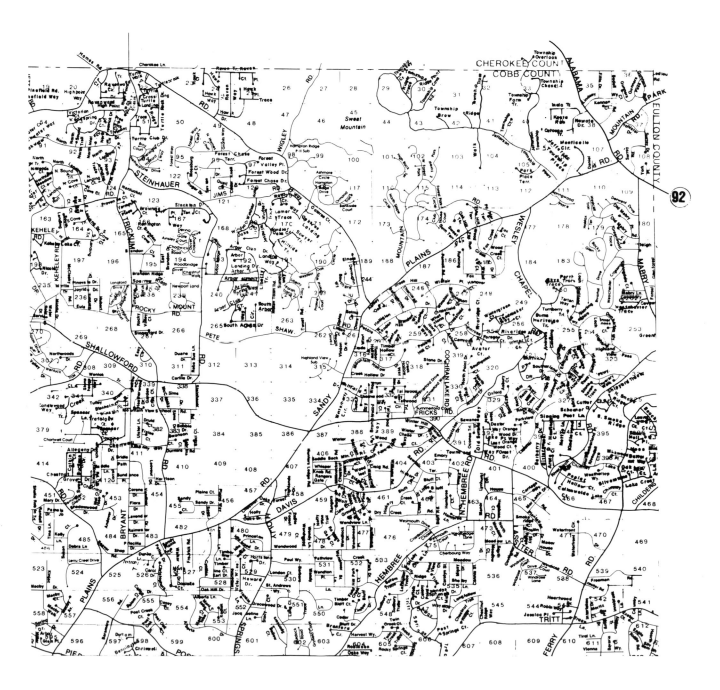

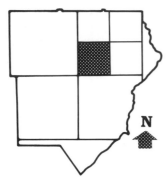

16th DISTRICT

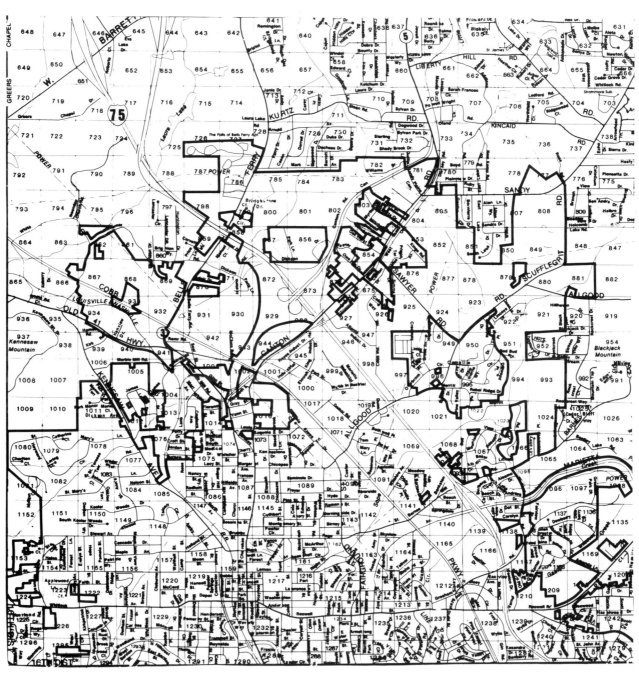

16th DISTRICT

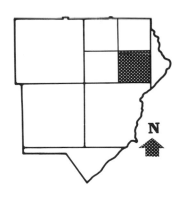

DISTRICT 16

District 16 occupies the northeast quarter of Cobb County. The land is quite hilly and was never very populous until recently. The district contains several architectural and historical resources of importance to the county and a number of individual sites of lesser value. Most of the individual structures considered as historic resources are scattered throughout the district, located in close proximity to contemporary subdivisions and shopping centers. Those sites which have been surrounded by new developments, but left standing, have some chance of surviving, though most of them have lost their cultural/environmental and architectural contexts.

1. Perhaps the most valuable rural site is the Tritt family farm on Post-Oak Tritt Road, a century-old farm complex completely intact from the first outbuilding to the last, from the rain barrel beside the front porch to the gourd tree in the yard. The farm has been in the hands of the same family from its origin to today and bears the distinct imprint of the slow rural evolution which marked Cobb County until the very recent past.

2. Marble Mill Road between Church Street Extension and Elizabeth Street represents several historical developments in Cobb County history. Marble Mill Road is the main street for the community bearing the name Elizabeth, which sits on the outskirts of Marietta, and as such is one of the more fully developed unincorporated crossroads centers in Cobb. Elizabeth grew up in association with two separate but related industrial activities--the L & N Railroad and the surrounding manufacturers. Marble Mill Road consists of a collection of residential structures from the late 19th and early 20th century representing the heterogeneity of pattern, income level, and style which is common to small working-class communities which are not company owned and operated. The street lends itself well to the creation of an historic district because it has so few intrusions.

3. Marietta Campground. This site has been in continuous use as a religious meeting ground since the first period of settlement in Cobb County. The complex contains a variety of structures dating from the nineteenth century to the recent past. The tabernacle, the academy, the walkways and burial grounds, and many of the woodframe "tents" combine to create a very special visual and cultural environment in the midst of an otherwise wholly contemporary scene along Roswell Road. Although religious camps and revival centers are and have been numerous in Georgia, this one is particularly long-lived and has many more structures attached to it than is normally the case.

4. Bishop Lake Subdivision. (See District 1.) The largest portion of this 1936 platted subdivision lies in District 16, including the oldest road segments associated with the subdivision.

5. Rural architecture. The 16th district is rich in remnant rural architecture; approximately 60 houses of 19th century and turn-of-the-century vernacular styles have been identified, scattered throughout the district. The styles include predominantly hall-and-parlor, double-pen, Victorian "L" and pyramidal hip-roofed forms and are to be found along Lower Roswell Road, Sewell Mill Road, Bells Ferry, Hawkins Store Road, Trickum Road, Sandy Plains, and Shallowford Road. Some have been absorbed into subdivisions. (In one instance, on Trickum Road, the 19th century house serves as an office for the development.) Many are simply isolated dwellings, some in excellent repair, some not. None of the identified dwellings is a "high style" house, that is, one with a great deal of architectural detail such as on the fine Victorian houses in Acworth, Marietta, and Kennesaw or even on some of the rural houses in the western section of the county. With few exceptions (the Robert McAfee house, the Davis-Cook house, the Mitchell-Dickerson house, and the Latimer-Prance house), these buildings have little individual significance. As a group, however, they demonstrate the modest rural character of this part of Cobb County from its earliest

settlement until the recent past. At least six buildings identified as historic structures in earlier surveys have been lost from this part of the county; more are obviously in the way of newer developments. Where possible, these houses should be incorporated into new residential developments, or recorded if they must be removed for new construction.

6. Unidentified rock retaining wall. These remnants run through several subdivisions in the northern section of the District. They appear to be a liner for an old road bed of indeterminate age and function but are now used as a dividing line between two different subdivisions. They are in no danger of being demolished, though they are overgrown.

7. The only sites in the 16th district listed in the National Register of Historic Places are the two historic districts in Marietta. No sites have as yet been designated by the Cobb County Historic Preservation Commission as County Historic Sites.

DISTRICT 16

Land Lot	Description	Land Lot	Description
1		31	
2		32	
3		33	
4		34	
5		35	
6		36	
7		37	
8		38	D: 4245 Alabama Rd/Hwy 92
9	**		(dr 15-34A) + Garrett Cemetery
10	**	39	
11		40	
12		41	
13	** ps112 Bentley-McCleskey hs	42	
	5087 Canton Rd (GONE)	43	
14		44	Sweat Mtn
15	** mmp magnetite J.B. Knight Prop	45	Sweat Mtn
16	Willoughby/Sewell Property	46	Sweat Mtn
	(undeveloped county park site)	47	
17	Willoughby/Sewell Property	48	
	(undeveloped county park site)	49	**
18		50	**
19		51	
20		52	
21	**	53	
22	C: dnr187 parcel 1 Trickum Rd +	54	C: dr13/31 1855 Jameson Rd
	C: dnr188 parcel 2 Trickum Rd	55	C: dr13/30 1791 Jameson Rd
23		56	Willoughby/Sewell Property
24			(undeveloped county park site)
25		57	Willoughby/Sewell Property
26			(undeveloped county park site)
27	Sweat Mtn	58	
28	Sweat Mtn	59	Fowler-Hoy Cemetery
29		60	
30		61	

DISTRICT 16

Land Lot	Description	Land Lot	Description
62		102	
63		103	
64		104	
65	B: ps122 Gresham hs Shallowford Rd n side of rd about 1.25 mi w of Canton Rd	105	
		106	
		107	Garrett Family Cemetery
66	B: ps122 Gresham hs Shallowford Rd n side of rd about 1.25 mi w of Canton Rd	108	
		109	
		110	**
67		111	D: 4645 Sandy Plains (dr15-35A)
68		112	
69		113	
70		114	E: 3695 Mountain Rd (dnr189; dr15-36A)
71	dnr70 Bells Ferry Rd (GONE)		
72	**	115	
73		116	Sweat Mountain
74		117	Sweat Mountain
75		118	Sweat Mountain
76		119	
77		120	
78	Gresham Cem	121	
79	ps123 Gresham Cemetery on s side of Shallowford Rd about 1.9 mi w of Canton Rd	122	C: 4519 Steinhauer Rd. (dr16-17)
		123	
		124	
80		125	
81		126	C: dnr192(dr13-29) 4545 Kemp Rd
82	**	127	
83	B: ps141 Allen-Overcash hs Shallowford Rd	128	
		129	
84	B: ps141 Allen-Overcash hs Shallowford Rd	130	
		131	
85		132	Noonday + ps120 Battle of Latimer's Mill
86	Fowler Cemetery		
87		133	
88		134	
89		135	
90		136	
91		137	
92		138	** Tate Cemetery (destroyed)
93		139	
94		140	
95		141	
96		142	
97		143	
98	D: 4785 Wigley Rd. (dr4-23)	144	
99	Sweat Mtn	145	
100	Sweat Mtn	146	
101	Sweat Mtn		

Land Lot	Description	Land Lot	Description
147	dnr69 608 Shiloh Rd + Shiloh Road Burying Ground	187	
148		188	Sweat Mtn
149		189	Sweat Mtn
150		190	
151		191	
152		192	
153		193	Sweat Mountain Park
154	**	194	
155		195	C: dnr193 parcel 1 Trickum Rd
156	E: pioneer rock-walled roadbed remnants between Highland Trace & Country Plantation Subdivisions	196	
		197	
157	Noonday + Old Noonday Cemetery + ps120 Battle of Latimer's Mill	198	**
		199	** Keheley Mound (recent subdivision encroachment)
158		200	
159		201	
160		202	
161		203	
162	D: 4371 Keheley Dr (dr16-12)	204	Old Noonday Cemetery + B: ps107 (dnr199) Latimer-Prance hs Canton Rd s of Shallowford Rd junct + ps120 Battle of Latimer's Mill
163	C: 4420 Keheley Rd (dr16-10) + E: parcel 2, KeheleyDr (dr16-11)		
164		205	ps120 Battle of Latimer's Mill + [Latimore] Girls Cemetery + E: pioneer rock-walled roadbed remnants between Highland Trace & Country Plantation subdivisions
165	C: dr13-28 4487 Trickum Rd		
166			
167			
168	C: Steinhauer smithy, mill, and farm site + Sweat Mountain Park	206	E: pioneer rock-walled roadbed remnants between Highland Trace & Country Plantation subdivisions
169	Mabry Middle School Site (cemetery)		
170		207	
171		208	dnr195 (dr13/4) Hawkins Store Rd + dnr196 (dr13/1-3) Hawkins Store Rd
172	Sweat Mtn		
173	Sweat Mtn	209	
174		210	
175	C: dr13/32 3670 Mountain Rd	211	
176		212	C: 4349 Bells Fy Rd (dr12-37)
177	C: parcel 4, Wesley Chapel Rd (dr16-2) + Wesley Chapel United Methodist Church Cemetery	213	
		214	
		215	
178		216	
179		217	B: Powers cabin (dr11/33-37)
180		218	
181	Mabry Family Cemetery	219	
182		220	
183		221	
184	Burying Ground off Wesley Chapel Rd	222	
185		223	
186			

Land Lot	Description	Land Lot	Description
224		266	Kemp Cemetery
225		267	C: 2001 Stoney Ford (dr16-8)
226		268	C: dnr194 parcel 1 Trickum Rd
227		269	
228	New Noonday Cemetery + Latimer Cemetery + ps109 (dnr197) Noonday Baptist Church (not orig.struct.) Canton Rd at Noonday Cr .5 mi s of Shallowford Rd junct + ps120 Battle of Latimer's Mill + dnr198 Canton Rd	270	
		271	
		272	
		273	
		274	
		275	
229	ps120 Battle of Latimer's Mill	276	**
230		277	**
231		278	
232	Dawson Cemetery	279	
233	Dawson Cemetery	280	
234		281	**
235		282	
236		283	
237		284	C: dr12-35 3941 Bells Fy Rd + C: dr13-7 3861 Westmoreland, cor. Bells Ferry Rd
238			
239	C: dr16-15 4122 Steinhauer Rd		
240	C: dr16-14 4090 Steinhauer Rd	285	
241		286	
242		287	Mt. Beulah Cemetery
243		288	
244		289	
245		290	
246		291	
247		292	
248		293	
249	C: dr16-4 4104 Wesley Chapel Rd + cemetery	294	dr13/6
250		295	
251		296	
252	E: 1215 Mabry Rd (dr15-33A)	297	
253		298	
254		299	
255		300	
256		301	**
257		302	
258		303	
259		304	
260		305	
261		306	
262		307	
263		308	
264		309	
265		310	dr16/19-20 3357 Sandy Plains
		311	

Land Lot	Description	Land Lot	Description
312		357	
313		358	
314		359	
315		360	
316	C: 3357 Sandy Plains (dr16-20)	361	
317		362	
318		363	
319		364	
320		365	
321		366	
322		367	
323		368	
324		369	
325		370	
326		371	
327		372	
328		373	
329		374	
330		375	
331		376	
332		377	
333		378	
334	C: 3690 Sandy Plains (dr16-19) + Sandy Plains Park	379	
		380	
335		381	
336		382	
337		383	
338		384	
339		385	
340		386	** + B: ps113 Morris hs, intersection of Shallowford Rd and Sandy Plains Rd + C: Mtn View School, wood frame bldg (dr16-28)
341			
342			
343			
344	C: dnr200(dr13-21) 1585 Blackwell Rd	387	D: 3575 Sandy Plains (dr16-18) + C: Mtn View School, wood frame bldg (dr16-28) + Mt. Beulah Cemetery
345	C: dnr201(dr13-20) Blackwell Rd (Fellowship Baptist Ch.,) + dnr202 parcel 11 Ebenezer Rd		
		388	
346		389	
347		390	
348		391	B: ps127 County Justice of Peace Courthouse at intersection of Davis Rd with Shallowford Rd
349			
350			
351		392	
352	**	393	
353	**	394	E: 3465 Mabry Rd (dr15-31A)
354		395	
355		396	
356		397	

Land Lot	Description	Land Lot	Description
398		442	
399		443	
400	B: ps126(dr5-5 & dr16-7) Davis-Cook hs 3921 Shallowford Rd (GONE)	444	
		445	
401	C: 3801 Shallowford Rd (dr16-5) + C: 3855 Shallowford Rd (dr5-4)	446	
		447	
402		448	
403	C: 3495 Davis Rd (dr16-27)	449	
404		450	
405		451	
406	Davis Cemetery	452	
407		453	
408		454	
409		455	
410	C: dr13-27 3320 Trickum Rd	456	
411		457	
412		458	E: dr16-25 2850 Davis Rd
413		459	Davis Family Cemetery + C: parcel 3 Davis Rd, across from 3012 (3061?) (dr16-26)
414			
415	C: dr13-16 3381? Ebenezer Rd + C: dr13-17 3384? Ebenezer Rd		
		460	
416	C: dr13-18 3485 Ebenezer Rd	461	
417		462	mmp W.M. Davis Place (mica)
418		463	
419		464	
420	C: dr13-23 3331 Windridge Dr., cor. Blackwell Rd	465	
		466	Harmony Grove Cemetery
421		467	E: Harmony Grove Baptist Church (dr15-30A)
422			
423		468	
424		469	
425		470	
426		471	
427	Franklin-Hamilton Burying Ground	472	
428		473	
429		474	
430		475	
431		476	
432		477	
433	**	478	
434		479	
435		480	
436		481	
437		482	C: 3095 Sandy Plains (dr16-29)
438		483	
439		484	C: 2237 Beaver Shop Rd (dr13-15)
440	**	485	
441		486	

DISTRICT 16

Land Lot	Description	Land Lot	Description
487		534	
488		535	
489		536	
490		537	
491		538	
492	** + Shaw Park	539	
493	** + Shaw Park + Ebenezer Cemetery	540	
494		541	
495		542	
496		543	Mt. Zion United Methodist Church Cemetery
497			
498	C: dnr99(dr13-9) 3015? Bells Ferry Rd (see map) + dnr100(dr13-8) 3107? Bells Ferry Rd (see map)	544	
		545	
		546	
499		547	
500		548	C: parcel 1, Hembry Rd (dr16-22)
501		549	
502		550	
503		551	
504		552	B: ps124(dnr207; dr4-34) Holly Springs Church (and cemetery) 2851 Holly Springs Rd
505			
506			
507	**	553	
508		554	
509	**	555	
510		556	D: ps132 Mitchell-Dickerson hs, Post Oak-Tritt Rd (north side) between Barmore Rd and Sandy Plains Rd + New Sandy Plains Baptist Church Cemetery
511	ps116 Fight at McAfee's Crossroads		
512			
513			
514		557	New Sandy Plains Baptist Church Cemetery
516	Shaw Park		
517	Shaw Park	558	
518		559	
519		560	
520	Old Sandy Plains Cemetery	561	
521		562	
522		563	C: 2741 Morgan Rd (dr13-24) + 2325 Morgan Rd (dr13-25)
523			
524		564	
525		565	Blackwells
526		566	Ponder Family Cemetery
527		567	
528		568	
529		569	
530		570	C: 2827 Bells Fy Rd (dr13-10)
531		571	**
532		572	**
533		573	

Land Lot	Description	Land Lot	Description
574	**	618	
575		619	
576		620	
577		621	**
578		622	**
579		623	
580		624	
581		625	
582		626	
583	B: ps108(dnr98) McAfee-Medford hs, 2595 Bells Ferry Rd at Roberts Rd (ghm: Robert McAfee hs)	627	
		628	
		629	C: dnr211(dr4-6) 2500 E. Piedmont Rd
584		630	Sandy Plains Cemetery
585	ps116 Fight at McAfee's Crossroads	631	
586		632	
587		633	
588		634	
589		635	
590		636	
591		637	
592		638	
593	Blackwell Cemetery	639	
594		640	** + E: ps125 Kirkpatrick's Mill, south of 350 Piedmont Rd on east bank of Noonday Creek
595	Sandy Plains		
596	** + Mayes Family Cemetery		
597		641	
598		642	C: 2480 Bells Fy Rd (dnr203/dr13-13)
599		643	
600		644	
601		645	
602		646	
603		647	
604		648	
605	D: Piney Grove Church (dr16-23); cemetery	649	
		650	**
606		651	
607	dnr208 5629 Post Oak-Tritt Rd	652	
608	B: Tritt Farm, parcel 1, Post Oak-Tritt Rd (dnr209; dr5-9+)	653	
		654	
609		655	
610	E: 2660 Johnson Ferry Rd (dr23-2)	656	Bells Ferry Park
611		657	Bells Ferry Park
612		658	
613		659	
614		660	
615		661	
616		662	
617		663	

Land Lot	Description	Land Lot	Description
664		710	
665		711	
666		712	
667		713	
668		714	
669	Burying Ground off Piedmont Road + C: dr13-26 Pinkney Dr (farm hs at end of street)	715	
		716	
		717	
670		718	
671		719	
672		720	
673		721	Greers Chapel Cemetery
674		722	
675		723	
676		724	
677		725	Burying Ground off Laura Lake Road
678		726	
679		727	
680		728	C: 1995 Bells Fy Rd (dr13-14)
681		729	
682		730	
683		731	
684		732	
685		733	
686		734	
687		735	
688		736	
689		737	
690		738	
691		739	
692		740	
693		741	
694		742	
695		743	
696		744	
697		745	
698		746	
699		747	
700		748	
701		749	
702		750	
703		751	
704		752	
705	Mount Arbor Baptist Church Cemetery	753	
706		754	
707		755	
708		756	D: Bishop Lake subdivision (dr23/3-14)
709			

Land Lot	Description	Land Lot	Description
757		804	
758		805	
759		806	
760		807	
761		808	
762		809	
763		810	
764		811	
765		812	
766		813	
767		814	
768		815	
769		816	
770		817	
771		818	C: parcel 1, Old Canton Rd, next to 1815 (dr16-24)
772			
773		819	
774		820	
775		821	
776		822	C: 3440 Sewell Mill (dr16-33) + C: 3460 Sewell Mill (dr16-34)
777			
778		823	
779		824	
780		825	
781		826	
782		827	
783		828	
784		829	
785		830	
786		831	
787		832	
788		833	
789		834	
790		835	
791		836	E: ** ps140 Ruins of Sewell Mill on Sewell Mill Road at Sope Creek
792			
793		837	
794		838	
795		839	
796		840	
797		841	
798		842	
799		843	
800		844	
801		845	
802		846	
803		847	
803		848	

Land Lot	Description	Land Lot	Description
849		896	C: 1495 Pine (dr16-35)
850		897	
851		898	
852		899	ps118 "Stop & Swap" (early pioneer community) at junction of Johnson Ferry Rd and Roswell Rd
853	Westoak: C: 1831 Westoak Dr (King?)		
854	Westoak		
855		900	
856		901	
857	Marietta	902	
858	Marietta	903	
859	C: 1521 Bells Fy Rd (dr12-19)	904	Bethlehem Primitive Baptist Church Cemetery
860			
861		905	
862		906	New Providence Baptist Church Cemetery
863	Noonday Baptist Extension Cemetery		
864		907	
865	** + kmnbp + opt	908	
866	kmnbp	909	
867	D: 1414 White Cir (dr12-20)	910	
868		911	C: 2856 Sewell Mill (dr16-31) + C: 2976 Sewell Mill (dr16-32)
869			
870	C: 1515 Bells Fy Rd (dr12-18)	912	C: 2681 Sewell Mill (dr16-30)
871		913	
872	Marietta	914	
873	Marietta	915	
874	C: 1388 Canton Rd (dnr205) + Marietta	916	
875		917	Blackjack Mtn
876		918	
877		919	Marietta Baptist Tabernacle Cemetery
878		920	
879		921	
880		922	
881		923	
882		924	
883	Wooten-Hodge Cemetery	925	
884	Blackjack Mtn	926	Marietta
885		927	Marietta
886		928	Marietta
887		929	Marietta
888		930	**
889		931	
890		932	
891		933	
892		934	opt
893	E: ** ps140 Sewell Mill Ruins on Sewell Mill Rd at Sope Creek	935	kmnbp (& Kennesaw Mtn) + opt
894		936	kmnbp (& Kennesaw Mtn) + opt
895		937	kmnbp (& Kennesaw Mtn)
		938	kmnbp (& Kennesaw Mtn)

Land Lot	Description	Land Lot	Description
939	kmnbp + opt	986	C: 2491 Roswell Rd (dr3-17)
940	opt + ghm: Johnston's Line East of Kennesaw	987	B: ps121 Old Marietta Campground + Campground Methodist Church Cemetery
941	opt	988	
942	C: 1090 Seal St (dr12-16)	989	
943	**	990	
944	Marietta	991	
945	Marietta	992	Blackjack Mtn
946	Marietta	993	Blackjack Mtn
947	Marietta	994	
948		995	
949		996	B: 1001 Allgood Rd (dnr212) + Marietta
950		997	Marietta
951		998	Marietta
952		999	Marietta
953		1000	
954		1001	Marietta/Elizabeth
955		1002	
956		1003	B: dr12/21-29 Marble Mill Rd between Elizabeth St &Church St Ext; proposed Elizabeth historic district of all pre-1940 houses, including but not limited to no.'s 106, 115,117, 118, 119, 136, 142 + D: dr12-17 Kelley's Ace Hardware,Church St Ext + D: 1397 Church St Ext (dr12-32)
957			
958	C: 2291 Sewell Mill Rd (dr4-5)		
959			
960			
961			
962	Antioch Methodist Cemetery		
963	Brown Family Cemetery		
964		1004	opt
965	Fullers Park	1005	
966		1006	C: 824 Kennesaw St (dr12-31)
967		1007	kmnbp (& Kennesaw Mtn)
968		1008	** + kmnbp (& Kennesaw Mtn)
969		1009	Marietta
970		1010	Marietta
971		1011	
972		1012	
973		1013	opt
974		1014	Marietta
975		1015	Marietta
976		1016	Marietta
977		1017	Marietta
978		1018	Marietta
979		1019	Marietta
980	** + Fullers Park	1020	Marietta
981		1021	Marietta
982		1022	Marietta
983		1023	
984		1024	
985			

Land Lot	Description	Land Lot	Description
1025	Blackjack Mtn	1073	Marietta
1026		1074	Marietta
1027		1075	Marietta
1028		1076	Marietta
1029		1077	Marietta
1030	C: 2271 Robinson Rd (dr20-2)	1078	Marietta
1031	C: 2511(?) Robinson Rd (no photo)	1079	Marietta
1032	C: 2621 Robinson Rd (dr3-14 & dr20-1)	1080	Marietta
1033	C: 2621 Robinson Rd (dr3-14 & dr20-1)	1081	Marietta
1034		1082	Marietta
1035		1083	Marietta
1036	C: parcel 1, Robinson Rd (dr20-3)	1084	Marietta
1037		1085	Marietta
1038		1086	Marietta
1039		1087	Marietta
1040	Bishop Family Cemetery	1088	Marietta
1041		1089	Marietta
1042		1090	Marietta
1043		1091	Marietta
1044		1092	Marietta
1045		1093	Marietta
1046		1094	Marietta
1047		1095	Marietta
1048		1096	
1049		1097	
1050		1098	
1051		1099	**
1052		1100	
1053	C: 3208 Robinson Rd (dr23-15)	1101	
1054		1102	
1055	D: 2930 Robinson Rd (dr3-13)	1103	
1056		1104	
1057		1105	
1058	Delk-Hunton Cemetery	1106	**
1059		1107	
1060		1108	
1061		1109	
1062	**	1110	**
1063		1111	
1064		1112	
1065		1113	
1066	Marietta	1114	
1067	Marietta	1115	
1068	Marietta	1116	
1069	Marietta	1117	
1070	Marietta	1118	
1071	Marietta	1119	C: 4068 Lower Roswell Rd (dr20-9)
1072	Marietta	1120	

Land Lot	Description	Land Lot	Description
1121		1168	dr19-33 Sope Creek Baptist Church
1122		1169	
1123		1170	
1124		1171	
1125		1172	Sewell Park
1126		1173	* * + Sewell Park
1127		1174	
1128		1175	** Sope Creek Cemetery (destroyed)
1129		1176	** Sope Creek Cemetery (destroyed)
1130		1177	
1131	**	1178	
1132		1179	
1133		1180	
1134	** + ghm: The March of McPherson's Army of the Tennessee to Roswell	1181	
		1182	
1135		1183	
1136		1184	
1137		1185	
1138	Marietta	1186	
1139	Marietta	1187	
1140	Marietta	1188	
1141	Marietta	1189	Dickerson Family Cemetery
1142	Marietta	1190	Dickerson Family Cemetery
1143	Marietta	1191	
1144	Marietta	1192	
1145	Marietta	1193	
1146	Marietta	1194	
1147	Marietta	1195	C: 3600 Lower Roswell Rd (dr20-8)
1148	Marietta	1196	C: parcel 1, Lower Roswell Rd at Pinehurst (dr20-6)
1149	Marietta		
1150	Marietta	1197	
1151	Marietta	1198	
1152		1199	
1153	Marietta	1200	
1154	Marietta	1201	Mayes-Sewell Cemetery
1155	Marietta	1202	
1156	Marietta	1203	
1157	Marietta	1204	Sewell Park
1158	Marietta	1205	Sewell Park
1159	Marietta	1206	
1160	Marietta	1207	
1161	Marietta	1208	
1162	Marietta	1209	Marietta
1163	Marietta	1210	Marietta
1164	Marietta	1211	Marietta
1165	Marietta	1212	Marietta
1166	Marietta	1213	Marietta
1167	Marietta	1214	Marietta

Land Lot	Description	Land Lot	Description
1215	Marietta	1256	
1216	Marietta	1257	**
1217	Marietta	1258	
1218	Marietta	1259	
1219	Marietta	1260	
1220	Marietta	1261	
1221	Marietta	1262	
1222	Marietta	1263	
1223	Marietta	1264	
1224	Marietta	1265	
1225	Marietta	1266	
1226	Marietta	1267	D: parcel 1, Shadowlawn Rd (dr27-16)
1227	Marietta	1268	
1228	Marietta	1269	
1229	Marietta	1270	C: 3031 Lower Roswell Rd (dr27-12)
1230	Marietta	1271	
1231	Marietta	1272	
1232	Marietta	1273	
1233	Marietta	1274	
1234	Marietta	1275	Barfield Memorial Cemetery
1235	Marietta	1276	
1236	Marietta	1277	
1237	Marietta	1278	
1238	Marietta	1279	
1239	Marietta	1280	Marietta
1240	Marietta	1281	Marietta
1241	Marietta	1282	Marietta
1242		1283	Marietta
1243		1284	Marietta
1244		1285	Marietta
1245		1286	Marietta
1246		1287	Marietta
1247		1288	Marietta
1248		1289	Marietta
1249		1290	Marietta
1250		1291	Marietta
1251	**	1292	Marietta
1252		1293	Marietta
1253	C: 3567 Lower Roswell Rd—see also LL 1254—(dr20-7)	1294	Marietta
1254	C: See LL 1253	1295	Marietta
1255	E: parcels 3 & 4, (#60?) Shadowlawn Rd (dr27-13)	1296	Marietta

17th DISTRICT

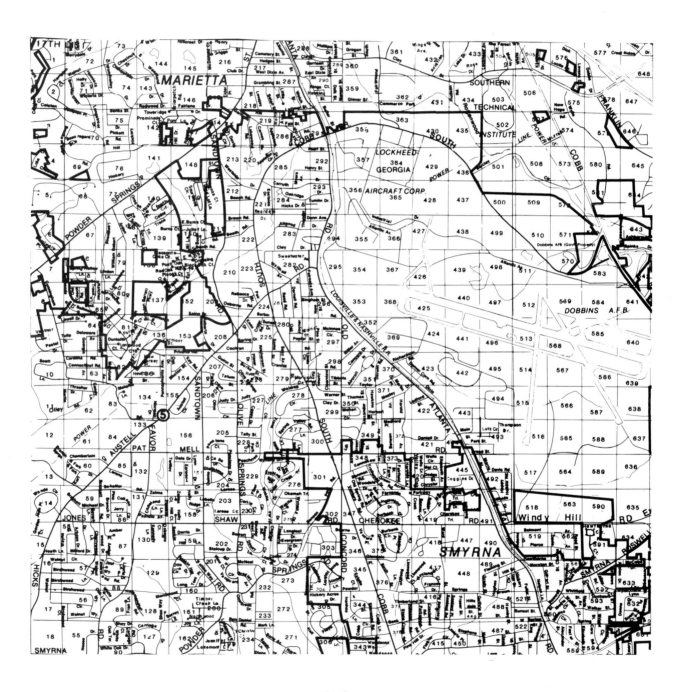

17th DISTRICT

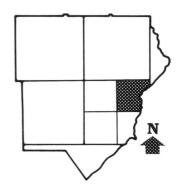

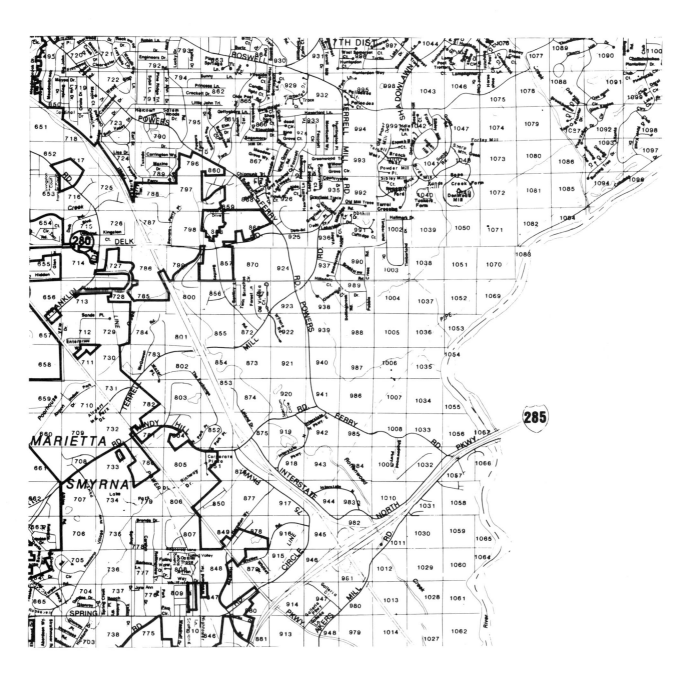

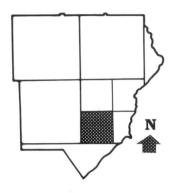

17th DISTRICT

N

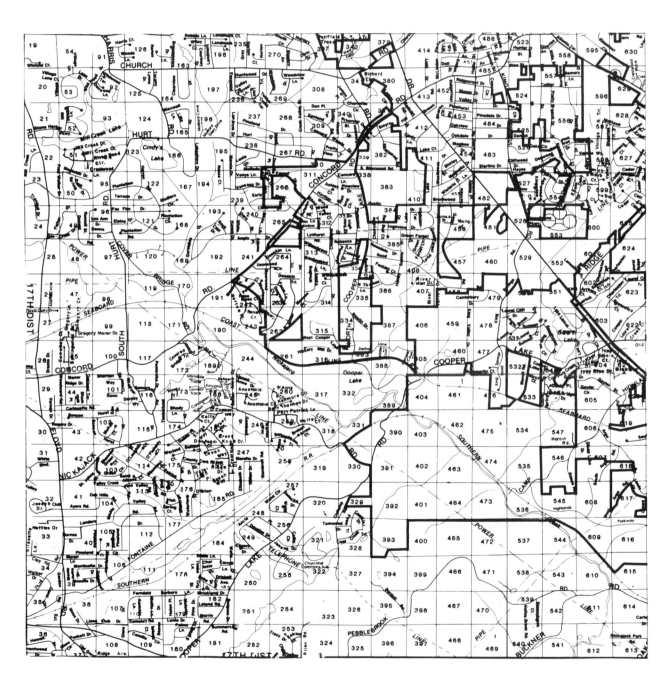

17th DISTRICT

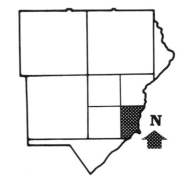

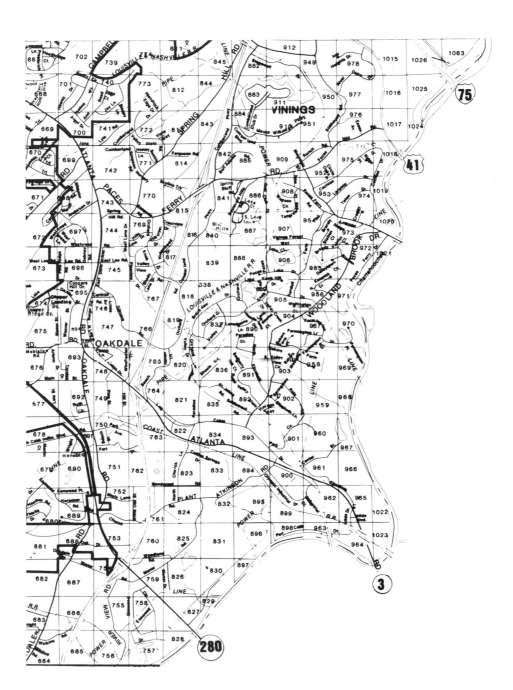

DISTRICT 17

District 17 occupies the southeast quarter of Cobb County and contains the densest 20th century development in the county, from early streetcar suburbs to the latest perimeter highrises. District 17 is traversed by all of the major transportation arteries which run through Cobb County, including Interstate highways 285 and 75, and state highways 3, 5, and 41, and all three of the major railroad lines which run through the county en route to Atlanta. District 17 bears the least resemblance to old rural Cobb County, and, except for the Concord Covered Bridge, the Sope Creek paper mills, Vinings village center and some important archaeological sites, most of the historic resources in District 17 relate to Cobb County at the turn of the 20th century and later.

1. The Concord Covered Bridge Historic District. This complex of structures includes the covered bridge itself, last in the county, associated dwellings and mill ruins which combine to create a wholly intact 19th century cultural environment. The Concord Covered Bridge district has already been accepted as the first Cobb County designated historic site and is already listed in the National Register of Historic Places.

2. Vinings. Vinings achieved its primary importance as a railroad junction in the late 19th century, though its roots are older. The historic center of Vinings bears the qualities of a village--a social and economic center on a smaller, less well-developed scale than a small town. The historic continuity of Vinings as a railroad junction and the architectural symmetry of its oldest buildings should lead to the creation of a small historic district.

3. Other National Register sites in the 17th District include the Sope Creek Paper Mill ruins on Paper Mill Road, the Carmichael House, and the Glover-McLeod-Garrison House (now a restaurant) on South Cobb Drive.

4. The last, best remnants of the Interurban Streetcar Line and associated developments are partially intact. This line connected downtown Atlanta and downtown Marietta, was established in 1905 and ran until 1947 when the trolley line was replaced by bus service. The interurban line was the longest such inter-city commuter streetcar line in the Southeast, and the only line of its kind in the state of Georgia. Most of the depots and stops were in Cobb County. The stations were located at Jonesville (where Lockheed is located), Fair Oaks , Smyrna, Hollywood, and Oakdale, with stops at major streets and intersections in between. What remains of the line are segments of residential development planned along the line on Atlanta Road, Log Cabin Road, Oakdale Road, and adjacent streets, the route of the line itself (still visible along the roadways), some bridge piers, and land cuts. The remnants of the Interurban line lend themselves to the creation of thematic district or a multiple resource area (MRA) which follows the route from the Chattahoochee crossing into Marietta.

5. The Bell Bomber Plant original buildings. The location of the Bell Bomber Plant changed the course of history in Cobb County. The original plant is intact and used by the Lockheed Corporation. The buildings do not yet meet the age criteria for listing in the National Register, but the historical value of the plant to Cobb County is indisputable.

6. Cooper Lake Road bungalows. A section of modest bungalows along Cooper Lake Road between Bankhead Highway and the railroad may have potential for historic preservation in the future as representative of Cobb County growth and settlement during the second quarter of the twentieth century. At present, they do not fully meet the age criteria for the National Register and do not represent as yet any compelling aspects of Cobb County history.

7. The Mable House. As the home of Mableton founder, Robert Mable, and as an excellent mid-nineteenth century architectural specimen, the Mable House is listed on the National Register of Historic Sites.

8. Mableton. See District 19.

9. As time passes, the residential developments which were erected in conjunction with the Bell Bomber plant in Marietta and on the outskirts of Marietta in Fair Oaks should receive attention as potential National Register districts. There are several segments of Fair Oaks which are very intentional subdivisions, some containing World War II style duplexes, others containing very modest minimal traditionalist cottages typical of the early and mid-1940s, which will have more historic meaning in another decade. These are noted now for what they are but they are not presently recommended for designation.

10. Assorted other identified structures in District 17 consist of mid-nineteenth century residences along Austell Road and Floyd Road, and Powder Springs Road. These are such heavily trafficked street that these sites are probably in jeopardy.

DISTRICT 17

Land Lot	Description	Land Lot	Description
1	Marietta	29	ghm The Extended Right + ghm The March to Sope Creek + ghm Site - Wm Moss hs + osr
2	Marietta		
3	Marietta		
4	Marietta	30	C: dnr243 parcel 2 of LL 31 on Floyd Rd + osr
5	Marietta		
6	Marietta	31	C: dnr243 parcel 2 Floyd Rd + osr
7	C: dnr223 parcel 36? Powder Springs Rd, north of junction with Cunningham Rd	32	osr
		33	osr
		34	osr + ghm + A: The Mable hs, N.R.
8		35	Mableton + B: 5487 Floyd Rd, proposed Mableton MRA, (dnr250; dr10-10) + C: no #, residence across from 5487 Floyd Rd. (dnr250)
9			
10			
11			
12		36	C: 5584 S. Gordon (dr10-18)
13		37	B: ps49 Mitchell hs, Old Gordon Rd (behind the public library on Gordon Rd) + ghm Turner's, Howell's, Baker's & Sandtown Ferries + osr
14			
15	C: 2500 Austell Rd (dr20-30)		
16			
17		38	Little Bethel Baptist Cemetery + Lions Park + osr
18			
19		39	osr
20		40	Mableton + A: ps48(dnr246) The Mable hs, N. R. 266 Floyd Rd. + Mable Cemetery + osr
21			
22			
23		41	osr
24		42	
25		43	
26		44	
27		45	
28	ghm Site - Wm Moss hs	46	

Land Lot	Description	Land Lot	Description
47		94	
48		95	
49		96	
50		97	
51		98	
52		99	
53		100	ghm Hood's Corps at Battle of Ruff's Mill
54		101	Old Clay Family Cemetery
55		102	
56		103	
57		104	
58		105	
59		106	
60		107	Lions Park
61		108	
62		109	
63		110	Fleming Cemetery
64		112	
65	Marietta	113	
66	Marietta	114	
67	C: dnr 222 Powder Springs Rd @ Longwood Rd + Marietta	115	Combee Cemetery
		116	
68	Marietta	117	A: Concord Covered Bridge H. D. N.R. dnr242 Concord Rd
69	Marietta		
70	Marietta	118	
71	Marietta	119	Concord Baptist Church Cemetery
72	Marietta	120	
73	Marietta	121	
74	Marietta	122	
75	Marietta	123	
76	Marietta	124	
77	Marietta	125	
78	Marietta	126	**
79	Marietta	127	
80	Marietta	128	
81	Marietta	129	
82	Marietta	130	
83		131	
84		132	
85		133	C: 2010 Austell Rd (dr23-16+)
86		134	
87		135	Marietta
88		136	Marietta
89		137	Fair Oaks Park
90		138	
91		139	Marietta
92		140	Marietta
93		141	Marietta

Land Lot	Description	Land Lot	Description
142	Marietta		Cooper Lake between Bankhead &
143	Marietta		Leland (dr9/28-35) + B/C: parcel 42,
144	Marietta		Cooper Lake (dr9-28)
145	Marietta	182	
146	Marietta	183	
147	Marietta	184	
148	Marietta	185	
149	Marietta	186	
150	Marietta	187	
151	Marietta	188	
152	Marietta	189	
153	Marietta	190	A: Concord Covered Bridge H.D.: **
154			ps19(dnr240) Concord Woolen Mill
155			Ruins 10 Concord Rd (on Nickajack
156			Creek) + dnr241A John W. Rice
157			Summer Cottage, N.R., across from
158			Ruff's Mill at 10 Concord Rd
159		191	A: ps25 Ruff-Milroy-Ivester hs,
160			Concord Rd about 3.3 mi. west of
161			Smyrna + Ruff Cemetery
162		192	
163		193	
164		194	
165		195	
166		196	**
167		197	
168		198	
169		199	
170		200	
171	A: Concord Covered Bridge H. D.:	201	
	ps46(dnr241) Concord Covered Bridge,	202	St. Jude's Episcopal Church Cemetery
	N.R. Concord Rd over Nickajack Creek	203	
	near Covered Bridge Rd + A: ps19	204	
	[Daniell] - Ruff's Mill (Concord Mills)	205	
172	A: Concord Covered Bridge H. D.;	206	
	ps28(dnr242) Gann-Hill hs 427	207	
	Concord Rd	208	
173		209	Marietta
174		210	
175		211	
176		212	
177		213	Marietta
178		214	Marietta
179		215	Marietta
180	B/D: pre-1940 residences along	216	Marietta
	Cooper Lake between Bankhead &	217	Marietta
	Leland (dr9/28-35)	218	Marietta
181	B/D: pre-1940 residences along	219	Marietta

Land Lot	Description	Land Lot	Description
220		267	
221		268	
222		269	
223		270	
224	Maloney Springs Cemetery	271	
225		272	
226		273	
227		274	
228	Smyrna	275	
229	Smyrna	276	Smyrna
230		277	Smyrna
231		278	
232		279	
233		280	Fair Oaks
234		281	Fair Oaks + cemetery
235		282	
236		283	
237		284	
238		285	
239	Smyrna	286	
240		287	Marietta
241	B: dnr 128 143 Concord Rd + Smyrna	288	Marietta
242	Smyrna	289	Marietta
243	Smyrna	290	Marietta
244	Smyrna	291	mrb + opt + cement arch bridge (GONE)
245		292	mrb + opt
246	Moss Cemetery	293	mrb + E: ps133 Sibley-Gardner hs "Cottage Hill" (Dobbins Air Force Base Officers' Club) + opt + cemetery (GONE)
247			
248			
249		294	mrb + opt
250		295	mrb + Barber Family Cemetery at Fair Oaks + opt
251			
252		296	mrb + opt
253		297	
254		298	
255		299	Olive Springs Cemetery + Clay Cemetery + Fair Oaks Cemetery
256			
257		300	
258		301	Smyrna
259		302	Smyrna
260		303	
261	Smyrna	304	Smyrna
262	Smyrna	305	Smyrna
263	Smyrna	306	
264	Smyrna	307	
265	C: dnr 239 200 Concord Rd + Smyrna	308	
266	Smyrna	309	
		310	Smyrna

Land Lot	Description	Land Lot	Description
311	Smyrna	356	Cemetery at the A.J.S. Gardner-Sibley hs (graves destroyed) + mrb + D: original bldgs, Bell Bomber Plant
312	Smyrna		
313	Smyrna		
314	Smyrna	357	mrb + D: original bldgs, Bell Bomber Plant
315	Smyrna		
316	Smyrna	358	mrb
317		359	Marietta
318	Cold Springs Park	360	Marietta
319		361	Marietta
320		362	Marietta
321		363	mrb
322		364	mrb + D: original bldgs, Bell Bomber Plant
323			
324		365	mrb + D: original bldgs, Bell Bomber Plant
325			
326		366	mrb + D: original bldgs, Bell Bomber Plant
328			
329		367	mrb
330		368	mrb
331		369	mrb
332		370	opt
333	Smyrna	371	
334		372	Smyrna
335		373	Smyrna
336	Smyrna	374	Smyrna
337	Smyrna	375	Smyrna
338	Smyrna	376	Smyrna
339	Smyrna	378	Smyrna
340		379	Smyrna
341	Smyrna	380	Smyrna
342	Smyrna	381	Smyrna
343	Smyrna	382	Smyrna
344	Smyrna	383	
345	Smyrna	384	Smyrna
346	Smyrna	385	Smyrna
347	Smyrna	386	Smyrna
348	Smyrna	387	Smyrna
349	Smyrna	388	
350		389	Dodgen Cemetery
351	D: WWII & 1940s housing along Miller, Concord, & Aircraft Dr—also in LL 352—(dr18/26-31)	390	
		391	
		392	
352	D: See LL 351 + mrb + opt	393	
353	mrb	394	
354	mrb	395	
355	mrb + D: original bldgs, Bell Bomber Plant	396	
		397	
		398	

Land Lot	Description	Land Lot	Description
399		446	Smyrna
400		447	Smyrna
401		448	Smyrna
402		449	Smyrna
403		450	Smyrna
404	C: Ry trestle bridge (dr9-27)	451	Smyrna
405		452	Smyrna
406		453	Smyrna
407	Smyrna	454	Smyrna
408	Smyrna	455	Smyrna
409	Smyrna	456	
410	Smyrna	457	
411	Smyrna	458	Smyrna
412	Smyrna	459	
413	Smyrna	460	
414	Smyrna	461	
415	Smyrna	462	
416	Smyrna	463	
417	Smyrna	464	
418	Smyrna	465	
419	Smyrna	466	
420		467	
421		468	
422	opt	469	
423		470	
424	mrb	471	
425	mrb	472	
426	mrb	473	
427	mrb	474	
428	mrb + D: original bldgs, Bell Bomber Plant	475	
		476	
429	mrb	477	** ps51 Site: Eaton hs, junction Kings Springs and Cooper Lake Roads
430	mrb		
431	Marietta	478	** ps51 Site: Eaton hs, junction Kings Springs and Cooper Lake Roads
432	Marietta		
433	Marietta	479	Smyrna
434	Marietta	480	Smyrna
435	mrb	481	
436	mrb	482	
437	mrb	483	Smyrna
438	mrb	484	Smyrna
439	mrb	485	Smyrna
440	mrb	486	Smyrna
441	mrb	487	Smyrna
442		488	Smyrna
443		489	Smyrna
444	Smyrna	490	Smyrna
445	Smyrna	491	Smyrna

Land Lot	Description	Land Lot	Description
492	Smyrna	540	
493	**	541	
494		542	** ps5 Pebblebrook Archaeological Site, school grounds of Pebblebrook High School, Buckner Rd. near Pebblebrook Rd. and Nickajack Creek
495	mrb		
496	mrb		
497	mrb		
498	mrb	543	**
499	mrb + Jonesville Cemetery	544	
500	Marietta/mrb	545	
501	Marietta	546	
502	Marietta	547	
503	Marietta	548	
504	Marietta	549	
505	Marietta	550	
506	Marietta	551	Smyrna
507	Marietta	552	Smyrna
508	Marietta	553	
509	Marietta/mrb	554	Smyrna
510	mrb	555	Smyrna
511	mrb	556	
512	mrb	557	Smyrna
513	mrb	558	Smyrna
514	mrb	559	Smyrna
515	mrb	560	Smyrna
516	mrb	561	Smyrna
517	mrb	562	
518	Smyrna/mrb	563	Smyrna/mrb
519	Smyrna	564	mrb
520	Smyrna	565	mrb
521	Smyrna	566	mrb
522	Smyrna	567	mrb
523	Smyrna	568	mrb
524	Smyrna	569	mrb
525	Smyrna	570	mrb
526	Smyrna	571	mrb
527		572	Marietta/mrb
528	Smyrna	573	Marietta
529	Smyrna	574	Marietta
530	Smyrna	575	Marietta
531		576	Marietta
532		577	Marietta
533		578	Marietta
534		579	Marietta
535		580	Marietta
536		581	Marietta/mrb
537		582	Marietta/mrb
538		583	Marietta/mrb
539	**		

Land Lot	Description	Land Lot	Description
584	mrb	631	Smyrna
585	mrb	632	Smyrna
586	mrb	633	Smyrna
587	mrb	634	Smyrna
588	mrb	635	mrb
589	mrb	636	mrb
590	Smyrna/mrb	637	mrb
591	Smyrna	638	mrb
592	Smyrna	639	mrb
593	Smyrna	640	mrb
594	Smyrna	641	mrb
595	Smyrna	642	Marietta/mrb
596	Smyrna	643	Marietta
597	Smyrna	644	Marietta
598	Smyrna	645	Marietta
599	Smyrna	646	Marietta
600	Smyrna	647	Marietta
601	Smyrna	648	Marietta
602	Smyrna	649	Marietta
603		650	Marietta
604		651	Marietta
605	Welcome Grove Baptist Church Cemetery	652	Marietta
606		653	Marietta
607		654	Marietta
608		655	Marietta
609		656	Marietta
610		657	Marietta/mrb
611	**	658	mrb
612	** + Nickajack Park	659	Marietta
613	cw	660	Marietta
614	cw	661	Marietta/mrb
615		662	mrb
616		663	Smyrna/mrb
617		664	Smyrna
618		665	Smyrna
619		666	Smyrna
620		667	Smyrna
621		668	Smyrna
622		669	Smyrna
623		670	Smyrna
624		671	Smyrna
625	Smyrna	672	Smyrna
626	Smyrna	673	
627	Smyrna	674	
628	Smyrna	675	
629	Smyrna	676	
630	Smyrna	677	
		678	

Land Lot	Description	Land Lot	Description
679		718	Marietta
680		719	
681		720	
682	** + cw	721	
683	Oakdale + cw	722	
684	cw	723	
685		724	Marietta
686		725	Marietta
687	cw	726	Marietta
688	cw	727	Haney Grove Cemetery
689		728	Marietta
690		729	Marietta
691		730	Marietta
692	B: Oakdale Rd between Hwy 3 & RR tracks—also in LL 693—all pre-1940 houses, possible contributing structures to potential Oakdale HD (dr18/1-9)	731	Marietta
		732	Marietta
		733	Marietta/Smyrna
		734	Smyrna
		735	Smyrna
693	B: See LL 692 + C: 4780 Atlanta Rd (dr17-33)	736	Smyrna
		737	Smyrna
694	Gilmore + B: Atlanta Rd between Cooper Lake Rd & Daniel: pre-1940 houses, possible contributing structures to potential Interurban HD—also in LL 695 (dr18/10-18)	738	Smyrna
		739	Smyrna
		740	Smyrna
		741	Smyrna
		742	
695	B: See LL 694	743	** + opt
696		744	** + opt
697		745	
698	opt	746	
699	Smyrna	747	
700	Smyrna	748	E: 2149 Peach Lane (dr17-35) + E: 4379 N. Log Cabin(dr17-36)
701	Smyrna		
702	Smyrna	749	
703	Smyrna	750	
704	Smyrna	751	
705	Smyrna	752	cw
706	Smyrna	753	**
707	Smyrna	754	
708	Smyrna/Marietta	755	
709	Marietta	756	
710	Marietta	757	
711	Marietta	758	
712	Marietta	759	
713	Marietta	760	**
714	Marietta	761	
715	Marietta	762	cw
716	Marietta	763	
717	Marietta		

Land Lot	Description	Land Lot	Description
764	** + ghm The Cumberland Army to Power's & Pace's Ferries + A: commercial bldgs @ Carmichael hs (dr17-30)	809	Smyrna
		810	Smyrna
		811	Smyrna
765	ghm The Cumberland Army to Powers' & Pace's Ferries	812	
		813	
766		814	
767		815	
768	opt	816	
769	opt	817	
770		818	opt
771		819	opt
772		820	**
773		821	** C: Paradise Shoals Rd & historic black settlement (dr)
774			
775	Smyrna	822	C: 4640 Atlanta Rd (dr17-28) + E: Collins Springs Bapt Church (dr17-26) + B: 2185 N Church, part of proposed Log Cabin HD (dr17-20) + B: 4711 N Church @ Eberhart (dr17-19) + B: 4666 N Church, part of proposed Log Cabin HD (dr17-18) + B: Log Cabin Rd between Woodland Brook Dr. & Carmichael hs N. R. (dr17/3-13+) + Collins Springs Cemetery
776	Smyrna		
777	Smyrna		
778	Smyrna		
779	Smyrna/Marietta		
780	Smyrna/Marietta		
781	Marietta		
782	Marietta		
783	Marietta		
784	**		
785	**	823	E: 4831 Church Rd (dr17-25) + cw
786		824	E: 4971 Church Rd (dr17-24) + E: Peaceful Valley Bapt Church (dr17-23)
787	Marietta		
788	Marietta	825	
789		826	
790		827	Hooper-McWilliams Cemetery + Riverview Memorial Park Cemetery
791			
792		828	
793		829	
794		830	
795		831	
796	Marietta	832	
797	Marietta	833	
798	Marietta	834	B: Log Cabin Rd between Woodland Brook Dr. & Carmichael hs N. R. (dr17/3-13+) + cw
799	Marietta		
800	**		
801	**	835	E: St. John's Rd & St. John's Church historic black settlement + Settlement Rd. (dr)
802			
803			
804	Marietta	836	
805	Marietta/Smyrna	837	opt
806	Marietta/Smyrna	838	
807	Smyrna	839	
808	Smyrna	840	

Land Lot	Description	Land Lot	Description
841	621 Paces Ferry Rd. - Miss Lois Gardner hs (dr)	885	Burt Adams B.S.A. Camp (GONE) + New Salem Methodist Church, Parcel 6, (GONE) + 19th & 20th century black settlement + Mt. Sinai Baptist Church (GONE) + Cemetery (dr + 2857 Paces Ferry Rd. Nellie Mae Rowe, folk artist, hs (GONE) (marker) (dr)
842	Burt Adams Boy Scouts of America Camp (GONE) + Burt Adams Rd. (dr)		
843	Burt Adams BSA Camp (GONE)		
844	**		
845	Smyrna		
846	Smyrna	886	
847	Smyrna	887	Vinings Cemetery
848	Smyrna	888	
849	Smyrna	889	**
850	Smyrna/Marietta	890	opt
851	Marietta	891	opt
852		892	C: 4641 Woodland (dr17-2) + opt E: Settlement Rd.
853			
854		893	B: Log Cabin Rd between Woodland Brook Dr. & Carmichael hs (dr17/3-13+) + cw
855	ghm 23d Army Corps to Sope Creek		
856			
857	Marietta	894	
858	Marietta	895	**
859		896	**
860	Marietta	897	
861		898	
862		899	
863		900	B: Log Cabin Rd between Woodland Brook Dr. & Carmichael hs (dr17/3 13+) + E: converted gas station on Old Hwy 3, next to #4892 (dr23-25) + ghm: Here Johnston's River Line Crossed Road + opt
864			
865			
866			
867			
868			
869	Marietta	901	B: Log Cabin Rd between Woodland Brook Dr. & Carmichael hs (dr17/3-13+) + C: 4750 Park Cir (dr17-14) + opt + cw
870			
871			
872			
873		902	opt
874		903	**
875	ps59 Buffalo Fish Town (site), east of I-75 near where Windy Hill Rd. crosses Rottenwood Creek	904	
		905	
		906	
876		907	
877		908	
878	Smyrna	909	Vinings + A: proposed Vinings HD + ps50 Pace's Cemetery (atop Vinings Mtn, aka Mount Wilkinson, Signal Mountain) + dnr 236 & 237 Paces Ferry Rd(see map) + ghm The 4th Corps at Vinings Station + B: Sanders-Robinson hs (Paces Ferry Rd. at R.R.)
879	Smyrna		
880	Smyrna		
881	Smyrna		
882			
883	Burt Adams B.S.A. Camp (GONE) (dr)		
884	Burt Adams B.S.A. Camp (GONE) (dr)		

Land Lot	Description	Land Lot	Description
910	Hardy Pace Cemetery-Vinings Mountain Cemetery + Burt Adams B.S.A. Camp (GONE)		(Old Post Office) (now Cottage Rose) + B: ps30(dnr232) Solomon K. Pace hs Vinings/Paces Mill Rd + 4040 Bldg. (now Vinings Bar) + B: ps61 Carter-Vanneman hs Paces Mill Rd near the Paces Ferry intersection + B: ps62(dnr233) Pace-Yarborough hs (now Old Vinings Inn) Paces Mill Rd + dnr234 Paces Ferry Rd + B: ps63(dnr235) Railroad Pavilion hs Mountain St + B: ps64 Section Chief's hs Ranch Rd + ghm Site: Hardy Pace's Residence/Howard's Headquarters
911	B.S.A. Camp (GONE)		
912			
913			
914			
915			
916			
917	**		
918	**		
919	**		
920			
921		953	B: 3025 Paces Ferry Rd
922		954	
923		955	
924		956	
925		957	** + Chambers Family Cemetery (GONE) Farmington Area
926	Ranch Rd., Vinings Spring (at Old Pavilion hs) + Mountain Rd.	958	**
927		959	**
928		960	cw
929		961	E: Elizabeth Lane between Hwy 3 & Park Cir (dr17/15-17)
930			
931		962	opt
932	E: 469 Sewell Mill Dr (dr3-11) + Terrell Mill Park	963	
		964	
933		965	E: Elizabeth Lane between Hwy 3 & Park Cir (dr17/15-17) + opt
934			
935		966	
936		967	cw
937		968	**
938		969	**
939	Osborn Cemetery	970	**
940		971	**
941	chat rec	972	**
942		973	
943	**	974	
944	**	975	**
945		976	** Stillhouse Rd + 4 Roses Bourbon Whiskey Distillery (GONE)
946			
947		977	** Stillhouse Rd mill-site (GONE)
948		978	
949		979	
950	** Stillhouse Rd	980	
951	** Stillhouse Rd	981	
952	Vinings + A: proposed Vinings HD + 2949 Paces Ferry Rd Vest-Hodge hs	982	
		983	

Land Lot	Description	Land Lot	Description
984		1023	** ps3 Site: Standing Peach Tree Village ("At confluence of Peachtree Creek and Chattahoochee River"—on west side of river, just north of Southern RR bridge at Cobb Co. Filtering Plant) + ps12 Montgomerys Ferry Site, Ga. 3 at the Chattahoochee River + opt
985	chat rec		
986	chat rec		
987	chat rec		
988			
989			
990			
991		1024	** + opt
992		1025	chat rec
993		1026	chat rec
994		1027	chat rec
995	C: Sardis Baptist Church (dr27-18) + Sardis Baptist Church Cemetery	1028	** + chat rec
		1029	** + chat rec
996		1030	chat rec
997		1031	
998		1032	
999		1033	**
1000		1034	** + chat rec
1001		1035	chat rec
1002		1036	chat rec
1003		1037	chat rec
1004	chat rec	1038	chat rec
1005	chat rec	1039	
1006	chat rec	1040	
1007	chat rec	1041	
1008		1042	
1009		1043	
1010		1044	
1011		1045	
1012	** + chat rec	1046	chat rec
1013	** + chat rec	1047	chat rec
1014		1048	chat rec
1015		1049	chat rec
1016		1050	chat rec
1017		1051	chat rec
1018	ps47 8-Gun Battery Site/Atlanta Campaign (in Cochise Subdivision at Cochise Dr. in Vinings—on ridge over looking Chattahoochee River) + ghm: The 4th Corps Posted Along the River	1052	chat rec
		1053	** + chat rec
		1054	chat rec
		1055	** + chat rec
		1056	** + chat rec
1019		1057	ps8(ghm) Powers Ferry Site, Powers Ferry Rd at Chattahoochee River
1020	** ps10 Paces Ferry Site, Paces Ferry Rd. at the Chattahoochee River + ghm: The Errant Pontoon Bridge: Pace's Ferry + ghm: The 4th & 20th A.C. Cross at Pace's Ferry		
		1058	
		1059	chat rec
		1060	chat rec
1021		1061	chat rec
1022		1062	chat rec

Land Lot	Description	Land Lot	Description
1063	chat rec + ps9 Cochran's (Cavalry) Ford, I-75 at Chattahoochee River	1080	chat rec
1064	chat rec	1081	
1065		1082	
1066		1083	
1067	** + ghm: The River Patrol & Cochran's Ford	1084	**
		1085	**
		1086	**
1068	** + chat rec	1087	** + chat rec
1069	** + chat rec	1088	
1070	** + chat rec	1089	
1071	chat rec + Scribner Cemetery	1090	
1072	chat rec	1091	
1073	chat rec	1092	
1074	chat rec	1093	
1075	chat rec	1094	
1076		1095	
1077	ghm Sope Creek Paper Mills + ghm The 23d Corps at Sope Creek	1096	
		1097	
1078	E: ** ps110 Ruins: Sope Creek Paper Mills, Paper Mill Rd at Sope Creek, east side of creek and south of bridge + ghm: Sope Creek Industries + chat rec	1098	
		1099	
		1100	A: Glover Machine Works (NR) (dr27-1) [Annexed to Marietta]
1079	chat rec		

Concord woolen mill ruins.

Concord Woolen Mill ruins.

Graves of Solomon and Penelope Pace on Vinings Mountain. Solomon Pace was the son of Hardy Pace, one of Vinings pioneer families.

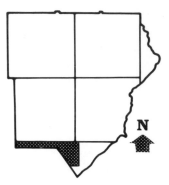

18th DISTRICT

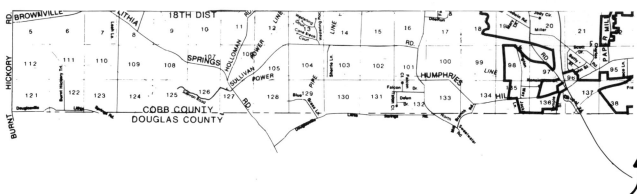

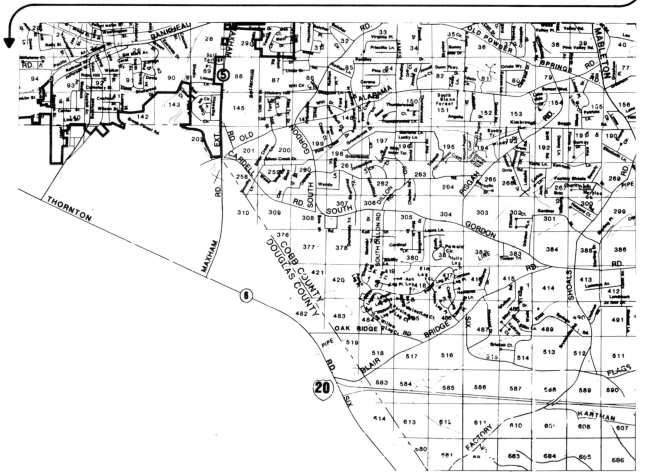

18th DISTRICT

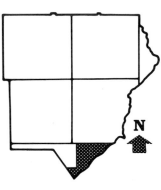

N

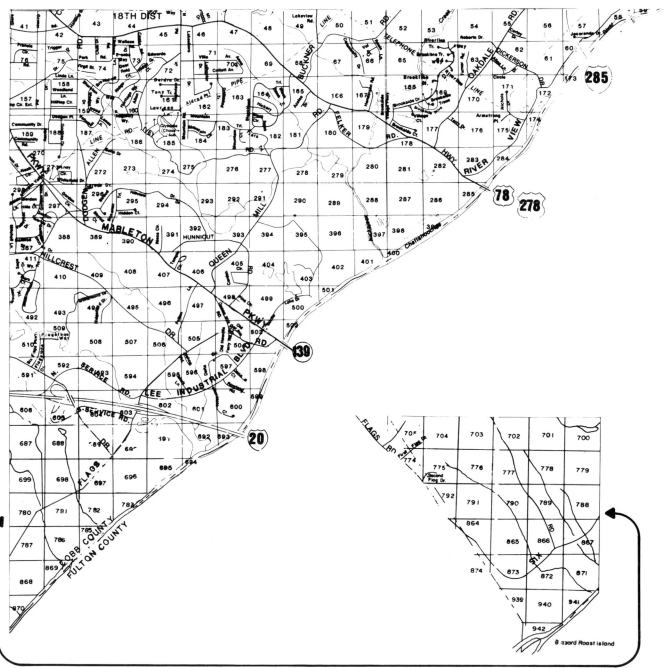

DISTRICT 18

District 18 occupies the southern tip of Cobb County and is primarily rural and industrial in character. The city of Austell is expanding into parts of district 18 as well as district 19. The district has few structural resources of valuable historical quality.

    1. National Register sites in district 18 include the Israel Causey House and Johnston's River Line.

    2. Remaining identified historic resources include some vernacular 19th century houses of the hall and parlor form, one probable log cabin which has been covered with asbestos siding, another log structure to which have been attached numerous additions, and two remnant water towers from industrial plants.

Land Lot	Description	Land Lot	Description
5		38	
6		39	osr
7	E: parcel 1, Brownsville-Lithia Springs Rd (dr9-13A)	40	osr + ghm The Mitchell hs + 5809 Gordon Rd.
8	E: parcel 9, Brown Rd (dr9-15A)	41	
9		42	Leland + ghm: Advance of the 17th A.C. Toward the River
10			
11		43	
12		44	D: 130 Bankhead Hwy (dr9-25) + D: 1051 Bankhead Hwy (dr9-26)
13			
14		45	D: bungalows on Bankhead Hwy between Allen Rd & Kitchens Rd (dr9-23)
15			
16			
17		46	D: gas station, Bankhead Hwy, SE corner Lakeshore (dr10-19)
18	Austell		
19	Austell	47	Mt. Harmony Church cemeteries + ghm: Georgia Militia on Turner's Ferry Rd.
20	Austell		
21			
22	Austell	48	Mt. Harmony Church cemeteries
23	Austell	49	
24	Austell	50	
25	Austell	51	
26	Austell	52	
27	Austell	53	
28	Austell	54	cw
29	Austell	55	cw
30	Austell	56	
31	Austell	57	
32		58	
33	Davis Chapel Cemetery	59	
34		60	
35		61	
36		62	cw
37			

Land Lot	Description	Land Lot	Description
63	E: 5811 Oakdale (dr10-21) + D: 5516 Oakdale (dr10-23) + cw	109	
64	**	110	
65		111	
66		112	
67		***	
68		121	
69		122	
70		123	
71		124	
72		125	
73		126	
74		127	
75		128	
76		129	
77	osr + ghm Toward the River	130	
78	osr	131	
79	C: 5875 Old Powder Springs Rd (dr8-16)	132	
80		133	
81		134	
82		135	Austell
83		136	Austell
84		137	Austell
85		138	Austell
86		139	Austell
87		140	Austell
88	B: ps15(dnr275A;dr7-20) Causey-Maxham hs N. R. 5909 Maxham Rd	141	Austell
89	Austell	142	Austell
90	Austell	143	Austell
91	Austell	144	Austell
92	Austell	145	Austell
93	Austell	146	
94	Austell	147	D: 1900 Old Alabama Rd (dr7-30) + Furniture City
95	Austell	148	D: 1776 Old Alabama Rd (dr7-28)
96	Austell	149	
97	Austell	150	
98	Austell	151	
99		152	
100		153	
101		154	C: dnr245 6025 Pisgah Rd
102		155	
103		156	osr
104		157	
105		158	
106		159	
107		160	
108		161	
		162	

Land Lot	Description	Land Lot	Description
163			Church (dr7-25) + E: parcel 1, corner
164			Alabama, Cardell, & Maxham (dr8-13)
165		202	** ps6 Sweet Water Town Site, junction
166	ghm Federals Halted by Johnston's River Line		Old Alabama and Maxham Roads
		***	
167		258	
168		259	
169	cw	260	
170	D: parcel 16, Oakdale (dr10-20) + cw	261	
171		262	
172		263	
173		264	
174		265	
175		266	Wallace Park
176		267	
177	ps45(ghm) Johnston's River Line (from Bankhead Hwy at Oakdale Rd northeastward to a point east of the W & A RR)	268	
		269	osr
		270	
178		271	
179		272	
180		273	
181		274	
182		275	
183		276	
184		277	cemetery
185		278	
186		279	
187		280	
188		281	cw
189	osr		
190	osr	282	D: parcel 8(?), Bankhead Hwy & Oakdale (dr8-17) (GONE) + ghm Johnston's River Line
191			
192			
193		283	
194		284	
195		285	ps11 Mayson-Turner's Ferry Site, at Bankhead Hwy & Chattahoochee River intersection
196			
197			
198		286	
199	E: water tower, Old Alabama Rd (dr8-14)	287	dnr253M Johnston's Line (NR), between Gordon Rd and Bankhead Hwy near Chattahoochee River
200	Shady Grove Church Cemetery		
201	** ps6 Sweet Water Town Site, junction Old Alabama and Maxham Roads + ps32 Causey Cemetery (aka Shady Grove Cemetery, and Community Church Cemetery), Old Alabama Rd east of Maxham Rd + C: Shady Grove	288	
		289	
		290	
		291	
		292	
		293	

Land Lot	Description	Land Lot	Description
294		404	
295		405	
296		406	
297		407	
298		408	
299	osr	409	
300	C: 6592 Factory Shoals (dr8-5) + osr	410	
301		411	E: Water tower, S Gordon (dr8-8)
302	Wallace Park	412	
303		413	osr
304		414	Mt. Pisgah Church Cemetery + Trinity Church Cemetery
305			
306	C: 1670 S Gordon (dr8-11)	415	
307		416	
308		417	
309		418	
310		419	
***		420	
376		421	
377		***	
378		482	
379		483	
380		484	
381		485	
382		486	
383		487	
384	Mt. Pisgah Church Cemetery	488	
385	D: 6699, 6689 Factory Shoals Rd (dr8-15) + osr	489	
		490	osr
386		491	
387	C: parcel 34, S Gordon, possible log cabin (dr8-10) + cw	492	
		493	
388	D: 289 S Gordon (dr8-7)	494	
389		495	
390		496	
391		497	
392		498	
393	Queen Cemetery	499	
394	**	500	
395	**	501	
396	** + dnr253M Johnston's Line (NR)	502	
397	cw	503	
398	dnr253M Johnston's Line (NR)	504	Howells' Cemetery
399		505	
400		506	
401	dnr253M Johnston's Line (NR)	507	
402	**	508	
403	**	509	

Land Lot	Description		Land Lot	Description
510			684	
511			685	
512	osr		686	
513			687	
514			688	
515			689	
516			690	
517			691	**
518			692	**
519			693	
***			694	
583	**		695	
584			696	
585			697	
586			698	**
587			699	
588	osr		700	
589	osr		701	
590			702	
591			703	
592			704	
593	**		705	Zion View Church Cemetery + osr
594			706	Zion View Church Cemetery
595			***	
596			765	**
597			766	**
598			***	
599			774	osr
600			775	** + osr
601			776	
602			777	**
603			778	
604			779	
605			780	
606			781	**
607			782	
608			783	
609	osr		***	
610	osr		785	**
611	osr		786	**
612			787	
613			788	
614			789	
***			790	**
680			791	
681	osr		792	osr
682	osr		793	
683			***	

Land Lot	Description	Land Lot	Description
863	osr	874	osr
864	** + osr	***	
865		939	
866	Griffith Cemetery	940	
867		941	**
868	**	942	** ps13 Baker's Ferry & Sand Town Ferry Sites, at southernmost tip of Cobb Co at Chattahoochee River (where Cobb, Fulton, & Douglas counties converge)
869 ***	**		
870	**		
871	**		
872	**	943	**
873	osr		

A section of Johnston's River Line, Confederate Civil War-era earthworks.

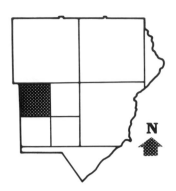

19th DISTRICT

N

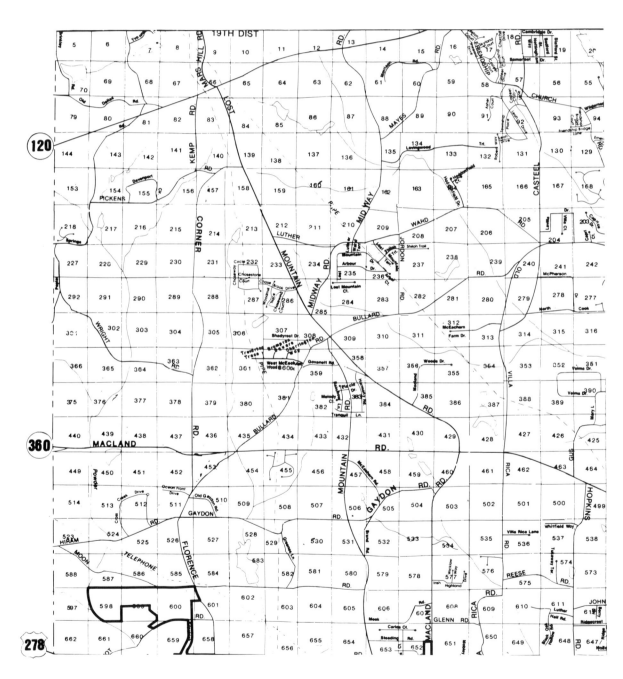

19th DISTRICT

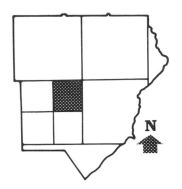

N

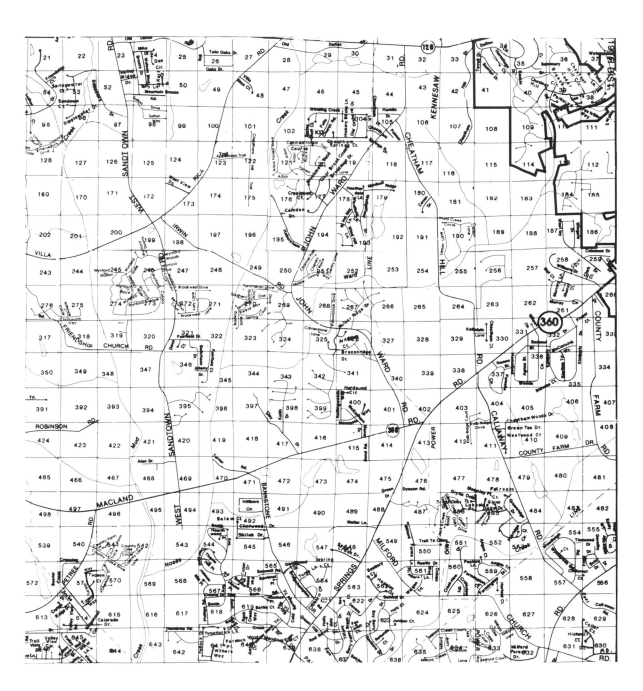

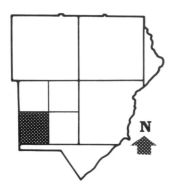

19th DISTRICT

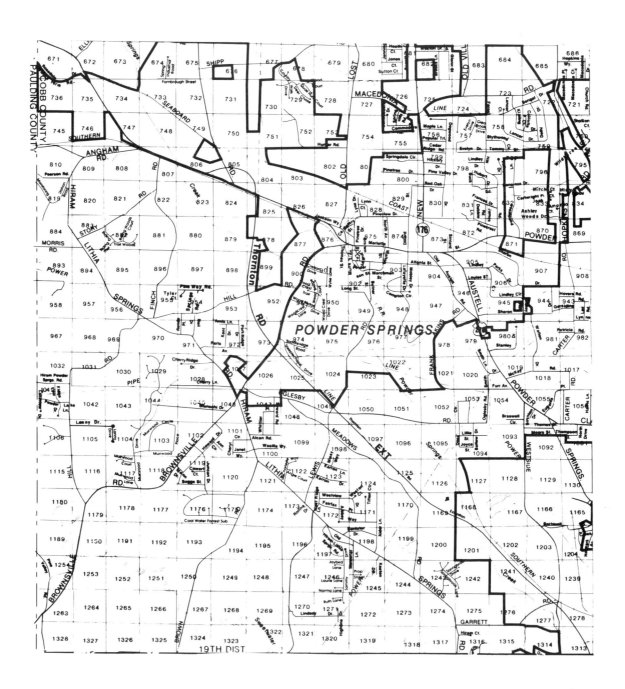

19th DISTRICT

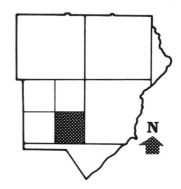

N

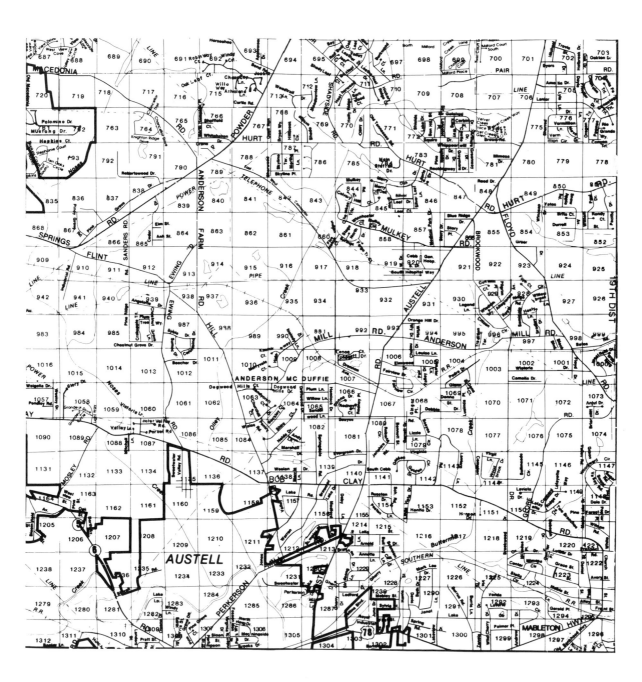

DISTRICT 19

District 19 occupies the southwestern quarter of the County and is predominantly rural in character. Industrial developments cluster around Powder Springs and Austell, and suburban developments spread north of those two towns. District 19 contains 4 sites listed on the National Register: the Cheney House, the McAdoo-Atkinson House, Midway Church, Clarkdale Mill and Village, and several other areas which lend themselves to historic district designations. Of these last, the Lost Mountain store on Dallas Road (at Lost Mountain Road), has been determined eligible for the National Register in an environmental review for road widening along Dallas Highway. Cobb County has agreed to acquire the Lost Mountain Store in the future.

1. Lost Mountain proposed designated Historic District. This small district would include the Lost Mountain Store, the adjacent residence, and the well house next to the store. The store itself is the only brick/trading/warehouse crossroads center in the County emanating from the rural period of Cobb County history and the largest of such early rural commercial structures left. The Lost Mountain district represents a different kind of rural development from that represented by other areas such as Vinings (village) or Macland (residential crossroads). Since the store building is unique in the county and also representative of a category of historic structure, it would warrant individual designation as an historic site.

2. Clarkdale. The Clarkdale historic district comprises the Coats and Clark Thread Mill and the adjoining village. Clarkdale is a fully intact planned mill village of late vintage, established in 1931. It reflects modernization of housing facilities (electricity and automobile garages) and stylistic differentiations between the mill workers' levels of employment. Architecturally, the proposed historic district is almost "perfect"--void of latterday intrusions and alterations to the structures. The area was added to the National Register in a procedure to redevelop the mill as an office/commercial complex.

3. Mableton. Mableton is a century-old railroad town with pre-Civil War origins. The community was laid out in the 1880s along the railroad tracks subdivided into business and residential lots. Highway development in the area has since moved the commercial centers away from the old town site leaving a largely intact small town. There is some potential for a historic district in Mableton, to include the early houses, the commercial buildings along Front Street, and the wooden "highway" bridge over the railroad tracks. Mid-19th century and early 20th century residential structures line Mable and Center Streets, Church, Front, and Floyd Streets, though not in uninterrupted succession. There are numerous recent intrusions in the old section, but the area is dense enough in historic resources to lend itself to a multiple resource designation if not an architectural district.

4. Macland community. Macland Road and the intersection of Macland with Lost Mountain Road contain numerous Victorian (late 19th century) buildings of considerable size and scale plus some more modest mid-19th century vernacular structures. These are widely spread, except for the buildings at the cross roads and would lend themselves to historic districting pending the determination of legitimate historical boundaries and the establishment of the history of the area.

5. The 19th district (like the 20th) is rich in rural vernacular architecture. Several roads have distinctive collections of rural structures which run the gamut from mid-19th century to mid-twentieth century styles. These roads include Corner-Florence, Old Lost Mountain Road, and Old Villa Rica Road. All three roads are agricultural areas, and their rural character is not jeopardized by current uses except as suburbanization spreads toward these areas. The styles represented in the 19th district include all endemic house forms--hall and parlor, double pen forms, saddle-

bag forms, extended hall and parlor, I-houses, pyramidal hip-roofed houses (small and large), and folk Victorians including "L's", gable-and-wing forms, and some very modest Queen Annes. These include some of the best examples of each style to be found in the county, including the only unaltered I-house in Cobb. Approximately one hundred structures exist in this district which fit these house form categories. Assorted early 20th century cottage and bungalow styles are also to be found in this district, but they are not of the quality and numbers of those found in the 18th district, and they do not cluster in sufficient locations to lend themselves to districting. The 19th District also contains a black agricultural area, the architecture for which includes some traditional rural styles, eclectic buildings, and contemporary structures.

6. Two house and mill combination sites, the Anderson and Perkerson house and mill sites, exist in the 19th district. The Anderson house has been severely altered, but the Perkerson house (an extremely large Georgia home) has not. Only the site of the Perkerson mill and minimal ruins for the Anderson mill exist. The farmhouse/mill combination in Cobb County history is better represented elsewhere in the county, (i.e., Sewell Mill, Paper Mill). Although early farmhouses are still relatively abundant in the 19th district, the Perkerson house is an exceptional structure, and the Perkerson family history sufficient to warrant attention to this site.

DISTRICT 19

Land Lot	Description	Land Lot	Description
5		28	ps69 Site: Grave of Chief Nose Dallas Rd, just east of the Villa Rica Rd inter
6			
7			section on west side of Noses Creek
8		29	
9	Lost Mtn	30	E: storefront, Old Dallas Rd (dr19-17) +
10	Lost Mtn		C: 1710 Old Dallas Rd (dr19-18)
11	Lost Mtn + dnr132 Dallas Rd	31	ghm: Federal, Confederate Lines, June
12	A: ps104(dnr133;dr15-13A) Midway Presbyterian Church N.R. 4635 Dallas Hwy, + C: parcel 2 on Dallas Hwy (dr15-11A)		22, 27, 1864
		32	kmnbp
		33	Marietta
		34	Marietta
13	A: ps104(dnr133;dr15-13A) Midway Presbyterian Church (and cemetery) N.R. 4635 Dallas Hwy, + dnr134 4609 Dallas Rd	35	Marietta
		36	Marietta
		37	Marietta
		38	Marietta
14		39	Marietta
15		40	Marietta
16	Midway Church Cemetery, N. R.	41	Marietta
17		42	kmnbp
18		43	kmnbp
19		44	
20		45	
21		46	
22		47	
23	osr	48	
24		49	
25		50	
26	C: no #, Old Dallas Hwy (dr15-8A)	51	
27	C: 434 Villa Rica Rd (dr20-13)	52	osr

Land Lot	Description	Land Lot	Description
53		102	
54		103	
55		104	
56		105	kmnbp + ghm McCook's Brigade
57		106	kmnbp
58	C: 470 Friendship Church Rd (dr20-22)	107	kmnbp + Cheatham Hill
59		108	kmnbp + Cheatham Hill
60		109	Marietta
61		110	Marietta
62		111	Marietta
63		112	Marietta
64	C: parcels 4 & 5 on Dallas Hwy (dnr132; dr15-7A)	113	Marietta
		114	Marietta
65		115	** + kmnbp
66	Lost Mountain (community); Lost Mountain proposed HD: parcels 4, 1, and 6; + B: ps82(dnr131, ghm) Lost Mtn Crossroads and General Store + Hs Dallas Rd at Lost Mtn/Mars Hill Rds + Lost Mtn (mountain)	116	** + kmnbp + Cheatham Hill
		117	kmnbp + ghm Five Federal Brigades
		118	kmnbp + Jones Memorial Church Cemetery
		119	
67		120	
68		121	
69		122	
70		123	
***		124	
79		125	
80	E: parcel 6 on Old Dallas Hwy (dr15-6A)	126	osr
81		127	
82		128	
83		129	
84		130	
85		131	
86		132	
87		133	
88		134	
89		135	
90		136	
91		137	
92		138	
93		139	
94		140	
95		141	
96		142	
97	** + osr	143	
98	**	144	
99	**	***	
100	C: 580 Villa Rica Rd (dr20-14)	153	
101		154	
		155	

Land Lot	Description	Land Lot	Description
156	C: parcel 1, Pickens Rd at Kemp (dr15-25A)	199	osr
157	C: 919 Corner Rd at Pickens Rd (dnr135; dr15-23A)	200	
		201	**
158		202	
159	C: parcel 2, Lost Mtn Rd (dr15-22A)	203	New Friendship Church Cemetery
160		204	
161		205	E: 3862 Luther Ward (dr21-28)
162		206	
163		207	
164		208	
165	E: 4170 Luther Ward (dr21-27)	209	
166		210	
167		211	
168	D: parcel 2, Friendship Church Rd (dr20-21)	212	
		213	
169		214	dnr136 1135 Corner Rd
170	**	215	
171	osr	216	
172	C: dnr111 2415 Stilesboro Rd + osr	217	E: parcel 3, Poplar Springs Rd (dr15-15A)
173	C: dnr143 985 Villa Rica Rd	218	
174	C: dnr142 parcel 1 Villa Rica Rd	***	
175		226	**
176		227	
177		228	
178		229	
179	kmnbp	230	
180	kmnbp + ghm Gen George H Thomas' Headquarters (In Field) Army of the Cumberland (F) June 24-July 3, 1864	231	C: 1135 (parcel 1) Corner Rd (dnr136; dr15-26A)
		232	
181	** + kmnbp	233	
182	** + kmnbp	234	
183	** + kmnbp	235	
184	Marietta	236	
185		237	
186		238	
187	kmnbp	239	
188	kmnbp	240	** dnr141 1299 Villa Rica Rd (GONE)
189	kmnbp	241	C: 1283 Villa Rica Rd (dr22-2) + dnr145 3830 Villa Rica Rd
190			
191	kmnbp	242	C: New Friendship Church Villa Rica Rd at Friendship Ch Rd (dnr144; dr20-20)
192	kmnbp		
193			
194		243	
195		244	
196		245	
197			
198			

Land Lot	Description	Land Lot	Description
246	ps23 Manning-Holcomb hs West Sandtown Rd, about .2 mi south of Villa Rica Rd (GONE) + osr	285	
		286	
		287	
247	osr	288	
248	**	289	
249	C: Steel and plank bridge on Old Dallas Rd (dr22-5)	290	
		291	
250		292	C: 363 Wright Rd (dr15-16A)
251	**	***	
252	**	301	
253	kmnbp	302	C: 5640 Wright Rd (dr15-17A)
254	E: ** ps138 Ruins: Greer-Ward hs west side of Cheatham Hill Rd just north of Ward (Nose's) Creek + kmnbp	303	
		304	
		305	C: 1570 Corner Rd (dr15-27A)
255		306	
256		307	
257	kmnbp	308	
258		309	C: dnr139(dr21-31) 1574 Bullard Rd
259	St. James Episcopal Church "Chapel of Ease" (ruins)	310	
		311	
260	St. James Episcopal Church "Chapel of Ease" (ruins)	312	
		313	
261	ghm Powder Springs Road June-July, 1864	314	D: parcel 2, Villa Rica & Casteel (dr21-29)
262	kmnbp	315	
263	kmnbp	316	
264	kmnbp	317	
265	** + kmnbp + ghm Battle of Kolb's Farm June 22, 1864	318	E: 1995 Friendship Church Rd (dr20-19)
266	** + kmnbp	319	
267		320	C: parcel 2(?), Friendship Church Rd (dr20-16) + osr
268			
269		321	dnr152 1570 Sandtown Rd + osr
270		322	
271		323	
272	osr	324	
273		325	
274		326	
275		327	C: 1605 Old John Ward (dr19-15) + kmnbp
276			
277		328	kmnbp
278		329	kmnbp
279		330	kmnbp
280		331	kmnbp + ghm Battle of Kolb's Farm June 22, 1864
281	C: dnr140(dr21-30) 1391 Bullard Rd		
282		332	
283		333	
284		334	O'Dell Park

Land Lot	Description	Land Lot	Description
335		377	
336	kmnbp	378	
337	kmnbp + Kolb Cemetery + ghm Battle of Kolb's Farm June 22, 1864	379	
338	B: ps80(dnr224) Kolb Farmhouse Powder Springs Rd at Callaway Rd + ps75 Battle of Kolb's Farm + dnr225 1585 Powder Springs Rd + kmnbp	380	E: no #, Bullard Rd near Brisbane (dr15-21A)
		381	
		382	
		383	
339	kmnbp	384	
340		385	C: 184 Lost Mtn Rd (dr21-32)
341	mmp I.B. Davis Prop. Gold Mine	386	
342		387	
343		388	
344	**	389	
345		390	
346		391	
347	ps24 Original site of Simpson Manning hs W. Sandtown Rd about 1.5 mi south of Villa Rica Rd (hs moved to Dist 20/LL 278) + osr + C: 1912 W. Sandtown Rd (dr20-15) + D: parcel 1, corner W. Sandtown & Friendship Church Rd (dr20-17)	392	
		393	
		394	osr
		395	osr
		396	**
		397	**
		398	
348		399	
349	E: parcel 3, Friendship Church Rd (dr20-18)	400	
		401	
350		402	A: ps89(dnr226,ghm: Wm. G. McAdoo's Birthplace) Young-McAdoo-Atkinson hs ("Melora") Powder Springs Rd near intersection with Macland Rd + Mt. Zion Church Cemetery N. R. + ghm Battle of Kolb's Farm June 22, 1864
351			
352			
353			
354			
355			
356		403	ps75(ghm) Battle of Kolb's Farm + dnr225 1585 Powder Springs Rd + kmnbp
357			
358			
359		404	
360		405	
361		406	
362		407	
363	C: dnr137 parcel 4 Corner Rd, near Wright Rd + D: parcel 1, Corner Rd (dr15-28A)	408	
		409	Al Bishop Softball Complex
364		410	Central Park (formerly Fairgrounds Park)
365			
366		411	
***		412	
		413	
375		414	
376		415	C: Macland Rd (no #, dr19-14)

Land Lot	Description	Land Lot	Description
416	B: ps92 Lane-Cofer hs Macland Rd, .5 mi east of Bankstone Rd + dnr146 2261 Macland Rd + C: 2250? Macland at Clay Rd (dr19-13)	461	
		462	dnr155 3731 Macland Rd
417		463	
418		464	
419		465	
420	** dnr151 2083 Sandtown Rd (GONE) + osr	466	
		467	
		468	
421		469	osr
422		470	** ps21(ghm) Site: Manning's Mill On Noses Creek, north of Macland and Bankstone Roads + osr
423			
424			
425		471	C: dnr148 parcel 10 Macland Rd + osr + C: corner Macland & Milford Ch Rd (dr19-9)
426			
427	dnr155? 3731 Macland Rd		
428	cemetery	472	B: ps93(dnr147) Camp-James hs Macland Rd, .2 mi east of Bankstone Rd
429	Macland + C: parcels 5, 6, 9, & 10, Lost Mtn & Macland (dr21-34)		
		473	
430		474	
431		475	
432		476	
433		477	
434		478	Central Park (formerly Fairgrounds)
435	C: 1980 Bullard Rd (dr15-20A)	479	Central Park (formerly Fairgrounds)
436	C: parcel 1, Macland Rd at Corner Rd (dnr138; dr15-19A)	480	
		481	
437		482	Central Park (formerly Fairgrounds)
438		483	Central Park (formerly Fairgrounds)
439		484	C: County Fairgrounds, parcel 1, Calloway Rd (dr20-31) + Central Park (formerly Fairgrounds)
440			
***		485	
449	D: parcel 2, Macland Rd (dr21-17)	486	
450		487	
451		488	
452		489	
453	C: dnr138(dr15-19A & dr21-18) listed under parcel l, 19-436, Macland Rd, N.W., at Corner Rd	490	
		491	
		492	osr
454		493	
455		494	
456		495	
457	C: dnr156(dr21-26) 2141 Old Lost Mtn Rd	496	dnr154 3131 Macland Rd
		497	
458		498	
459		499	C: parcel 7, corner Hopkins & Macland (dr22-4)
460	Macland + C: parcel 7, Lost Mtn Rd (dr21-35)	500	

Land Lot	Description	Land Lot	Description
501		549	C: 1934 Powder Springs Rd, @ Milford
502			Ch Rd (dr19-7)
503		550	
504	B: ps91 McEachern A&M Institute (l932 brick bldg) Lost Mtn Rd near Macland Rd	551	
		552	
		553	Central Park (formerly Fairgrounds)
505	E: parcel 7, Gaydon & McEachern (dr21-23)	554	Central Park (formerly Fairgrounds)
		555	
506	C: 2356 Old Lost Mtn Rd (dr21-25)	556	C: 2604 Austell Rd @ Dorothy (dr20-29)
507		557	
508		558	
509		559	
510	D: parcel 1, Bullard (dr21-19)	560	
511	D: parcel 9, Gaydon & Florence (dr21-20)	561	
		562	
512		563	Bethel Church Cemetery
513		564	
514		565	osr
***		566	
523		567	
524		568	
525		569	**
526		570	
527		571	
528		572	
529		573	
530		574	Jackson/Yarborough Property (undeveloped county park site)
531	C/D: parcel 16 & parcel 1, Old Mtn & Gaydon (dr21-22)	575	
532		576	
533	** ps91 McEachern A&M Institute (1930 wood frame bldg) Lost Mtn Rd near Macland Rd (GONE)	577	
		578	
		579	
534		580	
536		581	C: 4780 Moon Rd (dr21-11)
537		582	C: 4908 Moon Rd (dr21-12)
538		583	
539		584	C: 2600 Florence (dr21-16)
540		585	C: 2600 Florence (dr21-16)
541		586	
542		587	
543		588	D: 5698 Moon Rd (dr21-14)
544		***	
545		597	
546	C: dnr149 Sandtown Rd (see map) + osr	598	
547		599	
548	Bethel Church Cemetery	600	C: 5299 Moon Rd (dnr157; dr21-13)
		601	

Land Lot	Description	Land Lot	Description
602		645	
603		646	
604		647	
605	C: 4625 Moon Rd (dr21-10)	648	
606		649	
607		650	
608	E: 2771 Lost Mtn Rd (dr21-24	651	
609	C: 2800 Old Villa Rica Rd (dr21-36)	652	Powder Springs
610		653	
611		654	
612		655	
613		656	
614		657	
615	**	658	cemetery
616		659	Powder Springs
617	**	660	
618		661	
619		662	Powder Springs
620	Cheney Cemetery + osr	***	
621	A: ps33(dnr150,ghm: Schofield's Head-quarters, Home of Andrew J. Cheney) Cheney-Newcomer hs, N.R. Intersection of Bankstone and Powder Springs Rds + osr	671	Powder Springs
		672	Powder Springs
		673	Powder Springs
		674	Powder Springs
		675	Powder Springs
622		676	
623		677	
624		678	
625		679	
626		680	
627		681	Powder Springs
628		682	Powder Springs
629		683	Powder Springs
630	C: dnr221(dr19-3) 2860 Hicks Rd + Milford Church Cemetery	684	Powder Springs
		685	Powder Springs
631		686	
632		687	
633		688	
634		689	
635		690	
636		691	
637		692	
638	osr + ghm 16th A.C. to Roswell	693	
639	osr + ghm 16th A.C. to Roswell	694	
640		695	osr
641		696	osr
642	**	697	
643		698	
644		699	

Land Lot	Description	Land Lot	Description
700		753	
701		754	
702		755	Powder Springs
703	Milford Church Cemetery	756	Powder Springs
704		757	Powder Springs
705		758	Powder Springs
706		759	Powder Springs
707		760	Powder Springs
708		761	Powder Springs
709		762	Powder Springs
710		763	
711	osr	764	
712		765	C: 2752 Macedonia Rd (dr21-5)
713		766	
714		767	
715		768	
716		769	
717	E: Macedonia Bapt Church (dr21-6) + cemetery	770	
718	cemetery	771	** ps41(ghm: Ross' Headquarters) Site: Shaw hs East side of Sandtown Rd, at Shadyside & Hurt Rds, just east of Olley's Creek + osr
719			
720			
721	Powder Springs	772	
722	Powder Springs	773	
723	Powder Springs	774	
724	Powder Springs	775	dnr244 342 & 346 Austell Rd
725	Powder Springs	776	
726	Powder Springs	777	
727	C: 3269 Old Lost Mtn Rd (dnr160; dr21-7 & dr8-29)	778	Hurt Road Park
728		779	
729		780	
730		781	
731	Powder Springs	782	
732	Powder Springs	783	osr ghm
733	Powder Springs	784	osr ghm
734	Powder Springs	785	**
735	Powder Springs	786	
736	Powder Springs	787	
***		788	
		789	
745	cemetery	790	C: 2770 Macedonia Rd (dr21-4)
746	Powder Springs	791	
747	Powder Springs	792	
748	Powder Springs	793	Powder Springs
749	Powder Springs	794	Powder Springs
750	Powder Springs	795	Powder Springs
751	Powder Springs	796	Powder Springs
752		797	Powder Springs

Land Lot	Description	Land Lot	Description
798	Powder Springs	842	
799	Powder Springs	843	
800	Powder Springs	844	
801	D: 3595 Old Lost Mtn Rd (dr8-31)	845	
802	Powder Springs + C: 3600 Old Lost Mtn Rd, beyond city limits (dnr159; dr8-28) + D: 3460 Old Lost Mtn Rd, beyond city limits (dr8-30)	846	
		847	osr
		848	ps42 Sandtown Crossroads At intersection of Hurt, Austell, & Floyd Rds + ghm: "The Only Advantage of the Day" + osr
803	Powder Springs		
804	Powder Springs		
805	Powder Springs	849	
806	Powder Springs	850	
807	Powder Springs + E: trestle Ry bridge crossing Powder Springs Creek, edge of city limits (dr8-34)	851	** + Hurt Road Park
		852	
		853	
808		854	osr
809	D: parcel 1(?) Angham Rd @ Hiram-Lithia Springs Rd (dr8-24)	855	ps42 Sandtown Crossroads At intersection of Hurt, Austell, & Floyd Rds + osr
810 ***			
		856	
819		857	
820		858	
821		859	
822		860	
823		861	
824	Powder Springs	862	
825	Powder Springs	863	
826	Powder Springs + E: trestle Ry bridge across Lucille Creek, edge of city limits (dr8/25-26)	864	B: parcel 1, Anderson Farm Rd (dr21-3) + B/E: ps134 Anderson hs/Farm (dr20-36)
		865	
827	Powder Springs	866	E: 3070 Pine Grove (dr11-10) + D: 3120 Pine Grove (dr11-9)
828	Powder Springs		
829	Powder Springs	867	C: 3141 Pine Grove (dr11-8)
830	Powder Springs	868	**
831	Powder Springs	869	Powder Springs
832	Powder Springs	870	Powder Springs
833	Powder Springs	871	Powder Springs
834	Powder Springs	872	Powder Springs
835		873	Powder Springs
836		874	Powder Springs
837		875	Powder Springs
838		876	Powder Springs
839	B/E: Anderson hs/Farm Anderson Farm Rd, south of Powder Springs Rd at Macedonia Rd intersection (ps134; dr20-36)	877	
		878	
		879	
840		880	
841		881	

Land Lot	Description	Land Lot	Description
882		935	
883	C: 4015 Hiram-Lithia Springs Rd (dr8- 23) + D: Revival Bapt Church, Story Rd (dr8-36) + cemetery	936	
		937	
		938	
884		939	
***		940	
893		941	
894	cemetery	942	
895		943	
896		944	Powder Springs
897		945	Powder Springs
898		946	Powder Springs
899		947	Powder Springs
900	Powder Springs	948	Powder Springs
901	Powder Springs	949	Powder Springs
902	Powder Springs	950	Powder Springs
903	Powder Springs	951	Powder Springs
904	Powder Springs	952	
905	Powder Springs	953	
906	Powder Springs	954	
907	Powder Springs	955	C: dnr184(dr8-21) 4190 Hiram-Lithia Springs Rd + C: 5264 Hill Rd (dr8-37)
908	**		
909		956	C: dnr183(dr8-22) 4130 Hiram-Lithia Springs Rd
910	dnr158 3259 Powder Springs Rd		
911	C: 3989 Flint Hill (dr11-7)	957	cemetery
912		958	
913		***	
914		967	
915		968	
916		969	C: 5264 Hill Rd (dr8-19)
917		970	cemetery
918		971	
919	**	972	
920		973	
921		974	
922		975	
923	osr	976	
924	osr	977	**
925		978	
926		979	
927	osr	980	
928		981	
929		982	
930		983	
931		984	
932		985	
933		986	
934		987	

Land Lot	Description	Land Lot	Description
988		1029	
989	**	1030	
990		1031	
991		1032	
992		***	
993		1041	
994		1042	
995		1043	
996		1044	
997		1045	
998	osr	1046	
999		1047	
1000	Floyd + ps43 Site: Wm. Moss hs Concord Rd at Floyd Rd east of Concord Church + osr	1048	
		1049	
		1050	
1001	osr	1051	
1002		1052	
1003		1053	
1004		1054	
1005		1055	
1006		1056	
1007		1057	
1008		1058	**
1009		1059	
1010	D: 2472 Anderson Mill (dr11-4) + D: 2580 Flint Hill (dr11-3)	1060	
		1061	
1011	E: ** ps20 Ruins: Anderson's Mill, Flint Hill Rd just north of Anderson Mill Rd, on west side of Olley's Creek + C: 4446 Flint Hill (dr11-6)	1062	
		1063	
		1064	
		1065	
1012		1066	
1013		1067	
1014		1068	
1015		1069	
1016		1070	
1017		1071	
1018		1072	
1019		1073	ps14 Glore Cabin Glore Rd about .5 mi south of junction with Floyd Rd (GONE) + osr
1020			
1021			
1022		1074	
1023		1075	
1024		1076	cemetery
1025		1077	
1026		1078	
1027	C: 4435 Hiram-Lithia Springs Rd (dr9-8A)	1079	
		1080	
1028		1081	

Land Lot	Description	Land Lot	Description
1082		1132	D: 4860 Mosley (dr10-34) + D: parcel 4, Mosley (dr10-35) + E: parcel 1, Mosley (dr10-36)
1083			
1084			
1085		1133	
1086		1134	
1087		1135	Austell
1088		1136	
1089	D: 4650 Moseley Dr (dr11-2)	1137	
1090		1138	
1091		1139	
1092	C: dnr252 parcel 25 Old Austell Rd (Westside Rd)	1140	
		1141	
1093		1142	
1094		1143	
1095		1144	
1096		1145	
1097		1146	
1098		1147	
1099		1148	
1100	C: 4770 Hiram-Lithia Springs Rd (dr9-9A)	1149	
		1150	
1101	**	1151	
1102	C: dnr185(dr9-7A) 4756 Brownsville Rd	1152	
1103		1153	
1104		1154	
1105		1155	
1106	C: 4855 Hill Rd (dr8-18)	1156	
***		1157	Austell
1115		1158	Austcll
1116		1159	Austell
1117		1160	Austell
1118	E: parcel 1, Brownsville Rd (dr9-6A)	1161	
1119		1162	
1120		1163	A: Clarkdale HD (dr10/24-33) N.R.
1121	D: 4854 Hiram-Lithia Springs Rd (dr9-10A) + E: 4893 Hiram-Lithia Springs Rd (dr9-11A)	1164	A: Clarkdale HD (dr10/24-33) N.R.
		1165	A: Clarkdale HD (dr10/24-33) N.R.
1122		1166	
1123		1167	
1124		1168	
1125		1169	
1126		1170	
1127		1171	
1128		1172	
1129		1173	
1130		1174	
1131		1175	
		1176	
		1177	

Land Lot	Description	Land Lot	Description
1178	E: parcel 3, Brownsville Rd (dr9-5A)	1225	
1179	E: parcel 5, Brownsville Rd @ Hill Rd (dr9-4A) + D: parcel 4, Brownsville Rd (dr9-3A) + D: parcel 1, Brownsville Rd (dr9-2A)	1226	
		1227	
		1228	
		1229	
1180		1230	B: ps22 Perkerson hs & mill Just outside Austell city limits on Perkerson Rd at bridge over Sweetwater Creek
***			
1189			
1190		1231	Austell
1191		1232	Austell
1192		1233	Austell
1193		1234	Austell
1194		1235	Austell
1195		1236	Austell
1196		1237	Austell
1197	C: 5103 Holloman Rd (dr9-18A)	1238	
1198		1239	
1199		1240	
1200		1241	
1201		1242	
1202		1243	
1203		1244	
1204	A: Clarkdale HD (dr10/24-33) N.R.	1245	
1205	A: Clarkdale HD (dr10/24-33) N.R. + Coats & Clark Property (undeveloped county park site)	1246	
		1247	C: 5260 Holloman Rd (dr9-20A)
		1248	
1206	A: Clarkdale HD (dr10/24-33) N.R.	1249	
1207	Austell	1250	E: parcel 1, Brown Rd (dr9-16A) + C: parcel 1, Brown Rd (dr9-17A)
1208	Austell		
1209	Austell	1251	
1210	Austell	1252	
1211	Austell	1253	
1212	Austell(?)	1254	
1213		***	
1214		1263	
1215		1264	
1216		1265	
1217		1266	
1218		1267	
1219		1268	
1220		1269	
1221		1270	
1222	Mableton + Mableton MRA (proposed) + E: parcel 15 (4320?) Peak St (dr9-36) + B: 1031 (1042) Center St (dnr251; dr10-3) + cemetery	1271	mmp Corundum mine
		1272	
		1273	
		1274	E: 5490 Hiram Lithia Springs Rd (dr9-12A)
1223			
1224		1275	dnr253 3909 Garrett Rd

Land Lot	Description	Land Lot	Description
1276		1297	
1277		1298	
1278		1299	
1279	Austell	1300	
1280	Austell	1301	Austell
1281	Austell	1302	Austell
1282	Austell	1303	Austell
1283	Austell	1304	Austell
1284	Austell	1305	Austell
1285	Austell	1306	Austell
1286	Austell	1307	Austell
1287	Austell	1308	Austell
1288	Austell	1309	Austell
1289	Austell	1310	Austell
1290		1311	Austell
1291		1312	Austell
1292		1313	Austell
1293		1314	Austell
1294		1315	
1295	Mableton + Mableton MRA (proposed) + B: 1034 Center St (dr10-5) + B: stores, Church & Front Sts (dnr247; dr10-7) + B: 960 Front St (dnr248; dr10-6) + B:106 Front St (dnr249; dr10-9) + B: 1028 (1025) Center St (dnr251; dr10-4) + B: 1006 Mable (dr10-12) + B: 5425 Daniel St. (dr10-13) + B: 5491 Church St (dr10-14) + B: wood railroad bridge, Floyd St (dr10-17) + D: 928 Bankhead Hwy (dr10-8)	1316	dnr253 3909 Garrett Rd
		1317	
		1318	
		1319	
		1320	
		1321	mmp Corundum mine V.H. Stansill
		1322	
		1323	
		1324	
		1325	
		1326	
		1327	
1296		1328	Pleasant Hill Church Cemetery

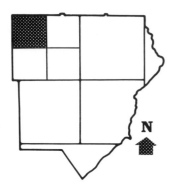

20th DISTRICT

N

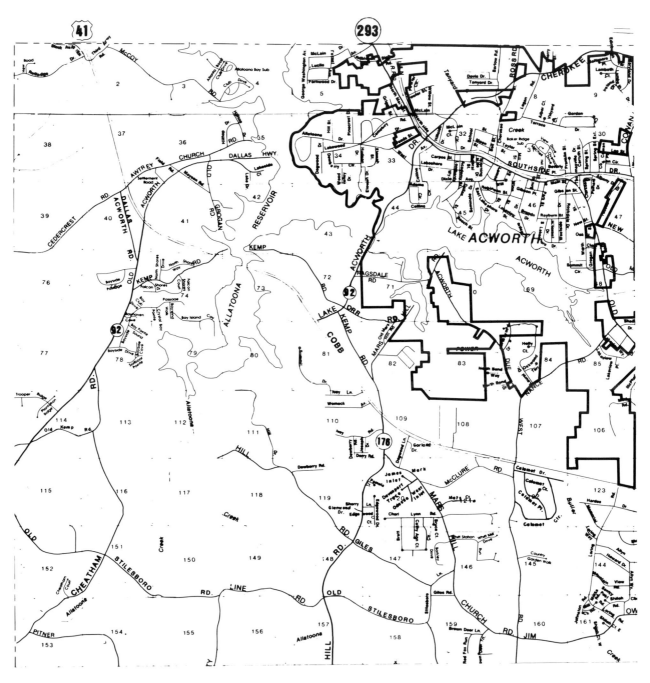

20th DISTRICT

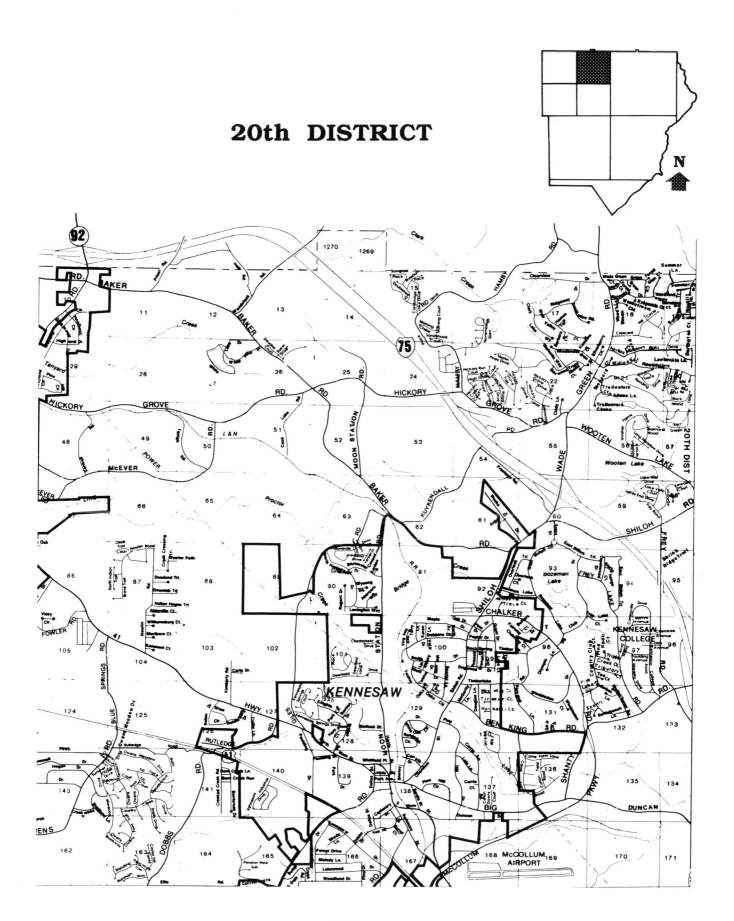

20th DISTRICT

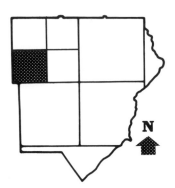

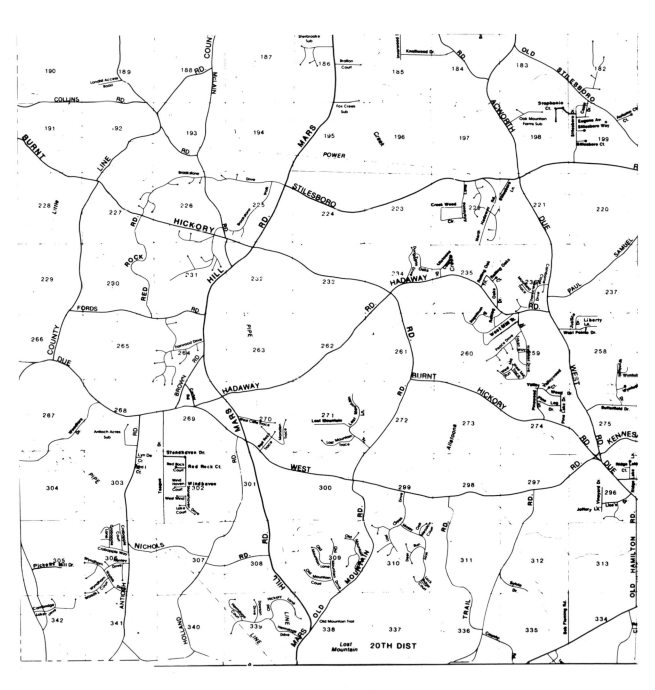

20th DISTRICT

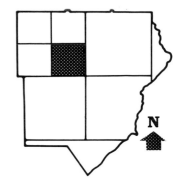

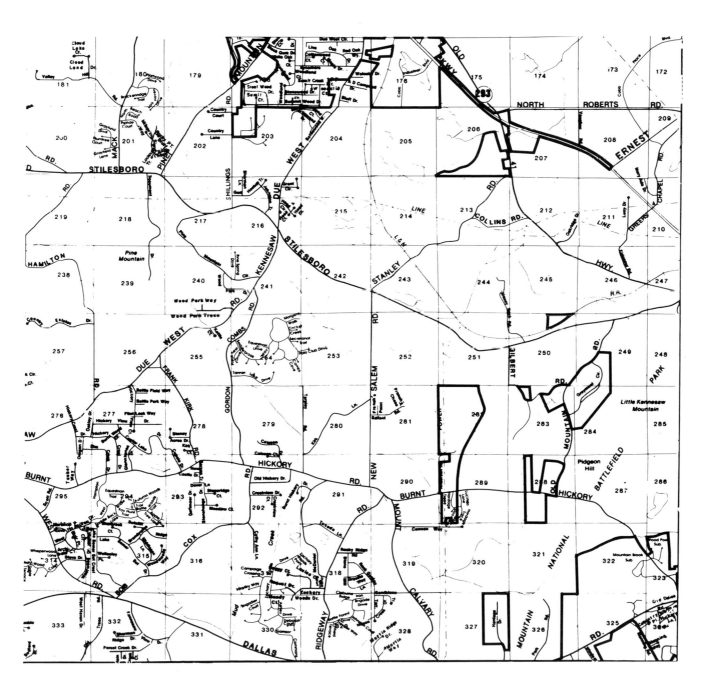

DISTRICT 20

District 20 occupies the northwest quarter of Cobb County and is heavily mixed in its current land uses. Sections of the District are rural; sections are dominated by the expanding communities of Acworth and Kennesaw. A large portion of the 20th District comprises the Lakes Allatoona and Acworth recreation areas. The district contains three sites listed in the National Register of Historic Places: the Kennesaw Multiple Resource Area, the Braswell-Carnes House, and the Gilgal Church Battlefield site.

1. District 20 has the most abundant collection of rural farm and farmhouse architecture in Cobb County, much of which is found along five main roads: Mars Hill Church Road, McLain Road, Old Stilesboro Road, County Line Road, and Old Sandtown Road. Of these, McLain Road bears the closest resemblance to an old "country road," and might bear designation as an historic district, pending the establishment of a reasonable history relevant to the McLain family and a set of legitimate historic boundaries. The other roads have more architectural discontinuities present along their edges. Remnants of the Due West and Red Rock communities might constitute Multiple Resource Areas with sufficient historical research and legitimate historic boundaries. Several individual structures warrant individual designation within these communities: e.g., the Wise-Guess House; the Peters-Davenport House and outbuildings; the Orr-Smithwick House; the House-McLain House; the Dickson-Lovingood House; the Green/Bullard House; and the Lattimore Farm. In addition, the Mars Hill Community Center (former Red Rock School) is one of the few rural school buildings remaining in the county and one of the few community centers to undergo a minimum of alteration. (The Nickajack Community Center has undergone little alteration, but was not a school building.)

2. Resources for historic archaeology are also particularly strong in the 20th District because of Civil War activity, the prior record of archaeological activity in association with the empoundment of Lake Allatoona, and the loss of a number of previously identified historic sites over the past few years (e.g., the Faith Church, the McClain House, and sites identified by the Department of Natural Resources numbered 123, 124, 126, and 129--All of which were mid-nineteenth century farm sites).

Land Lot	Description	Land Lot	Description
1		11	
2	C: 6000 McCoy Rd (dr13-33) + C: 5892 McCoy Rd (dr13-35) + C: 6872? McCoy Rd at Hwy 41 (dr13-36) + C: 4875 Hwy 41 (dr13-37 & dr14-1)) + C: Rutledge House, Hwy 41 at Rutledge Dr (dr20-24) + dnr1 Hwy 41 & Hwy 3 (see map) + ar + osr	12	
		13	C: 5070 Woodstock (dr1-12) + C: 3106 Baker Rd (dr1-15)
		14	
		15	
		16	
		17	
3	ar	18	
4	** + ar	19	
5	ar	20	
6	Acworth	21	**
7	Acworth	22	
8	Acworth	23	
9	Acworth	24	
10	Acworth		

Land Lot	Description	Land Lot	Description
25	C: dnr68(dr1-29) parcel 2 Hickory Grove Rd + C: 2191 Hickory Grove Rd (dr1-32)	67	dnr66 parcel 4 New McEver Rd + Acworth
26	Hickory Grove Church Cemetery	68	Acworth
27	Hickory Grove Church Cemetery	69	Acworth
28		70	Acworth
29	Acworth	71	Acworth
30	Acworth	72	C: 5127 Kemp (dr2-16) + C: 5040 Kemp (dr2-17) + larp + ar + osr + ** 1832 farm site
31	Acworth		
32	Acworth	73	** + ar + osr + 1832 farm site
33	Acworth	74	** + ar + osr
34	Acworth	75	ar + ghm The Wm Nickols hs
35	** + ar	76	
36	ar	77	
37	osr	78	ar + C: 3767 Hwy 92 (dr14-3)
***		79	ar
39		80	ar
40	osr + cemetery (GONE)	81	C: 3697 Kemp (dr2-18) + ar + osr
41	** + ar + osr	82	Acworth
42	** + ar + 1832 farm site	83	Acworth
43	Acworth	84	Acworth
44	Acworth	85	Acworth
45	Acworth	86	Blue Springs + ** + opt + C: 3740(?) Old 41 (Hwy 293) (dr14-34)
46	Acworth		
47	Acworth	87	
48	C: 4256 Cantrell (dr1-23)	88	
49	C: off Cantrell facing L&N tracks (dr1-27)	89	
		90	Kennesaw
50	Hickory Grove Church Cemetery	91	
51	Hickory Grove Church Cemetery	92	Kennesaw
52		93	Kennesaw
53		94	
54	**	95	
55		96	
56		97	
57		98	Kennesaw
58		99	dnr74 parcel 97 + Kennesaw
59		100	Kennesaw
60	Kennesaw	101	Kennesaw
61	Kennesaw	102	
62	ghm Site: Moon's Station	103	C: dnr73(dr1-35) Old 41 (SR 293, see map) + opt
63	ghm Site: Moon's Station		
64		104	** ps100 Andersonville Post Office Site About 1.5 mi north of Kennesaw on Old 41 Hwy at Blue Springs Rd + C: 3395 Old 41/Hwy 293 (dnr72; dr2-2) + E: old bus station, Hwy 293 at Blue Springs (dr20-26) + D: gas station, Hwy 293 at
65	**		
66	C: 3341 McEver (dr1-25) + C: 3299 McEver (dr1-26) +		
**			

Land Lot	Description	Land Lot	Description
	Blue Springs (dr20-27) + opt	145	
105	opt	146	C: 4646 Giles Rd (dnr101; dr6-7) + B: parcel 8, Mars Hill Community Center (Red Rock School) (dr6-8) + E: parcel 22, Stilesboro Ln, corner Mars Hill Church Rd (dr6-10)+ Mars Hill Cemetery + osr
106	Acworth		
107	C: 3522 Due West (dr2-10)		
108	Acworth		
109	Acworth		
110	ar		
111	ar + C: parcel 6, Hill Rd (dr14-30)	147	
112	ar + C: parcel 4, Hill Rd (dr14-31)	148	C: 2901 Mars Hill (14-27) + ar
113	ar + C: parcel 28, Cheatham Rd (dr14-5) + parcel 3, Cheatham Rd, corner Cheatham Dr (dr14-6)	149	** + ar + 1832 farm site
		150	** ghm: Site - Mason's Bridge + ar + 1832 farm site + C: bridge over Allatoona Creek (dr14-10)
114			
115		151	** + ar + D: parcel 9, Cheatham Rd (dr14-11)
116	ar		
117	** + ar	152	B. 6390 Old Stilesboro (dr 14-7)
118	** + ar	153	** + ar + C: 2586 Pitner (dr14-14)
119	C: parcel 9, Hill Rd (drn6; dr14-28) + ar	154	** + ar
120	Mars Hill + B: ps143(dr6-12) Peters-Davenport Hs 3280 Mars Hill Church Rd + C: 3132 Mars Hill Rd (dr14-33) + C: 3131 Mars Hill Church Rd (dr6-11) + osr	155	B: ps139(dnr5; dr7-16 & dr14-22) Wise-Guess hs (burned: GONE) Corner Old Stilesboro & County Line Rd + C: 2531 McLain Rd (dnr4; dr14-21) + ar
121	C: no #, across frm 4421 McClure (dr2-13) + osr	156	C: 5281 Old Stilesboro (dr14-23) + ar
122		157	C: parcel 9, Mars Hill & Old Stilesboro (dr14-24) + ar
123			
124		158	C: parcel 2, Old Stilesboro Rd (Stilesboro Station) (dnr102; dr6-6) + dnr103 2601 Stilesboro Rd + osr
125			
126	Morgan Hill Cemetery + opt	159	C: dnr106 2591 Mars Hill Church Rd + C: parcel 4, Old Stilesboro & Stilesboro Ln (dr6-2) + E: parcel 9, Mars Hill Church Rd (dr14-37) + osr
127	Kennesaw		
128	Kennesaw		
129	Kennesaw		
130	Kennesaw	160	E: 2610 Acworth-Due West Rd (dr6-13) + ghm: Durham hs + C: 4150 Jim Owens Rd (dr14-35) + D: parcel 19 (2516?) Acworth-Due West Rd (dr14-36)
131			
132	** 1832 farm site		
133	**		
134	** 1832 farm site		
135	** 1832 farm site	161	
136		162	
137	Kennesaw	163	
138	Kennesaw	164	
139	Kennesaw	165	Kennesaw + C: 2675 Pine Mtn Rd (dr6-24)
140	Kennesaw		
141	Kennesaw	166	Kennesaw
142		167	Kennesaw
143		168	** + opt
144		169	

DISTRICT 20

Land Lot	Description	Land Lot	Description
170	** 1832 farm site	200	C: parcel 1, Stilesboro Rd (dr6-22) + D: parcel 7, gas station @ Stilesboro & Old Stilesboro (dr6-20)
171			
172	**	201	ghm Pine Mountain
173	**	202	
174	**	203	
175	Kennesaw	204	
176	Kennesaw	205	
177	Kennesaw	206	Kennesaw
178	Kennesaw	207	Kennesaw
179	E: 2110 Pine Mtn Rd (dr6-25)	208	Kennesaw
180		209	
181		210	** + ghm: Brushy Mtn Line
182	D: 3875 Old Stilesboro Rd (dr6-18)	211	** + opt + Brushy Mtn Line
183	E: 4066 Old Stilesboro Rd (dr6-19) + B/E: 2346 Acworth-Due West Rd (dr6-14) + ghm Route of Polk's Corps	212	D: roadside bldgs on Old Hwy 41 (dr19-31) + C: Old Hwy 41 at Collins Rd (dr19-30) + ps101 Kennesaw Town (Cherokee Village Site) .5 mi NW of Marietta near Old Hwy 41 at Noonday Creek + ps74 Battle of Noonday Creek + opt
184	B: ps137(dnr104 "Old Stilesboro Station") Orr-Smithwick hs 4633 Old Stilesboro Rd + C: dnr105 parcel 6 Acworth Due West Rd (see map) + D: 4531 Old Stilesboro Rd(dr6-3) + mmp V. N. Mabry Prospect Mica mine + osr	213	ps101 Kennesaw Town (Cherokee Village Site) .5 mi NW of Marietta near Old Hwy 41 at Noonday Creek
185		214	** (unmarked cemetery)
186		215	
187	E: ** ps144 Ruins: McLain hs County Line Rd NE of junction with McLain Rd + ar	216	E: parcel 1 (2045?) Stilesboro Rd (dr6-26)
188	Allatoona (community) + B: ps142(dnr3; dr14-20) House-McLain hs McLain Rd north of junction with County Line Rd + ** dnr2 Faith Church (GONE)/Site of Old Allatoona Church (ghm) County Line Rd	217	ghm Lt Gen Leonidas Polk Killed at Pine Mtn
		218	Pine Mtn
189		219	D: parcel 4, Paul Samuel Rd (dr6-21)
190	**	220	
191	**	221	** ps81 Kemp-Born's Mill (site) Acworth-Due West Rd (about 2 mi north of Due West School) on Allatoona Creek + ps106 Mt. Olivet Church Site + ghm: Stilesboro-Sandtown Cross roads + osr
192	E: 2085 Pitner (dr14-15)		
193	C: dnr107 1940 McLain Rd + D: 1965 Pitner (dr14-16)		
194		222	
195	C: 2591 Mars Hill Rd (dr7-7)	223	** 1832 farm site
196		224	
197	osr	225	Piney Grove Church Cemetery
198	D: 2048 Acworth-Due West Rd (dr6-16) + osr	226	
199	D: 3681 Old Stilesboro Rd (dr6-17)	227	ghm: Dallas-Acworth Rd + ghm: James Foster hs, Old Burnt Hickory Rd
		228	dnr120 parcel 5 County Line Rd

Land Lot	Description	Land Lot	Description
229	dnr121 parcel 1 County Line Rd + dnr122 County Line United Methodist Church County Line Rd	261	B: ps90 Davis-Markle hs Intersection of Old Mtn Rd & Burnt Hickory Rd + C: 659 Old Mtn Rd (dnr127; dr7-18) + ghm: Davis' Cross Roads + ghm: Logan's 15th A.C. Line
230	dnr121 parcel 1 County Line Rd		
231		262	
232	C: dnr118(dr6-33) 5375 Burnt Hickory Rd	263	
		264	ps103 Red Rock Settlement Vicinity Hadaway & Due West Rds + B: ps135 Country General Store (Terry's) Mars Hill Rd at Ford's Rd intersection (Mars Hill Community) + B: ps136 Terry-Croker hs Mars Hill Rd at Brown Rd intersection
233			
234	** 1832 farm site		
235			
236	osr		
237			
238			
239	C: cannery, Dallas Rd at Villa Rica (dr19-19) + Pine Mtn + ps102 Pine Mtn Memorial	265	
		266	E: dnr122(dr6-22) County Line United Methodist Church & Cemetery County Line Rd + ghm: Hood & Hardee Withdraw E. to R.R.
240			
241			
242	** dnr111 2415 Stilesboro Rd (GONE) + C: dnr112 Stanley Rd, at Stilesboro Rd + C: 1289 New Salem (dr19-26)	267	** dnr123 Due West Rd (GONE)
		268	E: 5759 Due West Rd (dr6-35)
243	C: dnr108 1460 Stanley Rd + C: Stanley Rd/Dock Green Rd (dr19-28) + ** (unmarked cemetery)	269	ps103 Red Rock Settlement Vicinity Hadaway & Due West Rds + ** dnr124 Hadaway Rd, near intersection of Mars Hill Rd (GONE)
244			
245		270	C: parcel 1, Hadaway Rd (dnr125; dr15-5A)
246	** + kmnbp + ghm: Federal 15th Corps + opt	271	**
247	ps4(ghm, opt) Peachtree Trail + kmnbp	272	** + ** dnr126 Old Mtn Rd (GONE) + C: dnr127 parcel 3 Old Mtn Rd
248	** + Kennesaw Mtn + kmnbp	273	
249	Marietta	274	ps79 Battle of Gilgal Church
250	Marietta	275	ps79 Battle of Gilgal Church + B: ps65 Dickson-Lovingood hs Acworth-Due West Rd, .6 mi NW of Due West School + E: 805 Acworth-Due West Rd (dr6-30) + C: 760 Acworth-Due West Rd (dr6-29) + osr
251	C: dnr110 parcel 3 Stilesboro Rd		
252	C: dnr109 parcel 1 Stilesboro Rd		
253	C: 1187 New Salem (dr19-24) + ghm: Hardee's Salient		
254			
255			
256	ps78 Battle of Pine Mtn	276	** + E: 740(?) Kennesaw-Due West Rd (dr6-27) + ps78 Battle of Pine Mtn
257	ps78 Battle of Pine Mtn		
258	C: 751 Acworth-Due West Rd (dr6-31) + osr	277	ps78 Battle of Pine Mtn
259	C: Acworth-Due West Rd & Hadaway, originally parcel 2—now 55 (dnr116; dr6-32 & dr7-5)) + C: dnr117 Hadaway Rd + ** dnr118 5375 Burnt Hickory Rd (GONE) + osr	278	E: ps24 Simpson Manning hs (new location) 835 Frank Kirk Rd, NW + C: Frank Kirk hs (dr20-35)
		279	
260			

Land Lot	Description	Land Lot	Description
280	B/E: 242 Kirk Lane, the Lattimore Farm (dr19-22 & dr20-33)/ps76 Battle of Lattimore's Farm + ghm Hardee's Salient	312	
		313	** dnr129 Old Hamilton Rd (GONE) + Oregon Park
281		314	osr
282	Marietta	315	** dnr115 Old Sandtown Rd (GONE)
283	Marietta	316	D: 3030 Bob Cox Rd (dr22-7)
284	Marietta	317	
285	Marietta	318	**
286	kmnbp	319	**
287	Marietta	320	** + kmnbp
288	Marietta	321	kmnbp
289	C: 1888 Burnt Hickory Rd (dnr274) + knbfp + Marietta	322	Marietta
290	dnr113 Burnt Hickory Rd + ghm Gen. O. O. Howard's Headquarters	323	Marietta
		324	Marietta
291	dnr114 Braswell-Carnes hs, N.R. Burnt Hickory Rd, near intersection with McDaniel Rd	325	Marietta
		326	Marietta
		327	Marietta
292	**	328	
293		329	
294		330	ps77(ghm: Mud Creek Line) Battle of Mud Creek Dallas Rd at Mud Creek, just east of the Sandtown Rd
295	C: parcel 4, Acworth-Due West (Old Sandtown) Rd & Scott Rd (dr22-10 & dr7-1) + osr	331	osr
296	Due West(ghm: Due West Community) + ps79 Battle of Gilgal Church + osr + E: parcel 14, Acworth-Due West (Old Sandtown) Rd (dr22-8) + B/E: Due West Community Center (dr6-28) [moved 200 yds. E to N si. Kennesaw Due West Rd.]	332	ghm(osr) Old Sandtown Rd + ghm Darby Plantation + cemetery + D: old gas station, Dallas Hwy (dr22-11)
		333	**
		334	B: 3910 Dallas Rd. SW (across frm Casteel Rd): Green-Bullard hs/ Green Plantation (ps70; dnr128; dr15-9A)
297	ps79 Battle of Gilgal Church N. R.	335	E: Mayes hs, 4101 Dallas Hwy (dr15-10A & dr20-23)
298		336	**
299	**	337	Lost Mtn
300	**	338	Lost Mtn
301	C: Holland Rd, no # (dr15-2A)	339	**
302		340	
303		341	dnr130 65 Antioch Rd
304		342	mmp Mason Mine (gold), 1906 Stamp Mill, Cyanide plant (closed 1906)
305			
306	C: parcel 2, Antioch & Nichols Rds (dr6-36)		
307	C: 5730 Nichols (dr15-1A)		
308			
309			
310			
311	**		

INCORPORATED AREAS

Data presented in this section are drawn from the DNR and Secrist surveys; due to the scope of this project, no resurvey of the incorporated cities was possible. The information presented herein cannot, therefore, be presumed to be accurate in every detail. It is hoped that a comprehensive historic sites surveys can be undertaken for every incorporated city in Cobb County in the very near future.

ACWORTH

Academy St.
    4471
Bell St.
    no # (church, dnr20)
    no # (across from church, dnr21)
Carnes St.
    no # (south side between Academy &
          Federal, dnr50)
    4465
    4451
    4558
Church St.
    4561 (ps98 Acworth Presbyterian Church)
Collins Ave.
    no # (dnr35)
    no # (NW corner Collins/Lakeshore,
          dnr36)
Collins Cir.
    no # (dnr37)
Dallas St.
    4424
    4430
    4438
    4446
    4452
    4468
    4543
    4553
    4527
    4544
    4536
    4526
    4520
Highway 293
    gas station D: 293 at Toccoa (dr20-25)
Lemon St.
    no # (dnr57, residence, corner Lemon &
          Willis)
    4531
    4521

    no # (dnr59)
    no # (dnr63, commercial)
Logan Rd.
    117
    4765
    4839
Lombardy Way
    4523 (ps97 Smith Lemon-Nichols hs)

N. Main St.
    no # (residence by church parking lot,
          dnr39)
    5001
    4989
    no # (residence at corner N. Main &
          Carnes, dnr42)
    4947
    4929
    4897
    no #s (commercial block on south side of
          N. Main extending west from
          Dallas, dnr60)
    no #s (commercial block on south side of
          S. Main between Dallas and Lemon
          Streets, dnr61)
S. Main St.
    no # (commercial bldg. at NE corner of
          S. Main & Dallas, dnr62)
Maple Dr.
    no # (dnr64)
Mars Hill Rd.
    3343 C: (dr2-19)
    3385 E: Mars Hill Pres. Ch. (dr2-20)
Northside Dr.
    4810
    4784
    4610 (ps96/dnr9: Moore(?)-Shuford-
          Abbott hs)
    4588
    4572

ACWORTH

4490
4476
4462
4438
no #   (dnr16)
4418
4488
no #   (dnr19, residence, corner N'side &
        Bell)
no #   (dnr22, now or formerly Boyce Mfg.
        Co.)
Old McEver Rd.
    366 C: (dr1-20, dnr66)
    3495 C: (dr1-24)
    3581 D: at Cantrell (dr1-21)
Ragsdale
    D: 4144 (dr2-7)
    D: 4146 (dr2-5)

Southside Dr.
    no #   (dnr 23, now or formerly Boyce
            Mfg. Co.)
    no #   (dnr29, residence)
    4294
    no #   (dnr32)
    no #   (dnr33)
    no #   (dnr34)
Taylor St.
    4217
Willis St.
    205
    200   (ps95/dnr56: Lemon-Nichols hs)
Street(s) Unidentified
    dnr24
    dnr25
    dnr65 (st.# 4480)

AUSTELL

Bankhead Hwy.
    D: 2471 (dr7-19)
Broad St.
    no #   (dnr261, NE corner Broad & Joe)
    no #   (dnr262, row of commercial struc-
            tures on north side of Broad
            between Powder Springs Rd. &
            Perry St.)
Jefferson St.
    no #   (ps56/dnr266: Shelverton hs,
            also now or formerly the Firehouse
            Restaurant & Lounge, SW corner
            Jefferson & Spring) (GONE)
    2898
    no #   (dnr267, north side of Jefferson
            across from Medlock intersection &
            between 2898 & 2860)
    2860
    no #   (dnr267, SE corner Jefferson &
            Medlock, across from 2860)
Love St.
    5895 (ps57/dnr263: Austell Presbyterian
            Church)
Mozley St.
    2737 (ps55: Lithia Springs Hotel)
Mulberry St.

5925 (ps54: Austell-Davis hs)
Old Marietta Rd
    no #   (dnr254)
    no #   (dnr255)
    no #   (dnr257)
Spring St.
    5915
    5928
    5938
    no #   (dnr269, SW corner Spring & Rose
            Hill)
    5994
    no #   (dnr271, NE corner Spring &
            Cochran)
    6050
    no #   (dnr272, south of & adjacent to
            6050)
    6070
    6082
    6083
Sweetwater St.
    2688 (ps58/dnr256: Methodist parson-
            age)
Washington St.
    no #   (dnr258, NE corner Washington &
            Mulberry)

AUSTELL

no # (dnr258, 2nd hs east of
  Mulberry on north side of
  Washington)
no # (dnr259)
no # (dnr260, SE corner Washington &
  Powder Springs Rd.)
no # (dnr260, 2nd hs east of Powder
  Springs Rd. on south side of
  Washington)

no # (dnr260, 3rd hs east of Powder
  Springs Rd. on south side of
  Washington)
no # (dnr260, 4th hs-5th bldg.-east
  of Powder Springs Rd. on south
  side of Washington)
Street(s) Unidentified
  dnr263 (4 structures)
  dnr264 (4 structures)
  dnr265

KENNESAW

Big Shanty Rd.
  2838
Cherokee St.
  no # (ps67: Big Shanty Museum, near
    RR tracks)
  no # (dnr74, SE corner Cherokee &
    Dogwood)
  no # (dnr75, NE corner Cherokee & Pine
    Hill)
  no # (dnr75, SE corner Cherokee & Pine
    Hill, beside 3068)
  3068
  3066
  3008
  no # (dnr76, across street from 3008)
  2985
  2950
  2913
  2885? (dnr79 & dnr77 same)
  no # (dnr80)
  no # (dnr81, church)
  2870
  no # (dnr85, railroad station)
Harris St.
  no # (dnr88, south of & adjacent to
    2908)
  2908
  2934
  no # (dnr88, north of & adjacent to
    2934)
  no # (dnr89, NW corner Harris &
    Whitfield)
  no # (dnr89, SW corner Harris &
    Whitfield)

no # (dnr89, 2nd hs south of
  Whitfield on west side of Harris)
Hawkins Store Rd.
  no # C: Roberts Hs (dnr196; dr13-2)
  no # C: Benson House (dnr195; dr13-5)
Highway 293 (see also Old US 41)
  no # (dnr93, chapel)
Lewis St.
  no # (dnr91, south of junction with Hwy
    293)
  no # (dnr91, south & east of junction
    with Hwy 293)
Main St.
  no # (dnr86, commercial structures at
    SW corner Main & Cherokee)
  no # (dnr87, commercial structures)
S. Main St.
  no # (dnr 92)
Old US 41 (see also Hwy 293)
  no # C: near Giles Rd (dr1-33)
  3057 C: (dr1-34)
Pine Mtn. Rd.
  no # (B: ps71: Roberts-Gilbert hs,
    between Stilesboro& Hwy 41)
  2675 (C: dr6-24)
Shiloh Rd.
  3814 B/C: Shiloh U. Meth. Ch. (dnr71;
    dr1-8 & 12-33)
Shirley Dr.
  2881
  no # (ps99/dnr84: Carrie-Fowler hs,
    NW corner Shirley& Cherokee,
    adjacent to 2881)

KENNESAW

Summers St.
  2741
  no #   (dnr95)
  2689
  no #   (dnr97)
Wade Green R.
  no # B/E: Mt. Zion AME Ch. (dr12-34)

Watts Dr.
  no #s (ps68: Site of Camp McDonald,
        west of Main St. on both sides of
        Watts)
Whitfield Pl.
  no (dnr90, NE of junction with N. Main)

MARIETTA

Alexander St.
  31
  no #s (dnr424, 2 structures south of &
        adjacent to 31, across from Cagle's
        Gym)
Atlanta St.
  30
  31
  36
  42
  54
Barnes Mill
  E: 1117 (dr19-32)
  D: no #, D.O.T. bldgs. at Barnes Mill & Hwy
  41 (dr19-36)
Camp St.
  248
Campbell Hill St.
  395
  398
  401?   (see dnr280)
  403
  404
  411
  412
  419
  420
  421
  426
  431
  432
  437
  438
  444
  445
  454
  460

  462
  611?   (see dnr280)
Cherokee St.
  1031
  660
  484
  452
  446
  440
  429
  419
  405
  402
  393
  392
  381
  380
  367
  362
  357
  347
  337
  323
  321
  239
  201
  200
  183
  177
  169
  130   (GONE?)
  107
Church St.
  907   B: Elizabeth United Methodist
            Church, contributing to Elizabeth
            H D (dr12-36)
  453

441
429
411
409
401
383
366
365
358
355
352
346
343
340
334
331
328
322
316
308
297
290
289
284? (dnr327, south of & adjacent to 290)
281
276
268
262
250
no # (dnr333, now or formerly the Full
    Gospel Church)
236
228
218
212
202
192
189
180
172 & 170 (under same roof)
no # (dnr345, south of & adjacent to 170/
    172, at NE corner Church & Lemon)
148
120
no #s (dnr389, commercial structures at
    NW corner Church& Mill)

Cole St.
147

no # (dnr394, residence south of &
    adjacent to church at 147)

Depot St.
no # (dnr397, formerly Marietta Railroad
    Station)
no # (dnr398, Kennesaw House Block,
    east side of RR tracks, between
    Depot & Whitlock)

Dobbs St.
130
no #s (dnr388, 2 warehouses on south side
    of Dobbs across from 130)

Gresham Rd.
no # E: Sope Creek Bapt. Ch. (dr19-34)

Haynes St.
no # (dnr393, church at SW corner
    Haynes & Lemon)
no # (dnr393, residence south of &
    adjacent to church at corner Haynes
    & Lemon)

Holland St.
136
126
120
116
112

Kennesaw Ave.
no # (dnr281)
no # (dnr282, just SE of St. Ann's Rd.)
no # (dnr283, "Oakton")
505? (dnr284)
no # (dnr285)
435
no #s (dnr287, 2 residences)
363
359
354? (dnr335, Birney hs)
348
345
343
340
327
321
315
303
298
no # (dnr297)
288

MARIETTA

285		Maple Ave.
282		158
274		137
271		129
268		121
267		109
264		108
256		103
243?	(dnr304, SW corner Kennesaw & Maple)	98
		97
230		94
Lawrence St.		93
198		89
214		84
250		79
268		Margaret St.
280		108
288		116
no #	(dnr409, west of & adjacent to 313)	Maxwell St.
313		81
321		McDonald St.
324		43
329		76
332		77
341		89
346		99
349		131
354		134
376		145
387		Northcutt Rd.
422		no # (dnr366)
425		Oakmont Dr.
433		39
434		N. Park Square
Lemon St.		no #s (dnr395, commercial structures
171		between Church & Cherokee)
Locust St.		S. Park Square
226		no #s (dnr401, commercial structures
218		between Powder Springs & Winters)
213		no #s (dnr402, commercial block bordered
210		by S. Park Sq., Atlanta, Anderson, &
209		Winters)
206		W. Park Square
202		no #s (dnr399, commercial structures
201		between Whitlock & Depot)
196		no #s (dnr396, commercial structures
195		between Depot & Mill)
187		

MARIETTA

Polk St.
   205
   46
   50
   60
   405
   80
   84
   90
   94
   96
   100
   no # (dnr360)
Powder Springs St.
   26
   32? (dnr430, structure south of &
       adjacent to 26)
   no # (dnr431)
Radium St.
   86
   92
   106
   114
   122
   128
   134
Rose Lane
   547
   555
   561
Roswell St.
   180
Sessions St.
   14
   15
   17
   18
   21
   22
   25
   26
   29
   30
   35
   315
   472
Stewart Ave.
   90

   102
   112
   119
Tramell St.
   55
   39
   31
   25
   no # (dnr384, between 19 & 25)
   19
   15
Washington Ave.
   no #s (dnr403, commercial block bordered
         by Washington, Waddell, Anderson,
         & Atlanta)
   190? (dnr413, SE corner Washington &
         Haynes)
   216
   222? (dnr415, west of & adjacent to 236)
   223
   231
   236
   241
   247
   248
   253
   260
   261
   272
   273
   274
   275
   279
   288
   289
   no # (dnr420, Marietta National Military
         Cemetery)
   301
   331
   351
Whitlock Ave./Hwy. 120
   no # (dnr361, SW corner Whitlock &
         Powder Springs)
   43
   57
   65
   no # (dnr362, north side of street; 60?)
   81

MARIETTA

95
96
201
267? (dnr368, south side of Whitlock, near Cleburne intersection)
282
298
335? (dnr370, SW corner Whitlock Ave. & Whitlock Dr.)
446
462

475
no # (dnr374)
no # (dnr375)
no # (dnr376)
Street(s) Unidentified
dnr387 (commercial structures bordered by Polk, RR tracks, and ....?)
dnr400 (commercial block bordered by Whitlock, Powder Springs, Anderson, & RR tracks)

POWDER SPRINGS

Atlanta St
4388
4365
4335
4321
4302
4299
Brownsville Rd.
no # (ps52: Powder Springs Pavillion, near junction with Hwy 278)
Dallas Hwy.
4494
no #s (D: roadside bldgs LL 826, dr8-33)
Jackson Way
Powder Springs Primitive Baptist Church C: south side of road near Old Lost Mtn Rd intersection (dnr161; dr8-27)
Marietta St.
4491
4481

no #s (dnr165, commercial structures north & south sides of street)
no # (dnr166)
no # (dnr167)
no # (dnr168)
4380
4371
4366 (B: ps53/dnr171: Scott-Rice hs)
4355
4293
4284
4279
4270
4263
4220
4207
Unidentified Street(s)
LL 807 E: trestle Ry bridge across Powder Springs Creek (dr8-34)
LL 826 E: trestle Ry bridge across Lucille Creek (dr8/25-26)

SMYRNA

Atlanta St.
no # (dnr231)
Gilbert St.
no #s (dnr227, 2 residences at NW corner Gilbert & Powder Springs; may face RR tracks)
Powder Springs St.
no # (dnr228, SW corner Powder Springs & Gilbert; may face RR tracks)

Roswell St.
1316
1312
1308
Spring St.
1359

PRESERVATION FINDINGS
AND OPPORTUNITIES

If the preservation movement is to be successful, it must go beyond saving bricks and mortar. It must go beyond saving occasional historic houses and opening museums. It must be more than a cult of antiquarians. It must do more than revere a few precious national shrines. It must attempt to give a sense of orientation to our society, using structures and objects of the past to establish values of time and place.

U.S. Conference of Mayors
With Heritage So Rich (1966)

FINDINGS

1. The single most important historical theme in Cobb County, the one which has national significance in terms of National Register status, is the Civil War. This has already been recognized by the development of the Kennesaw Mountain National Battlefield Park, the Big Shanty Museum in Kennesaw, the designation of Johnston's River Line as a National Register site, the abundance of markers which bear Civil War associations, and the archaeological sites which are also important for the information they may revel about the war. This theme provides a very strong base upon which to build the protection of other resources which are Civil War era resources and relate to the full socio-economic-cultural story.

A thematic or Multiple Resource Area approach to all Civil War era resources should be developed. This includes structures built immediately following the War, during Reconstruction, which were developed to replace lost structures, or were rebuilt exactly in the lost forms as a measure of continuity in the wake of wartime devastation, as well as those structures known to be present before or during the War. Known Civil War battlesites which lie outside protected areas should also be included. The point is not so much to illuminate the Civil War *per se* as to draw a total picture of what Cobb County was like at the time the War occurred.

The designation as Cobb Centennial houses of all mid-nineteenth century dwellings of certain types is recommended, especially those which represent a modest Greek Revival farmhouse, c1840-1870. A thematic National Register nomination or Multiple Resource Area submission for them is one possible approach. All industrial ruins of the mid-nineteenth century may be included in this Multiple Resource Area.

2. The entire corridor of the Atlanta-Marietta Interurban Railway should be marked and those sections of it which are its last best remnants should be indicated. These are the only 1910s to 1920s collections of "highstyle" bungalow architecture in the county, with the exception of a portion of Oakdale Road, which relates to the development of the Interurban Railway, and is part of the same period of development. The "best" architectural examples of the suburban development along the Interurban are in Smyrna, but the Log Cabin Road Atlanta Road segment is the next best, and the only portion which lies in unincorporated Cobb County. The Interurban Railway was a singular development in Georgia, and, because of that, has state level significance *viz* the National Register.

3. There are only a handful of legitimate log cabin buildings and building parts left in Cobb County. These are the oldest known structures in the county and deserve protection for their educational value if nothing else. They are as a group not in good condition; termite damage has affected, for example, the Power-Jackson log cabin, and the portion of the Hyde farm which is still in logs. These cabins are not the "best" nor most notable examples of their type in Georgia, but they are extremely rare. Therein lies their value. It ought to be against the law in Cobb to destroy a log cabin. They can be easily moved, but never replaced.

4. An important theme to Cobb County history is the development of transportation--railroad, streetcar, highway. The streetcar segment has already been discussed, but the railroad and highway segments are problematical. The matter of railroad development (around major stops and stations) is more a consideration for local municipalities than for the Cobb unincorporated sections. Marietta has done a splendid job of preserving its historic railroad connections, as has Kennesaw. Structures connected to the railroad in the outlying areas have more to do with sidings, bridges, and crossing markings. There are some good trestle bridges for the railroads still standing in Cobb, probably many more than could be surveyed from the roads, but otherwise the historical importance of railroads to the outlying areas is largely invisible. Sidings, warehouses and crossing markers have disappeared, if they ever existed.

For highway development, the historical record in preservable resources is even bleaker. The development of crossroads, of the Dixie Highway in particular, and in the county's own program of road paving, would have precipitated the creation of "roadside businesses"--gas/grocery stands, gasoline stations, general stores and warehouse/trade centers, tourist cabin motels, eateries, and the like. In Cobb County, these phenomena have been either eradicated by modern developments or replaced by more modern versions of the same businesses. Very few structures which could be considered "roadside" businesses related to highway development in Cobb have been identified. The best examples occur within the municipalities.

5. Churches. The quintessential "country church" resides all over Cobb County, but not very often in its pure form. Most country churches have been bricked or sided or both; most have added ells or new sanctuaries; many have other additions, such as louvered windows, or inappropriate front entrances which, architecturally, would disqualify them from listing in the National Register. There are a few good examples. These should be further documented and the congregations encouraged to understand and maintain the original architectural form.

6. Schools. Only a handful of buildings have been identified as actual or possible community school sites. The "one-room" school-house, or even the early county replacement for it, are an endangered species in the County. In some cases the community schools have been adapted for use as community centers, an appropriate and creative use, which has in some cases, unfortunately, rendered the original school form unrecognizable.

7. Industrial sites. The sites from the mid-nineteenth century, mentioned above, are mostly in ruins. Mill development in Cobb County is important locally, and deserves attention, though most industries developed within municipal areas. Clarkdale is a notable and important exception. Another industrial area is Elizabeth, just north of Marietta, where the industry has been rendered unrecognizable, but the related residential site has not, and Marble Mill Road between Church Street Extension and the old mill (now a chemical factory) warrants district nomination as well. In Fair Oaks a similar situation exists where a residential area was developed in conjunction with the air base across Atlanta Road. World War II housing, both government and what appears to be private cottage development are unique resources within the county. Reference is made specifically to the duplexes along Concord Road and Concord Drive, and the tiny suburban cottage subdivision along Aircraft Drive.

8. Some additional residential resources exist. Briefly they are as follows: an extensive number of folk Victorian and vernacular houses for the late 19th century; some bungalow neighborhoods (chiefly in Mableton and Leland), and the World War II housing mentioned above.

9. Twentieth century agricultural/industrial resources exist, but may be of lesser interest at present. Examples include a fully intact feed mill (now Kelly Ace Hardware) in Elizabeth, barns throughout the county, and early automotive repair shops in Mableton and elsewhere.

10. There is potential for historic districting in the unincorporated sections of Cobb: Vinings (already known), Mableton, Macland, Elizabeth, Lost Mountain (store and house); and some streets may have potential for rural preservation, such as McLain and sections of Old Stilesboro.

11. Two properties stand out as truly exceptional examples of rural 19th-20th century rural strongholds: the Tritt family place on Post Oak Tritt off Johnson Ferry Road, and the Hyde farm/Power family farm on Hyde Road off Lower Roswell. These properties offer an exceptional opportunity at rural preservation, and/or the creation of passive parks in an area which needs passive parks.

12. There are some examples of folk housing in Cobb County, but since this is not a folk county in the same way that an Appalachian county would be, these are not judged as important a resource as others. Still, they are a part of the whole picture. There is a question here, more than recommendation. Some could be included in the Civil War designation; others would have to be treated separately.

Lost Mountain Store, Dallas Highway at its intersection with Lost Mountain Road and Mars Hill Road.

BIBLIOGRAPHY

Anonymous. *A History of Cobb County -- The Indian Period.* (Unpublished material from the Cobb County Archaeology Department).

Austin, Richard L., et al., eds. *The Yearbook of Landscape Architecture: Historic Preservation.* New York: Van Nostrand, 1983.

Bryan, T. Conn. "The Gold Rush in Georgia," *The Georgia Review* (Winter 1955), pp. 398-404.

Cobb County Planning and Zoning Department. *Cobb County Data Report.* Marietta, Georgia: 1985.

Cobb County Planning and Zoning Department. *Cobb County Data Report.* Marietta, Georgia: 1986.

Cobb County Sesquicentennial Committee. *Cobb County Sesquicentennial.* Marietta: By the author, 1983.

Crimmins, Timothy J., Ph.D., et al. *Textile Mills in Georgia: A Cultural Assessment.* Atlanta, Georgia: Georgia State University Heritage Preservation Program, 1985.

Daniel, Pete. "The Transformation of the Rural South, 1930 to the Present," *Agricultural History* (July 1981), p. 23.

Federal Writers Project. *Georgia.* (American Guide Series). Athens: University of Georgia Press, 1940.

Fisher, James, "The Piedmont: Old and New." Atlanta 69th American Association of Geographers' Meeting. 1973.

Fundaburk, Emma Lila, and Mary Douglass Fundaburk Foreman, eds. *Sun Circles and Human Hands.* Luverne, Alabama: By the editor, 1981.

Garrett, Franklin M. *Atlanta and Environs.* Athens: University of Georgia Press, 1982.

Georgia Department of Agriculture. *Georgia Historical and Industrial.* Atlanta, Georgia: 1901.

Glore, L. Harold. *Bicentennial History of South Cobb County.* (unpublished manuscript, 1976).

Glore, L. Harold. *History of Mableton, Georgia.* (unpublished manuscript, 1968).

Healy, Robert G. *Competition for Land in the American South.* Washington, D.C.: The Conservation Foundation, 1985.

Holdes, Gerald L. "State Planned Trading Centers in Pioneer Georgia," *Pioneer American* 14 (1983), pp. 115-124.

Hudson, Charles M., ed. *Red, White, and Black: Symposium on Indians in the Old South.* Southern Anthropological Society Proceedings, No. 5. Athens: University of Georgia Press, 1971.

Hudson, Charles. *The Southeastern Indians.* Knoxville: University of Tennessee Press, 1980.

Jones, Charles C., Jr. *The History of Georgia, Vol. I: Aboriginal and Colonial Epochs.* Boston: Houghton, Mifflin and Company, 1883.

Kollock, John. "The Vale of Nacoochee," *Georgia Magazine* 10 (June-July, 1966) pp. 16-20.

Lewis, Thomas M. N., and Madeline Kneberg. *Tribes That Slumber: Indians of the Tennessee Region.* Knoxville: University of Tennessee Press, 1977.

Linley, John. *The Georgia Catalog: HABS: A Guide to the Architecture of the State.* Athens: University of Georgia Press, 1982.

Range, Willard. *A Century of Georgia Agriculture.* Athens: University of Georgia Press, 1954.

Scott, Thomas A. *Cobb County, Georgia, 1880-1900: A Socioeconomic Study of an Upper Piedmont County.* March, 1978. Dissertation for the Doctor of Philosophy Degree, University of Tennessee, Knoxville.

Sears, Joan N. "Town Planning in White and Habersham Counties, Georgia." *Georgia Historical Quarterly* 54 (1970), pp. 20-40.

Secrist, Dr. Philip L. *Historic Cobb County: Historical Inventory of Marietta and Cobb County.* Marietta: Cobb Landmarks Society, 1975.

Stilgoe, John R. *Common Landscape of America, 1580 to 1845.* New Haven: Yale University Press, 1982.

Stovall, Allen D., et al. *The Sautee and Nacoochee Valleys: A Preservation Study.* Sautee-Nacoochee Community Association, 1982.

Temple, Sarah Blackwell Gober. *The First Hundred Years: A Short History of Cobb County, in Georgia.* Atlanta: Cherokee Publishing Company, 1980.

Toomey, Noxon. *Proper Names of the Muskhogean Languages.* Hervas Labs of American Linguistics Bulletin No. 3, St. Louis, 1917.

U. S. Department of Commerce, Bureau of the Census, *United States Censuses of Population, Agriculture and Manufacturing: 1850-1980.*

Waters, John C. *Maintaining a Sense of Place: A Citizen's Guide to Community Preservation.* Athens: Institute of Commerce and Area Development, University of Georgia, 1983.

White, George. *Statistics of Georgia.* Savannah: W. T. Williams, 1849.

Wood, W. Dean, et al. *A Cultural Resources Survey of the Lost Mountain Transmission Line and Due West Substation.* Athens, Georgia: Southeastern Archaeological Society, 1986.